DO YOU HAVE A MINUTE?

AN AWARD-WINNING REAL ESTATE MANAGING BROKER
REVEALS KEYS FOR INDUSTRY SUCCESS

JOHN M. GIFFEN

DKG
Publishing
Group

ISBN: 978-1-7326912-0-9 (Paperback)
ISBN: 978-1-7326912-2-3 (Ebook)

Library of Congress Control Number: 2018911885

Front cover image by Hal Bergman
Cover and interior design: Doug Cordes
Author photo: Mark Denman

Printed in the United States of America.

First printing edition 2018.

DKG Publishing Group
P.O. Box 681355
Franklin, TN 37068-1355

www.DoYouHaveAMinuteBook.com
www.JohnGiffen.com

DEDICATED TO

*My father who always had
a minute or two for me.*

ACKNOWLEDGMENTS

This book is a result of over two years of gathering my many thoughts and ideas and putting them down on paper to share with the world. This has not happened without the encouragement and assistance of many people. I would like to thank my wife and best friend since college, Michelle, for putting up with me over these past two years as I wrote this piece of work. She has encouraged me every step of the way in the writing process. A special thank you to my children — Andy, Matt, and Elizabeth — who are an inspiration to me and always supportive of whatever I do in life. I also would like to extend my appreciation to Phillip Cantrell, the CEO/Founder of Benchmark Realty, LLC in Franklin, Tennessee, who provided me the opportunity to be the principal broker at Benchmark for several years and allowing me to be part of the company's phenomenal growth making it one of the largest independent brokers in the country. His knowledge, insight, and wisdom have been a great blessing to me over the years.

I also would like to thank my creative team: my editor, Mary Parker Bernard, who took my words and made them into a publishable book; Doug Cordes, who took his incredible skills in graphic design and created the book's front and back covers as well as the interior design and formatting, making my words visually appealing to the reader.

The risk management section in this book could not have been completed without the assistance of Cindy Grissom, CEO of Rice Insurance Services Company, LLC. I am grateful to her and Rice Insurance for providing me with valuable information on current risk management strategies for agents and brokers.

I could not have written this book without all of the agents I have had the privilege and honor of working with over the years. Their hard work, professionalism, and commitment to the ideals of our profession are amazing. Thanks, guys!

Finally, I want to acknowledge my parents, Dave and Bonnie Giffen, who were always loving, supportive, encouraging, and there for me when I needed them. Though they are no longer with us, their influence on my life is immeasurable, and not a day goes by that I don't think of them. Thanks, Mom and Dad!

"Hey, John! Do you have a minute?"

That's how it always begins. An agent knocks on my door with a puzzled look on their face. They come by just for a minute — or a few — with a question about their latest client or transaction.

"What's the best way to handle my client who has decided to back out of a contract two days before closing?"

"What if the client doesn't want a home inspection?"

"How should I write a business plan for my real estate practice?"

"How do I get qualified buyer leads?"

The questions are almost limitless. Many of them come up repeatedly, while every now and then an agent throws me a new one that I've not heard before.

I don't have all the answers, but I do have years of experience navigating the ups and downs of the real estate business. I believe I have learned enough to keep agents out of trouble.

WHY REAL ESTATE?

Although working as a real estate agent can be financially lucrative and it has certainly supported my family, the money wasn't the appeal for me.

I was drawn to this industry because of the professional and personal satisfaction it offers. We get a front-row seat during one of the most important milestones in a person's life: buying or selling a home. It's gratifying for me to help a young couple facilitate the complicated process of buying their first house. I enjoy coming alongside a growing family or single mother to help them sell their current property and find the ideal home for their special situation. It's fun to dream with empty nesters as they downsize and find that perfect spot to spend their retirement years.

The role of the real estate agent is an important one for the consumer. We are the professionals who are educated and experienced in walking with buyers and sellers in ensuring they have a place to call home.

SHEPHERDING THE SHEEP

A few years after I was licensed, I found myself always wanting to support and encourage other real estate agents by helping them work through complicated transactions and dealing with challenging clients. Soon after I received my real estate broker's license, I became a managing broker for an ERA franchise office in the Nashville, Tennessee, area.

Since then, I have worked as a managing broker for two nationally franchised companies and one independent firm. The latter is where I am now working as part of the senior management team overseeing several managing brokers, compliance, and branch office operations.

For the past several years, I have become more of a "shepherd of the sheep" in my role as a principal broker, manager, instructor, and mentor. A shepherd's primary responsibility is the safety and welfare of the flock. Shepherds tend to their herd by watching them, urging them along, and leading them to good pastures to graze when they are hungry. They are watching over the flock to ensure dangerous predators do not threaten any of the sheep under their care.

> *I honestly believe that what we do as real estate professionals makes a significant difference in how real property is transacted in this country.*

The role of a real estate managing broker is very similar to that of a shepherd. Like a shepherd, a good managing broker will watch over his or her agents, protecting them when needed, and encouraging them as they grow their businesses and address the needs of their buyer and seller clients.

I wrote this book because I want to help agents "get it right" the first time. After several years of overseeing hundreds of agents and their managing brokers and teaching numerous real estate continuing education classes, I decided I wanted to share some of the advice and counsel I have offered agents over the years.

I believe agents can be much more effective in working with prospects, clients, and customers if they truly know what to do when listing or selling a home. I would not have written this book if I didn't honestly believe what we do as real estate professionals makes a significant difference in how real property is transacted in this country.

As real estate professionals, we are asked to steward the most significant asset a person has: their home. This responsibility cannot be taken lightly. It requires expertise, insight, salesmanship, self-confidence, problem solving, patience, understanding, empathy, compassion, perseverance, and tenacity. The scope of this book contains tips and advice from me encompassing many of these attributes.

HOW TO USE THIS BOOK

I hope you'll find this book a valuable resource for navigating your business when working with clients, properties, and transactions.

It's not exhaustive, though, and should not replace the wisdom, insight, and counsel of an agent's principal broker. Always turn to your broker when issues and challenges arise, as the broker is the one responsible for your real estate license and professional conduct.

I wrote each chapter so it stands on its own. You don't need to read them in order, but I do encourage you to read all of them carefully. I wanted to make the book a very practical tool. Therefore, you'll find worksheets, charts, checklists, and templates for documents I use (and my agents use) with clients.

Real estate is becoming more complicated as each year passes. Increasingly impatient clients, poorly trained cooperating agents, complex sales transactions, and competition from large, national start-up real estate companies are forcing agents to "step up their game" and work harder than ever. The playing field has changed and will continue to evolve in the years ahead. This book will provide you with the tools you need to make sure you can have a thriving business in this industry for years to come.

YOU'RE INVITED TO STAY AWHILE

Since you, dear reader, and I likely don't know one another and will never work together, consider this book your invitation.

Go ahead. Stop by my office, poke your head in the door with a light knock, and ask, "Hey, John! I've got a question. Do you have a minute?"

Yes, I do. Come on in.

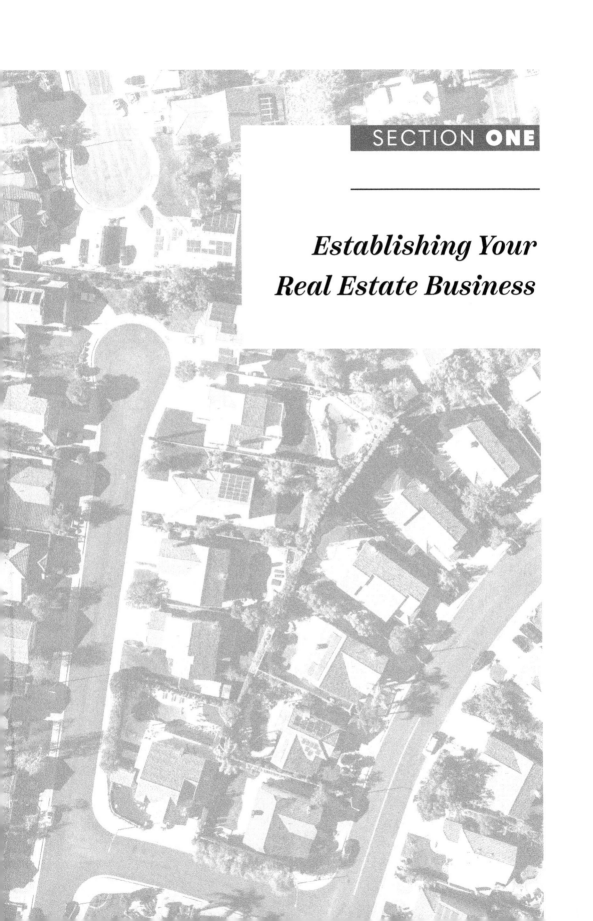

Establishing Your Real Estate Business

CHAPTER 1

What It Takes to Be Successful in Real Estate

"Success is neither magical nor mysterious. Success is the natural consequence of consistently applying the basic fundamentals."

— JIM ROHN

Many times during the week an agent will knock on my office door and ask how they can get their real estate business moving in the right direction. I ask them what they have been doing in their business to procure prospects and convert them to clients. The majority of the time I identify one common problem for everyone who seeks my advice: They forgot the fundamentals of what it takes to be a successful business owner and real estate agent.

Practicing real estate is a business enterprise, plain and simple. When I entered the real estate profession, one of the most difficult and challenging parts of the transition was going from a full-time job to being out on my own. I was not starting a new "job" but starting a small business. I was joining the ranks of the self-employed, realizing I would be working for myself and not for somebody else. It was both scary and exciting at the same time.

FIVE ATTRIBUTES OF SUCCESSFUL REAL ESTATE AGENTS

1. Disciplined
2. Motivated
3. Organized
4. Focused
5. Expert client advocate

As I ventured into this new reality, I needed to embrace what it meant to be solely responsible for the income that would keep a roof over my head and feed my family. Being independent and not having to "clock in" was a welcome change from my previous profession, but it also brought about new responsibilities, disciplined work behavior, and structured business practices to ensure my success. Without them, I would surely fail, and I would be back on the streets looking for employment.

FIVE ATTRIBUTES OF THE SUCCESSFUL REAL ESTATE AGENT

I soon learned after receiving my affiliate broker license there are five areas I needed to concentrate on to make it as a self-employed individual selling real estate: discipline, motivation, organization, focus, and client advocacy. These characteristics are the foundation of successful business people, including agents. Without them, agents will find themselves frustrated, discouraged, and defeated.

These five principles are the necessary elements of a successful real estate career. Your annual business plan (see Chapter 2) needs to be developed with these principles in mind. If you are struggling right now in getting your business in "forward motion" consider how you can make some needed changes in your real estate practice (and, in you) that will incorporate all five of these "pillars to success." Without them, you are like a ship without a rudder. You will remain where you are, just drifting along aimlessly.

SUCCESSFUL REAL ESTATE AGENTS ARE DISCIPLINED

Owning your own business requires great discipline. You need to develop routines that positively impact you and your business. Successful agents wake up early every morning and are ready to go to work by 8:00 a.m. They utilize every minute of the day, so no time is wasted. They understand what needs to be done and when it needs to be done. They follow routines consistently each day. They also do not let any issue go unaddressed, lest it morphs into a more significant problem. You will not prosper in this business unless you are disciplined.

TIME MANAGEMENT

How do you spend your time during the day? Are you using your time wisely? I ask these questions of agents who seem to be struggling in getting or retaining business. I've found that those who do not have their day well organized and laid out like a road map usually never make much progress in becoming productive. I believe productivity is tied to proper time management.

There are twenty-four hours in a day. No more, no less. Each day should be divided into "segments" or time blocks allowing a more focused approach to accomplish what needs to be completed during the day. Allow for flexibility, but try to do specific daily tasks at the same time each day, so a routine and discipline are formed.

SUCCESSFUL REAL ESTATE AGENTS ARE MOTIVATED

What motivates you as a real estate agent? Is it assisting buyers and sellers with their real estate needs? Is it the commission check you receive after a deal closes? Is it the thrill of the "hunt" in finding new prospects and converting them to clients? No matter what your motivation is, your production level corresponds directly to your motivation. To reach a level of sustained success in real estate, you must stay motivated.

How do you do this? Goals. Motivation and goals go hand-in-hand. Setting realistic and attainable goals fuels motivation. (I go over in-depth goal planning in Chapter 3.) As you reach goals, you become more confident and also more driven to reach the next one. Motivation keeps you moving forward so you do not become stagnant and unexcited about what you are doing.

SUCCESSFUL REAL ESTATE AGENTS ARE ORGANIZED

As an independent businessperson, you must have strong organizational skills. A disorganized business creates ongoing chaos for everyone associated with it—especially for you, the owner. Chaos impacts your sales production because you are always trying to figure out where things are and which way is up. If you find yourself unorganized, seek the assistance of someone who can get you organized so you can optimize your day and improve your productivity. Without organization, your business will never be what you want it to be.

TASK DELEGATION

Delegate certain tasks, which will help you with organization and time management. Don't try to do everything! One of the most important lessons I learned early in my real estate career was to surround myself with people who are experts at what they do and let them do it! One example is how agents handle transaction management.

Agents may find themselves caught up in the minutiae of all the little details involved with their transactions. Of course we should want to know what is happening with our listings, contracts, and closings, but an excellent real estate assistant can free up quite a bit of an agent's time by taking care of paperwork and the "little stuff." An assistant who is licensed adds more value to the equation.

If your business is growing, and you are micro-managing everything, how much time can you spend prospecting and finding new streams of revenue if you are trying to hunt down a piece of paper or a copy of a home inspection report?

SUCCESSFUL REAL ESTATE AGENTS ARE FOCUSED

Distractions in the real estate world are plentiful, and they come from all directions, including:
- Never-ending emails or phone calls from sales people or those wanting your time
- Lead generation sources attempting to convince you they have the best solution for finding prospects
- Agents and brokers inviting you to broker open houses
- Coaching companies enticing you to sign up for coaching
- Other brokerages attempting to recruit you
- People and non-revenue producing activities that steal time away from your business

We also spend too much time on things that make no significant impact on our business or the income it provides us. One example is over-involvement in REALTOR® associations and networking organizations.

You may be asked to serve on an association committee or organize a special event. Before you know it, you are invited to serve on the board of directors or leadership committee of the organization. This activity takes time out of your schedule, which will certainly impact your business. Stay focused on the goals you have set for your business, allocating your time accordingly.

DAILY PROSPECTING

You should be prospecting daily! Real estate agents are like farmers; if we do not continually plant seeds and tend to our "crops," a bounty cannot be harvested. A specific amount of time during the day should be spent on prospecting and developing your business. A minimum of two hours each day should be devoted to finding new business. Yes, a *minimum* of two hours!

It is essential to be consistent in both finding new clients and retaining those you served in the past. Develop "gatekeeper" relationships with attorneys, accountants, doctors, past clients, and others who are the most likely ones to refer buyers and

> *You should devote a minimum of two hours each day to prospecting.*

sellers to you. Create prospecting plans for For Sale by Owners, expired listings, targeted neighborhood areas, investors, international buyers, etc.

SUCCESSFUL REAL ESTATE AGENTS ARE CLIENT ADVOCATES OF THE HIGHEST EXPERTISE

The REALTOR® Code of Ethics and most state real estate commissions/boards require agents always to put the needs of their clients above their own. This does not mean giving away our services for free or lowering our commissions. It does say, however, that we do not make decisions based on how it will impact us financially.

If an agent always focuses on the money they can earn from a sale, they can never be considered a true professional in this industry. The money is secondary to doing a good job in finding a client a new home or selling their existing one. Our Code of Ethics has within it a foundation based on the Golden Rule: "Do unto others as you would have them do unto you." The client is king (or queen!); learn it and live it.

PROFESSIONAL EXPERTISE

The most successful real estate professionals are those who know the real estate market up, down, backwards, and forwards. They know their communities, current market statistics, and trends, and they are excellent negotiators. Agents making six-figure incomes are those who can provide valuable advice and insight to their clients. They also can guide their clients with ease through the confusing and ever-changing world of real estate.

Every real estate agent's aspiration should be to possess a character rooted in professionalism and integrity with a commitment to expertise in their industry.

WHAT YOU PUT IN IS WHAT YOU GET OUT

My late father always told me the more effort I put into something, the more results I will see from my efforts. The same is true for real estate agents.

You cannot expect to become a top producer unless you are willing to put the time and effort into your business. Success in real estate results from hard work, long days, time away from family, and making sacrifices regular "employees" don't experience. At times, you will want to give up because you don't see the results you expect.

Don't give into the temptation!

You will see positive outcomes if you consistently "stay at it" and see things through to the end. It may be a difficult road for you as you try to find clients, get new listings, and work tirelessly with buyers. However, that road can be more easily traveled if you are willing to be disciplined, motivated, organized, focused, and devoted to your clients and your industry.

CHAPTER 2

Your Business Plan: A Roadmap to Success

"The plans of the diligent lead surely to abundance, but everyone who is hasty comes only to poverty."

Carol*, an agent who had been in our firm for several years, approached me in the hallway outside of my office one afternoon and asked if I had a minute to speak with her. I said I did and we went into my office to meet.

She said her business was floundering, and she was not sure if she should retire her real estate license and seek full-time employment.

Carol had been a multi-million-dollar producer for several years but appeared to have lost her real estate "mojo" over the previous couple of years. A substantial part of her business came from leads supplied by the human resources department at her husband's company. Unfortunately, he left his position at the company to become a consultant. Her regular "supply line" dried up.

I asked Carol if she had a written business plan for her real estate practice. She said she did not. I encouraged her to sit down and write one as soon as possible and bring the first draft to me for review. After the two of us made a few changes, she was ready to execute her plan. Over the next several months I encouraged

---

* *All names of individuals have been changed to protect their privacy.*

her to stay focused and follow the plan as she prospected for new clients and reengaged with old ones.

Her plan worked. Carol once again achieved a level of production that allowed her to make a comfortable income and have a bright future in the business.

A BUSINESS PLAN — A CRITICAL TOOL FOR YOUR SUCCESS

I could not have attained the level of success selling real estate if I didn't have a business plan in place. A business plan allows you to have a "road map" for your real estate business. It is a document summarizing the operational and financial objectives of your business and contains the detailed plans and budgets showing how the objectives are to be realized.

You are the CEO of your business. Successful CEOs and business owners have a plan for their business. Without a plan for how you are going to succeed as an agent, failure is almost guaranteed.

When I wrote my first business plan, I had no idea what I needed to include. After asking other agents and doing some research on my own, I learned the primary components of a business plan should contain several elements: a mission and vision statement, a SWOT (strengths, weaknesses, opportunities, and threats) analysis for my competitors and me, specific and quantifiable goals and objectives (including prospect lead generation), marketing for listings as well as personal promotion and advertising and long-term client follow-up, and the systems and processes I would utilize to operate my business.

The first business plan I created was the most difficult one, but in subsequent years it became easier because I laid the foundation in that first plan.

As you begin writing your real estate business plan, remember the guidelines below. It should:
- Be an active document
- Be short and sweet
- State what you want to accomplish and how you plan to achieve it
- Flow out of your mission and vision statements
- Be used to assist with your monthly, weekly, and daily planning
- Specify how you define and measure your sales production goals that will allow you to grow your business and sustain it

beyond the next closing or two

CREATING A REAL ESTATE BUSINESS PLAN

The following are the various sections of the business plan I created to operate my real estate business:

1. DEFINE MISSION AND VISION STATEMENTS

I know this may sound a little odd, but creating a vision and mission statement will lay the groundwork for how you will operate your business. It should also reflect your personal and professional principles and ideals.

A *mission statement* describes what you want to accomplish now with your business and how you get there. A *vision statement* outlines what your business will look like as you grow it.

MY REAL ESTATE MISSION STATEMENT

"I am committed to providing the highest level of professional real estate services to my clients supported by my many years of experience and expertise in meeting the needs of buyers and sellers in Middle Tennessee. Our client and transaction management services, technology, and personal attention allow us to understand your particular needs and exceed your expectations."

MY REAL ESTATE VISION STATEMENT

"Our real estate practice will continue to be a driving force in the Middle Tennessee market by providing the technology, support, and services to meet the needs of our buyer and seller clients."

---

2. PERFORM A SWOT (STRENGTHS, WEAKNESSES, OPPORTUNITIES, AND THREATS) ANALYSIS

This is a critical section of your business plan. You need to determine your strengths and weaknesses. Answer these questions to get started:

- Do you have the necessary selling skills to be successful in real estate?
- What areas are you weak in and what do you need to do to strengthen them?
- What will set you apart from your competition?
- Will you specialize in a particular geographic area or demographic group?
- What will be the one niche of business you will most likely see consistent results?
- What could impact your business?
- How can you expand your real estate practice?
- Where do you see yourself in six, twelve, and twenty-four months?

3. SET REALISTIC AND ATTAINABLE GOALS

I tell agents the real estate business is either "feast or famine." We are selling houses like they are going out of style (in an "up" market) *or* we are "listening to crickets" because sellers and buyers are not coming forward to sell or purchase a home (in a "down" market).

To keep your business sustainable, set specific, realistic, and attainable goals you would like to achieve in the weeks and months ahead. The key words here are "specific" and "attainable." You may have lofty and ambitious goals, but you need to be able to sell some real estate in order not to starve. Don't make your goals complicated or out-of-reach. You should feel confident you can meet them with some effort and focused attention. (See Chapter 3 for more on setting goals.)

4. DEVELOP A STRATEGIC PLAN OF ACTION

Now that your goals are set, how will you reach them? What strategies will you employ that will bring the results you want?

For example, to work with first-time homebuyers, you may consider developing and hosting a first-time home buying seminar that will outline everything involved in purchasing a home. Or, if you are working with baby boomers, you may want to partner with family estate attorneys or assisted-living communities to help seniors and their families with their real estate needs.

Be specific about how you are going to carry out each business objective and refine your methods as you go along. Remember it's best to use the "rifle" approach (precise and defined) and not the "shotgun" (scattered and undefined) approach to build your business.

5. CREATE A TIME FRAME FOR YOUR GOALS AND STICK TO IT

You cannot achieve your goals unless you put a timeline in place to finish them. If one of your goals is to acquire a professional designation or training certificate, how long will that take you? How many months to identify fifty good prospects to add to your database?

No matter what time frame you set for your goals you will need to measure your progress. Refer back to each goal or objective every month to see how you are doing. Ask your principal broker to hold you accountable for achieving your goals, or consider hiring a real estate coach who can guide you in developing and growing your business.

6. DEFINE YOUR SOURCES OF BUSINESS

How will you get your business? Which sources will you utilize to find business? Will these sources be individuals you know, broker leads, electronic lead generation, For Sale by Owners (FSBOs)?

The most common source of buyer and seller leads is your sphere of influence (SOI). Your SOI comprises people who know, love, and trust you. The foundation of my business was built on people in my sphere who knew other people who could use my services. Remember, your sphere includes the individuals you see on a regular basis at church, at work, or in your neighborhood. If you treat them right, they will always be dependable for referrals of prospective clients.

Other sources to consider are e-leads from the internet, targeted geographic areas, open houses, foreclosures, FSBOs, and old-fashioned door knocking. Trust me, knocking on doors still works. No matter what sources you put into your business plan, they need to be streams of business that can produce good fruit for you. You need business sources that can consistently fuel your business.

7. USE SYSTEMS AND PROCESSES TO SUPPORT YOUR BUSINESS

You will need specific systems and processes in place to grow your business. You must have a good CRM (customer relationship manager) system to manage your database and transactions. Programs such as Top Producer, Wise Agent, and Contactually are some of the more popular ones on the market and charge a monthly subscription fee. In addition to a CRM, you should have software programs on your computer such as Microsoft Word, Excel, Outlook, and Power-Point for correspondence, email, presentations, etc. Almost everyone utilizes these four programs to conduct business on a daily basis.

Whatever system you use, make sure you understand what it can and cannot do for your business. The last thing you want to do is waste money on a program or software that you never use or doesn't meet your needs.

8. MEASURE YOUR SALES SUCCESS

Your business plan needs to be quantified. You need to know where you have been, where you are, and where you are going!

Routinely, you need to examine how your business is perform-ing as compared to everything you laid out in your business plan. You should "check-in" with yourself at least quarterly to make sure you're following the tactics you laid out in your plan.

YOUR REAL ESTATE BUSINESS PLAN

I want to help you create your real estate business plan right now.

Use the following worksheets to evaluate your production thus far and to record your future sales goals. I've also included a sample real estate business plan, so you can see what it looks like complete. You'll also find a blank business plan template at the end of the chapter. Adapt this template or use it as is to write out your own business plan.

PREVIOUS YEAR'S PRODUCTION

Complete each item noted below. After you have completed this exercise, you will be able to know what you need to do to meet your production goals.

A. Income for prior 12 months: _____

B. Number of closed transactions in last 12 months: _____

C. Number of buyer-controlled sales in last 12 months: _____

D. Number of listings sold in last 12 months: _____

E. Dollar volume closed in the last 12 months: _____

F. Average commission per closing for prior 12 months: _____

G. Average sale price over the past 12 months: _____

H. Number of listings taken in the last 12 months: _____

I. Number of buyer contracts written in the last 12 months: _____

J. Number of listing appointments for the last 12 months: _____

K. Number of buyer appointments for the last 12 months: _____

L. Listings closed to listings taken %: _____
(number of listings closed for the past 12 months divided by the number of listings taken for the past 12 months)

M. Buyers closed to buyer appointments %: _____
(number of buyers closed for the past 12 months divided by the number of buyer appointments for the past 12 months)

N. Prequalification conversion %: _____
(number of listings taken for the past 12 months divided by the number of listing appointments taken for the past 12 months)

O. Prequalification conversion %: _____
(number of buyer clients created [i.e., signed buyer agency agreement or committed to work with you] for the past 12 months divided by the number of buyer appointments for the past 12 months)

MY ANTICIPATED PRODUCTION
MOVING FORWARD

		Year	Month
1.	What is my desired income level?	_____	_____
2.	Average commission per closing for the last 12 months *(F. from above):*	_____	
3.	Number of closed transactions required: *(#1 divided by #2)*	_____	

4. Number of closed transactions in last 12 months:
   (B. from prior page)

   _____ _____

5. Percentage increase required:
   ([#3 minus #4] multiply by #4)

   _____

6. What is my average sale price? *(G. from prior page)*

   _____

7. What is my dollar volume closing goal?
   (#3 multiplied by #6)

   _____ _____

8. Percentage of closed transactions that are buyer-controlled sales: *(C from prior page divided by #4)*

   _____

9. Percentage of closed transactions that are listings sold:
   (D. from prior page divided by #4)

   _____

10. Number of listings closed goal: *(#3 multiplied by #9)*

    _____ _____

11. Number of buyer-controlled sales closed goal:
    (#3 multiplied by #8)

    _____ _____

12. Percentage *(M. from prior page)*

    _____

13. Percentage *(L. from prior page) This should be a minimum of 80% - target of 95%.*

    _____

14. Calculate the number of buyer broker agreements you will need to meet your buyer unit closing goal:
    (#11 divided by #12)

    _____ _____

15. Calculate the number of listings taken needed to meet listings closed goal: *(#10 divided by #13)*

    _____ _____

16. Conversion percentage: *(Number of listings taken divided by listing appointments) (N. from prior page) This should be a minimum of 60% - target 80%*

    _____

17. Conversion percentage: *(Number of buyer clients created divided by # buyer appointments) (O. from prior page)*

    _____

18. Number of listing appointments you will need:
    (#15 divided by #16)

    _____ _____

19. Number of buyer appointments you will need:
    (#14 divided by #17)

    _____ _____

NECESSARY SALES PRODUCTION

1. Number of listing appointments I will need: (#18)   _____

2. Number of my listings closed goal: (#10)   _____

3. Where did my listings come from last year?   _____
   Examples: Past clients, referrals, FSBOs, etc.

4. Number of buyer appointments I will need: (#19)   _____

5. Number of buyer-controlled sales closed goal (#11)   _____

6. Where did my buyers come from last year?   _____
   Examples: Your "for sale" signs, past clients, referrals, e-leads, etc.

Now, you need to gather the information from this exercise to determine how you will reach your production goals. Answer the following questions so you can complete your business plan for the next twelve months.

1. Who will be my clients?
2. Why will they choose me?
3. What services will I provide them?
4. How will I provide these services?
5. What geographic area(s) will I work?
6. How will I cover this area(s)?
7. How will I market to my seller prospects?
8. How will I market to my buyer prospects?
9. How will I market to my past clients?
10. How will I market to my gatekeepers?
11. How will I market to my networking groups?
12. What systems will I need to reach my goals?
13. What are my specific goals for the next twelve months?
14. What action plan will I implement to accomplish these goals?
15. Are there areas of improvement on which I need to focus?

A SAMPLE REAL ESTATE BUSINESS PLAN

Agent Alice

MISSION STATEMENT: *To have a business that is constantly growing and improving in order to assist our clients in meeting their real estate goals ... all supported by world-class customer service and technological innovation.*

VISION STATEMENT: *To be a driving force in the local real estate market by providing the technology, support, and services to meet the needs of our buyer and seller clients — all while giving back to our community.*

STRENGTHS: *Knowledge of the local market area; five years of real estate experience; multi-million-dollar producer, numerous professional develop-ment designations and training certificates.*

WEAKNESSES: *Working with investors, foreclosures, and For Sale By Owner (FSBO) sellers.*

OPPORTUNITIES: *Growing economy in the local area; new construction representation; relocation opportunities.*

THREATS: *More real estate companies emerging in the market; top pro-ducers are also marketing to my target areas; rapid change in real estate industry technology.*

MY GOALS: *Invest in a good contact management system; hire a contract to close assistant; begin developing daily goals; earn a couple of NAR designations.*

MY PLAN OF ACTION: *Develop and host a first-time home buying sem-inar; work with retirement centers in assisting the senior citizens and their families with their real estate needs.*

TIME FRAME: *First-time home buying seminar within six months; earn my Seniors Real Estate Specialist designation within four months; reach $5 million in sales production by December 31st.*

SOURCES OF BUSINESS: *First-time home buyers, seniors, sphere of influence referrals, online lead generation.*

MY REAL ESTATE BUSINESS PLAN

MISSION STATEMENT:

VISION STATEMENT:

STRENGTHS:

WEAKNESSES:

OPPORTUNITIES:

THREATS:

MY GOALS:

MY PLAN OF ACTION:

TIME FRAME:

SOURCES OF BUSINESS:

SYSTEMS AND PROCESSES I NEED FOR MY BUSINESS:

3

Using the 1-7-30 Goal-Setting Method

"A goal properly set is halfway reached."

When I earned my real estate license, one of the first pieces of advice I received from my principal broker was to establish a written business plan with specific goals and objectives. After meeting with him, I remember sitting down and doing just that. I wrote out a detailed plan and listed all the goals I wanted to reach in my first year selling real estate.

My goals centered around the number of prospects I needed to add to my database, the prospects whom I wanted to convert to clients, the volume of business I needed to sell to survive, and the various streams of revenue for my business. These goals were long-term and part of a twelve-month strategy to get me up and going in the business. Many of them were pretty ambitious, but I was confident I could reach them.

At the end of my first year in the business, I reviewed my list and discovered I only reached about 55 percent of my original goals. I had a great first year and made a decent amount of money, but I did not accomplish everything I set out to do. I was frustrated at not being able to do a better job of checking items off my goals list.

After talking to my broker and several veteran agents, I discovered I was concentrating more on reaching long-term goals than trying to accomplish shorter, more attainable goals. I soon realized I had to change my methodology for goal setting and focus on goals that were short-term.

1-7-30 GOAL-SETTING

Focusing on realistic and attainable goals is critical when establishing business and personal goals. These types of goals are always shorter and much less complicated. Shorter-term goals allow you to zero in on what needs to be done *now* to meet them.

Set these goals in one-day, seven-day, and thirty-day segments. I call it the "1-7-30 Goal-Setting Method." Consider the following examples for these three types of goals.

Shorter, achievable goals allow you to remain more productive and grow your business faster.

ONE-DAY GOALS

These goals are high-priority, immediate, and should be reached between twelve and twenty-four hours. Every morning, or the previous evening, write down what you want or need to accomplish in the day ahead. Ask yourself:

- How many calls will I make to prospects?
- How many calls will I make to past clients?
- What follow-up should I do with my current listings or active contracts?
- What items in my transactions need to be addressed?

Remember to also list any personal items that need to be accomplished during the day.

SEVEN-DAY GOALS

Not as urgent as one-day goals, these goals may incorporate some of the one-day goals you set. They should address larger issues or projects you need to accomplish in the next seven days.

An example of a seven-day goal might be developing a new marketing or promotional piece for your business, meeting with your broker on how to work with relocation clients, or planning a broker or public open house.

THIRTY-DAY GOALS

Thirty-day goals are a little longer-term, but they are still within reach. Maybe you need to take a class to obtain continuing education credit for license renewal, build a new website for your business, or create a marketing plan to work with a particular demographic group.

These goals are a bit more complicated and broader in scope than the others, but they can easily be met.

EFFECTIVE GOAL TRACKING

Goals are worthless if they are not accurately measured, so you need to track your progress with each one. It is important to see how you are doing and determine why you did or did not reach them.

Tracking goals allows you not only to look at what you can mark off your list, but it also gives you an indication of how productive you are during a day, a week, and a month.

START GOAL-SETTING NOW

You may have goals you would like to accomplish in the next three, five, and ten years. Long-term goals are not all bad. However, shorter, achievable goals allow you to remain more productive and grow your business faster.

Focusing on long-term goals creates more stress since you may feel as if you have a long way to go to reach them. Longer-term goals also take your attention away from what needs to be addressed now or in the not-too-distant future.

Start tomorrow morning — or better yet — this evening, on one-day goal setting. Sit down, grab a pen and a piece of paper, and write down what you need to accomplish tomorrow, next week, and by the end of the month.

Keep track of what you wrote and see how well you did in checking items off the list.

CHAPTER 4

Creating a Daily Plan of Action That Leads to Success

"Plans are of little importance, but planning is essential."

In real estate, we find ourselves facing numerous tasks every single day. Our business requires us to work on prospecting, personal marketing, listing management, transaction management, overseeing the activities of current sellers and buyers, and other important responsibilities. At times, we are running in different directions trying to get everything completed before the end of the day.

I discovered years ago that my productivity increased — and my business goals were more likely to be achieved — if I had a list of things I needed to do each day. To that end, I always have an action plan in place before I start my workday.

CREATING A DAILY ACTION PLAN

Write it the night before. I used to write my list of "to-do" items early each morning. I felt this was the best time to put it together. However, I always had items from the previous day that were not completed. Many times, I forgot to carry over incomplete items to my "today" list. Moreover, I was feeling the stress of the day in the early morning when I created my plan.

Several years ago, I started putting my "tomorrow together today." I found that when I wrote down what needed to be done the night before, I was more relaxed so I could be focused on what I needed to accomplish. It helped me quite a bit.

Prioritize your list. List the most important items needing attention at the top of your daily action plan. Many of the things we do in real estate are time-sensitive. The clock is always ticking to meet contract deadlines. You should have all of the various performance dates associated with contract contingencies marked on your calendar. The ones coming due need to be a top priority as you begin your workday.

Work on the first item on your list first thing in the morning. The most important item you need to accomplish during the day should be the number one item on your list. Once you tackle this "big" item, you will have a sense of satisfaction, impacting the remainder of the tasks needing attention.

Don't put too many items on your list. Be realistic about what you can get done each day. Remember, there are only twenty-four hours in a day. Action items contained on long lists tend to "carry over" to the next day or following days. You need to be comfortable with what you write down and confident you can get everything accomplished during your day.

WHAT SHOULD BE IN YOUR DAILY ACTION PLAN

Include follow-up items from the previous day. Anything you could not get accomplished the day before should be on your list.

Listing and contract action items should be a two-part section. Designate one for listings and one for active contracts. For current listings, review the marketing plan you created for each one. Check to see which items in the plan need to be addressed. For contracts, look at your list of performance dates in your transaction file and mark down the ones that are coming due in the next day or so. Also, list any paperwork that needs to be submitted to your broker for document compliance review.

All prospecting action items need to be listed. As I note in Chapter 6, you need to prospect at least two hours every day. Your list should include:

1. The telephone calls you need to make to your prospects — especially your "A" prospects
2. Face-to-face appointments you need to schedule with past clients to keep in touch and possibly ask for a referral

3. Follow-up "thank you" or "it was great to see you" notes you need to handwrite

Your business will not grow unless you are organized in how you prospect. Having a priority list of prospecting activities written down will allow you to be more successful in acquiring new business.

Include marketing action plan items. Real estate agents do two types of marketing: personal and property. In this section, note which marketing activities in the two categories need to be accomplished today. You may also want to include any postings you need to create for your social media sites such as Facebook, Twitter, Instagram, LinkedIn, etc.

Review the day's activities. I added this section to my daily action plan as a summary of my day's activities. I always want to see how well I did in getting everything from my list completed. It also provides me with an opportunity to "grade" myself on the day's productivity and note what I could do better to remain on track with my business.

Use the template I created to write your own Daily Plan of Action. Make it a habit to start each day with an intentional plan for action.

MY DAILY PLAN OF ACTION

FOLLOW-UP ITEMS FROM YESTERDAY
(Note: Do not allow items to be carried over for more than one day.)

☐   ☐
☐   ☐
☐   ☐
☐   ☐

LISTING AND CONTRACT ACTION ITEMS

Listings	Contracts
☐	☐
☐	☐
☐	☐
☐	☐

PROSPECTING ACTIVITIES

Calls to be Made	Face-to-Face Appointments to Schedule	Follow-up Notes to Write
☐	☐	☐
☐	☐	☐
☐	☐	☐
☐	☐	☐

MARKETING ACTIVITIES TO BE ACCOMPLISHED

Social Media Postings

END OF DAY REVIEW

Summary of the Day

CHAPTER 5

Get Over It —
You Are in Sales

"Everyone lives by selling something."

I have been selling since I graduated from college in 1984. For many years after college, I was an account manager for three prominent consumer packaging companies in the South, and I owned a small printed packaging brokerage company in Nashville. When I started my first job, I had no idea about sales techniques and practices. My college degree is in business administration (marketing and management), but I never learned how to sell during my undergraduate years.

In fact, I was not seeking a sales position upon graduation. I wanted to find a good management training program and grow with a reputable company. Selling was the last endeavor on my job list. Why? Because my impression of a salesperson was not a good one. I always thought of salespeople as aggressive and overbearing. I did not want to try to push a product or service onto someone who probably didn't need it. Surely, there was something better out there for me.

The job market in the early- to mid-1980s was not strong, and finding a job was challenging. After several interviews, rejections, and no offers, I worked at the college from where I just graduated as a recruiter. I did that for a short period until I interviewed for a packaging company in Louisville, Kentucky. I must have done well in the initial interview as they asked me back for a follow-up meeting.

After this second meeting, my prospective employer sent me to a company specializing in human resources consulting and psychological testing. I was put through a battery of tests and a few one-on-one interviews. Apparently, the results from the assessment were good because I received a telephone call from the sales manager of the company offering me a job. I accepted the position and started two weeks later. Again, I had no idea how to sell, but the company promised to teach me. They saw something in me that I did not see in myself.

I went through an extensive training period for six months before I was allowed to hit the road to sell anything. My training included understanding the technical side of commercial printing as well as learning how to prospect and close deals effectively. During those initial six months, I discovered that selling is a science. It requires organization, discipline, excellent communication skills, and, most importantly, perseverance. Those who succeed are people who can comprehend the concepts of selling, practice them over and over, and execute them on an ongoing basis. Fortunately for me, the success I have had over the years is due to learning how to sell and make a living at it.

> *Selling is a science that requires organization, discipline, excellent communication skills, and most importantly, perseverance.*

FROM SELLING BOXES TO SELLING HOUSES

Practicing real estate is a second career for many. It is for me. Prior to getting my real estate license, I was in the printed paperboard packaging industry selling folding cartons to national consumer products companies. I sold boxes to companies who manufactured everything from auto parts to toothbrushes. It was a pretty demanding job, but I learned a great deal about selling and building strong customer relationships. However, it was not going to last forever.

In 2003, due to changes in the economy (and my desire to find a more challenging and fulfilling opportunity), I decided to change careers and entered the real estate profession. The selling skills I learned in my previous occupation allowed me to pretty much "hit the ground running."

THE TWO-YEAR REALITY

I want you to understand that the heart of what we do as real estate professionals is selling. Not only do we sell real estate, but we also sell our expertise, our education, our experience, and ourselves to seller and buyer clients. Clients benefit from our know-how and can-do attitude, and they lean on us to guide them through their real estate transaction. Unfortunately, not all real estate agents are successful, and around 80 percent will leave the profession after their second year in the business. Why? Read on.

The real estate industry is notorious for its turnover. It may be because the agents don't realize what they are getting themselves into, or they are unable to survive on a low income after they receive their real estate license. According to the National Association of REALTORS®, the average income for a REALTOR® has remained at less than $50,000 for the past several years.

> *About 80 percent of real estate agents will leave the profession after their second year in the business.*

Fifty thousand dollars is the average income, meaning that more than 1.1 million agents are making less than that. Some are making below the U.S. poverty level (which at the time of this writing is $12,140 for a household of one; a household of four is $25,100). This statistic is pretty scary when you think about it.

So, why is the industry turnover so high and the income level so low? I believe the real reason is that most real estate agents have no idea how to sell.

THE BASICS OF SELLING

Successful agents know the four necessary elements of selling, summed up as AIDC:

- **Approach** – establish and build rapport with the client;
- **Identify** – discover the wants and needs of the client;
- **Demonstrate** – show the client how you can meet their wants and needs; and
- **Close** – get them to sign on the "dotted line" so you can represent them as their listing agent or buyer's agent.

These four concepts are the foundation of selling and can be taught and learned with the right training and coaching. Sadly, most managing brokers do not spend the needed time and money to provide adequate sales training for their affiliates. As a result, we see more and more agents hang up their licenses because they don't know how to prospect for new clients and capture business successfully.

To safeguard against becoming one of the "many fallen" in the real estate profession, you must be willing to hone your selling skills and do so on an ongoing basis. If your broker is not providing you with the necessary training to "hunt, kill, and drag home" new business, you need to find other avenues to learn how to do it.

GETTING SALES TRAINING

A Google search for "real estate sales training" returns more than 600 million results and includes numerous seminars, conferences, webinars, coaching programs, podcasts, and more. Select one that has a good reputation, and, more importantly, one that can show they have helped agents see good results from their training.

And then start learning how to sell.

I initially trained with Dale Carnegie Training. Dale Carnegie is one of the largest training companies in the world and has been in business for more than 100 years. Their systems have worked for millions of sales professionals. (This is *not* an endorsement for Dale Carnegie, by the way. I share my story only because their programs helped me remove the obstacles that were in my way to become a successful sales professional. There are other good sales training companies who can do the same type of training as Dale Carnegie.)

For those who know me, I come across as a Type-A extroverted person with lots of energy. I am not afraid to speak my mind or stand in front of an audience of hundreds of REALTORS® speaking on a specific topic or teaching a continuing education class. However, what many of my friends and colleagues don't know about me is that, before I started selling, I was an introvert and struggled to talk to people, let alone try to persuade them to buy a product or service. In fact, I avoided speech class in college until my last semester before graduation! Interacting with others terrified me.

My employer in Louisville sent me to a series of Dale Carnegie courses. One of the results of the tests conducted during the interview stage showed I had the ability to learn how to sell, and I could be successful at it. Don't ask me why, as I never saw the results of their evaluations. But, the company felt it was worth the time and money to send me to Dale Carnegie to learn how to be confident and determined in the way I spoke and acted in front of prospective clients.

During the first few classes I enrolled in, they gave me the necessary tools to use the four elements of selling: AIDC. I had a great team of teachers as well as a coach who kept me accountable and taught me a great deal about the art of selling. I learned methods in cold calling, lead generation, client management, and more that still benefit me to this day. I truly believe I would not be where I am today if I had not taken those classes many years ago.

Over the years I participated in other sales training events to sharpen my skills and learn new concepts in selling. In my third year as a real estate agent, I went through a great program called Integrity Selling. Their program is specifically designed for real estate agents and provides specific ways to increase business through a systematic approach.

I have also seen and listened to other selling experts at national, state, and local REALTOR® association conferences and events. Look online or ask your fellow agents or principal broker for training opportunities where you can sharpen your sales skills. You can never have too much training!

Through sales training, I overcame fear, apprehension, shyness, and lack of self-confidence to become successful at selling products and services to those who have a need. Whether you use a company like Dale Carnegie or not, you need to find a training program (with coaching) that can work for you. Trust me, it will be worth your time and money. Don't become part of the 80 percent who leave our industry.

KEY POINTS ON SELLING

Recognize today's real estate selling environment. Selling is not an event, but a process. It also is not an art, but a science. So many factors come into play in selling. The real estate industry is ever-changing. Being well versed in current national and local real estate market conditions, industry trends, technology, federal and state governmental regulations, and other issues allows agents to be in the best possible position to sell their value proposition to the client.

Know your sales goals and measure your performance. You need to set specific goals to get where you want to be, and you must track your progress along the way and make improvements where needed. You should have a section in your business plan that quantifies your sales goals for the next twelve months. (See Chapter 2.)

Discover and listen to your client's needs. You cannot sell anything to a client if they do not have a need for what you are trying to sell to them. Identifying the "pain" a client has regarding their real estate needs can move you ahead of your competition. If you can show the client you can sell their home for the highest amount in the shortest period, you will probably win them over. You also must be able to *listen* to your client. Many opportunities have been lost when an agent did not hear what the client needed.

Present yourself as a consultant, not a salesperson. As a real estate professional, you are a consultant, not a salesperson. In your efforts to procure a new listing or a new buyer, you need to represent yourself as someone a prospective client can see providing them with advice and wise counsel through the entire real estate transaction process. You are the expert who can find solutions and guide them from start to finish. You should always come across as non-threatening and easy-going. Be natural in how you relate to the prospect, but be professional in your presentation.

Know your local real estate market. All real estate is local. I cannot overstress the importance of agents knowing the state of the local real estate market. You should be well versed in areas of your city, county, and region that are selling well, as well as the other areas that are underperforming. What are the trends among the properties sold during the past six months, the past year or two, and what direction is the market heading? A good agent will know absorption rates, current property tax rates and impact fees, the latest new construction projects, and proposed residential developments, etc.

> *Your unique value proposition is what makes you stand out in the crowd. It is the key to your success as an agent.*

Know your unique value proposition. Your value proposition is probably the *most important* element of selling real estate, especially as the market continues to evolve and adapt to numerous technological and generational changes. You are one of many real estate agents in your market. Your unique value proposition is what makes you stand out in the crowd. It differentiates you from your competitors and demonstrates how you are different, superior, and most skilled in offering buyers and sellers the highest service in the sale or purchase of a home. Your value proposition lies at the heart of how you market yourself and your services. It is the key to your success as an agent.

If you have a strong value proposition, you will find that

your business will grow as others will want you to list their home or have you assist them in finding their next one. What is your unique value proposition? Think about it. Take the time to develop a very succinct one and then make sure you communicate it to your prospects as you seek out new business.

Don't promise what you can't deliver. If you tell a client you can get their house under contract within thirty days, you better have a signed Purchase and Sale Agreement in hand before the clock strikes midnight on the thirtieth day. A cardinal sin in selling is when a salesperson promises a client they can accomplish something but cannot deliver on that promise.

I always obey the adage, "It's better to under-promise and over-deliver!" I believe one should always be upfront and honest with clients. Many variables in our industry are out of our control. If you under-promise a client, but over-deliver for them, you will not only keep your clients happy, but you will probably also see them become a client for life.

Accept rejection as a part of the selling process. In any type of sales, a salesperson will receive more rejections than orders. The same is true in real estate.

Rejection happens and is part of the selling process. Be prepared for it. Train yourself to handle and treat it as a necessary step to get to the next opportunity. Many sales trainers say rejection gets you closer to a "win."

WHAT'S YOUR UNIQUE VALUE PROPOSITION?

Your value proposition is probably the most important element of selling real estate. Here's my unique value proposition:

- Proven results and honest guidance from beginning to end
- Superior negotiation expertise
- Exceptional customer service
- We take the "trauma and drama" out of the real estate transaction
- Advanced internet and technology tools for property searches
- Professional client transaction management system
- Superior client communication

To find your unique value proposition, ask yourself:

- What sets me apart from the competition?
- Is it the success I've had in marketing homes?
- Am I skillful in managing the details of a transaction?
- Am I a good negotiator?

When a prospective buyer or seller is not willing to work with you, it rarely has anything to do with you personally. Set emotional boundaries, so you are not impacted by the prospect's rejection. When they do say "no" to you, remember your professionalism and be courteous to the prospect. You never know; they may seek your services in the future.

FOLLOW-UP AND STAYING IN TOUCH WITH PAST CLIENTS

One reason real estate agents fail in this business is they do not stay in touch with their past clients on an ongoing basis. We work extremely hard in our prospecting efforts to procure buyers and sellers, but we do very little to make sure they remember us after the transaction closes. Why?

I believe we become too involved in taking care of current prospects, clients, and transactions, and forget the importance of staying in touch with those whom we served in the past and who will more than likely need our services in the future.

A year or two into this business I learned the importance of staying in touch with clients. One Saturday morning, I was driving in a Nashville neighborhood where I assisted a young couple a year earlier purchase their first home. As I passed their home, I saw a "For Sale" sign in the front yard. Sadly, it was not one of my signs. I was shocked and very disappointed.

Why didn't they call me? Didn't they know I was their agent? Apparently, not. Why would they use someone else?

The reason was simple. I did not stay in touch with them after they moved into their home. It was my fault.

OUT OF SIGHT, OUT OF MIND

According to the 2017 National Association of REALTORS® *Profile of Home Buyers and Sellers**, only 12 percent of buyers and sellers use the agent who represented them in their last real estate transaction. That means 88 percent did not. This statistic confirms the fact the majority of real estate professionals have become "stealth" agents and disappear from their past client's radar and find themselves "out of sight, out of mind."

I believe it is vital agents regularly stay in touch with their clients after everyone leaves the title attorney's closing table. A good client appreciation program including periodic mailings, telephone calls, emails, in-person "drop by" visits, etc. will ensure you stay in front of clients on an ongoing basis.

Remembering your client's birthdays and anniversaries as well as births of children, job promotions, and other special occasions

---

*   *National Association of REALTORS® 2017 Profile of Home Buyers and Sellers* will be remembered by them. This is a great way to let them know you still care about them and are always available if they ever need you. Put a reminder system in place in your contact management program or calendar so you know when you should reach out to a past client. Remember, you always want to be the "real estate agent for life" for your clients. Good follow-up after the sale will make this happen!

SELLING IS THE SECRET TO SUCCESS

After these many years in real estate, I believe that I made a good decision to change vocations.

In my first year, I closed more than $1.5 million in sales and earned the "Rookie of the Year" award at my real estate firm. My production increased year over year, and I was blessed to see the fruits of my labor with millions of dollars of real estate sold, all involving happy and satisfied clients.

There's no doubt in my mind, though, that I owe much of my success to one crucial skill — selling. Could I have enjoyed the same level of professional productivity if I had not had the proper sales training early on?

Absolutely not.

It's been that important to me.

CHAPTER 6

The Importance of Prospecting

*"Keep your sales pipeline full by prospecting
continuously. Always have more people to
see than you have time to see them."*

— BRIAN TRACY

Successful agents with six-figure incomes hunt for new opportunities every single day. They utilize effective prospecting systems and processes to find new clients.

Unfortunately, most agents prospect "on the fly" and tend to prospect only when they are in need of new business. When we are busy listing and selling homes, we forget about prospecting.

Consistent prospecting, supported by good, new business marketing plans, is critical to the survival of your business! Prospecting is a *proactive* activity. Unfortunately, we usually prospect as a *reaction* to the shortage of business.

I believe this attitude and practice towards prospecting is the reason why so many agents experience ups and downs in their businesses.

> *Prospecting is a proactive activity. Unfortunately, we usually prospect as a reaction to the shortage of business. Successful agents with six-figure incomes are those who are hunting for new opportunities every single day.*

EXAMINE YOUR PROSPECTING ACTIVITIES

If you are not seeing the sales results you want, the following ideas will help you evaluate your prospecting efforts and what you should do to get your business back on track. Discuss each one with your principal broker, team leader, or sales coach, so they can counsel you on where you need to focus your time and spend your money to grow your business and your income.

PROSPECT EVERY DAY

Your sales production is directly related to the amount of time you spend on prospecting for new business. Prospecting is a fundamental principle of sales and should be the highest daily priority, with other activities following behind. Top producers always have prospecting blocked out on their daily schedule. You should prospect for new clients at least two hours a day. Carve out specific times in your calendar to go after new business.

As you review your schedule from the last week or two, take a close look at how much prospecting you did. You will probably be surprised at how little you accomplished. Maybe you didn't do anything to generate more business. Don't worry. You are not alone.

Sales production is directly related to the amount of time you spend on prospecting for new business. Prospecting should be the highest daily priority, and you should prospect for new clients at least two hours every single day.

Most agents spend more time working *in* their business than *on* their business. Looking at your calendar now should give you motivation to whittle out time for daily prospecting.

How do you find the time to prospect? Review the last five days in your schedule to determine if there is something that might be consuming the majority of your time. If you discover certain activities are taking too much of your time and attention, you need to reorder your priorities. Prospecting should be number one.

PROSPECT WITHIN YOUR SPHERE OF INFLUENCE (SOI)

How many people do you know? If you have not created a list of individuals who are in your sphere of influence (SOI), you need to develop one today! Your sphere is made up of the people who are most likely to ask you to represent them in the sale or purchase of a home or provide you with the names of people who might need an agent. Your SOI is the number one source for referrals!

Make sure you develop effective marketing programs that keep you "front and center" with your sphere of influence on an ongoing basis. Remember the old phrase "out of sight, out of mind"? You can become a stealth real estate agent if you are not staying in touch with the people who know you.

PROSPECT THROUGH MAILING CAMPAIGNS, NEWSLETTERS, AND POSTCARDS

If you have not recently sent something to one or more of your prospect groups or geographic target areas, plan on putting a new mailing or email campaign together today. Strategic mailing campaigns utilizing postcards, newsletters, and other printed materials can be very effective in reaching your prospects. This is a great way to "touch" potential clients and generate leads.

AIN'T BROKE? DON'T FIX IT!

Future success is built on past success. Look at one marketing project you implemented in the past that was successful and brought you additional business. Try to replicate whatever you did then for what you need to do now. It may only require a little updating on your part. Don't "reinvent the wheel" if the prospect campaigns of the past worked to generate business for you.

DO YOU HAVE A DESIGNATED FARM AREA?

"Farming" — and I don't mean the kind you do with tractors and livestock — is still a valuable prospecting strategy for real estate agents. Whether you focus on a geographic area or a specific group of people, you need to be consistent in how you prospect.

Determine the size of your farm group and how often you want your farming campaign to contact them. Be consistent in the marketing you do for your farm areas or farm groups. As a "farmer," you will need to plant "seeds" and nurture them to see results.

Buyers and sellers from farming areas do not appear overnight. Be patient because it will take time before you see your efforts begin to pay off.

UNREPRESENTED SELLERS: FOR SALE BY OWNERS (FSBOS)

Unrepresented sellers can be an excellent source for both buyers and sellers (I go into this more in-depth in Chapter 26). If you recently contacted a FSBO, follow-up with them to see if you can help them sell their home or purchase their next one if they are remaining in the local area. If they are not staying in town, offer to find them an agent in the city they are moving to and pick up a referral fee from that agent.

HERE'S AN EFFECTIVE PROSPECTING TIP!

In the next few days, send handwritten notes to ten of your past clients with the following message:

CLIENT NAME:

I hope you and your family are doing well! I just wanted to drop you a quick note to let you know how much I appreciated you allowing me to assist you with your real estate needs. My business is built on referrals from past clients and others I personally know. If you know of someone who is considering selling or buying a home, please pass my card on to them. I will provide them with the same level of service I provided you! I really would appreciate it!

Warmest regards,

YOUR SIGNATURE

BROKER OR PUBLIC OPEN HOUSES

When was the last time you held an open house? I believe open houses still provide value for agents. I was skeptical of open houses for a long time and would only hold one if the seller requested it.

Then, I sold two listings after a buyer walked in the door and toured the house. These two sales convinced me open houses actually do work. Hold an open house for one of your listings or a listing belonging to another agent. Because those who walk through the front door could be potential clients, open houses are good prospecting activities.

SCORING YOUR PROSPECTING EFFORTS

How are you doing with prospecting? What score, on a scale of one to ten, would you give yourself? Be honest as you answer that question, and consider what you can do to improve your efforts.

Prospecting is the lifeblood of your real estate business. If you are not spending enough time each day going after new business, you will find yourself gasping for air when the selling season slows down or the market begins to turn down.

If your pipeline is full and seeds have been planted, though, you'll be equipped to handle most any storm that comes your way.

CHAPTER 7

Overcoming Fear and Rejection in Selling Real Estate

"If you want to conquer fear, don't sit home and think about it. Go out and get busy."

— DALE CARNEGIE

When one of my agents, Will, came to talk to me, he was extremely frustrated with his productivity level. He told me he closed seven deals during the past twelve months but knew he had to increase his production if he wanted to remain in the real estate business.

After talking to him for a little while, I discovered he was not focused on prospecting for new business. In fact, he was not prospecting at all. Apparently, Will's seven closings originated from his neighbors and close friends at church.

I asked him what was preventing him from picking up the phone and making the necessary calls to prospective buyers and sellers. He admitted he was terrified of rejection and could not face the fact that someone might say "no" to him. Will's fear overwhelmed him to the point of paralysis.

Why do salespeople experience fear? Some experts point to the public perception of a salesperson. Many see salespeople as being pushy, rude, intrusive, abrasive, and artificial. Others believe they are obnoxious, arrogant, and dishonest and focus only on the money they can earn. As professional real estate agents, we work hard not to be in the same category as a snake oil salesman.

Originating in the 1800s, the snake oil salesmen were disreputable people who tried to make money from unsuspecting prospects by selling them fake cures derived from concoctions similar to Chinese snake oil.

Real estate agents are far from these peddlers of years past! We must see ourselves as professionals who assist buyers and sellers with their most significant asset — their home. Unfortunately, however, when we pick up the phone or knock on a door, we often feel the prospect will view us as just another charlatan trying to hawk a magic potion.

Boost your self-confidence. To be successful in residential real estate sales, you have to believe in two things: yourself and the services you will provide a buyer or seller. I always tell agents you have to sell yourself before you can sell your client. Fear usually kicks in when we believe we are going to fail even before we start. We won't be able to get off ground zero with a prospect if we are fearful and lack confidence.

Many people are predisposed to look at what can go wrong instead of what can go right. If rejection is the first thing you

> *Fear usually kicks in when we believe we are going to fail even before we start.*

think about when making a call, your attitude will reflect it. Your attitude is everything! Approach every call knowing you have what the prospect needs to sell or purchase their home. You possess the education, experience, and know-how to shepherd them through the transaction from beginning to end. You have successfully done it for others, and you can do it for them. You need to believe you can do it because you can!

Turn lemons into lemonade. One of my early sales managers gave me a suggestion that has helped me up to this day. He advised I ask myself, "What is the worst thing that can happen when a prospect says 'no'?" The answer is nothing. That's right — *nothing*! You will not be harmed when someone says "no" to you. They are not going to track you down and make your life miserable. They will just say "no."

That doesn't need to be the end of the conversation with them, though. Try to turn a "no" telephone call from a "lemon" to "lemonade." In other words, change the objective of the call from being unilateral — focused on them — to a bilateral one where they might be able to help you.

For example, if they say "no" to you, consider asking them if they know of someone who could use your services. They might have a friend, neighbor, or work colleague who is considering selling or buying a home. Explain to them the foundation of your business is built on referrals. You might get a referral from the person who just said "no" to you! Now, that's an awesome thought, isn't it?

Accept rejection as a normal prospecting element. Not everyone you approach about working with you as their agent is going to say "yes." More than likely, they are going to say "no." In fact, statistics show the majority of sales calls will end in rejection.

Professional salespeople are used to rejection. They know it is part of selling and are prepared for it when it happens. They also don't take rejection personally. Rejection as a statement on the agent as a person appears to be one of the biggest prospecting issues among agents today.

When a person says "no," it could have nothing to do with the agent but be caused by a bad experience with a previous agent, financial issues, bad timing, or the way they feel the day of the call. Top producers accept "no" and move on to the next person in their database or prospect group. They do not give up! It is part of doing business.

Know your value proposition and hone your selling abilities. Working on these areas will make you a more accomplished real estate sales professional, which will help you overcome the fear of rejection.

Overcoming fear can be challenging. Knowing what you are selling and how it can benefit the prospect is critical to boosting your self-confidence and keeping fear of rejection away.

Rejection, however, is inevitable. As long as you are able to accept it as a regular part of prospecting, you should be able to move forward and take the ones who say "yes" and turn them into clients for life. And, who knows, the person who said "no" might say "yes" at some point in the future!

CHAPTER 8

Where Art Thou Database?

"No business can succeed in any great degree without being properly organized."

— JAMES CASH PENNEY

Once you've chased down new leads, helped clients buy and sell a few homes, and built up your prospect pool, you need a way to store and use that information. I'm always surprised at the number of agents I speak with who say they do not have a structured system in place to keep up with those with whom they have done business in the past or might do business in the future.

One of the first questions I fire back to agents who come to me looking for advice on getting more business is, "How are you using your database of clients and prospects?" That's when I get a glazed-over look and sheepish expression, followed by an admission that they don't have a database — or at least an *organized* one.

And no — old, smudged legal pads with scribbled-out notes don't count.

To be successful in this business, you must have a database that is organized, categorized, and systematized containing the names of people who have the potential to do business with you or refer others to you who need your services. Management of your contacts is vital if you want to sustain your real estate business beyond the current selling season.

> **Keep notes from your conversations with clients and prospects in your database. It is almost impossible to remember specifics of what was said if it is not written down.**

CREATING A DATABASE

Developing a prospect and client database is not difficult. It requires some work on your part, as you will need to decide who should be in it and gather their necessary contact information, so you are able to stay in touch with them on a regular basis. The essential contact information for each prospect should include four pieces of information:

1. Name (and the name of their significant other)
2. Primary mailing address
3. Telephone number
4. Email address

Once you have their information, it will be time to develop a contact record for them. A contact record is like a file folder. The record is used to note each time you contact a prospect or client by phone, email, snail mail, or other means. You can also write notes about your conversation or meeting for later reference, if needed. It is almost impossible to remember specifics of what was said if it is not written down.

NO MORE EXCUSES!

When I speak to agents about why they don't have a database, I hear all types of excuses. To make it in this business, you must eliminate those excuses, change your mindset, and shift the self-talk.

1. I don't know that many people.	Change to	1. I know more people than I think.
2. I don't want to impose on my friends and family.	Change to	2. My friends and family are those who love, trust, and believe in me!
3. People know I am a real estate agent.	Change to	3. Not everyone knows I am a real estate agent.
4. I don't know how to build a contact database.	Change to	4. I am going to learn how to build my contact database.
5. I have no idea how and where I will find the information for that many people.	Change to	5. I will hunt down the information for all of my contacts!

DATABASE ORGANIZATION

First, you need to understand that an organized database and a mailing list are different. A mailing list includes names and addresses that usually are not qualified or defined beyond a geographic location or demographic group. A database is much more structured with detailed contact information and grouped by level of importance. Most databases usually have two to three groupings identifying them based on the probability of conversion from prospect to client.

How many groups within a database do you need? It depends on how you are going to use the data in your business. You may have one group of people you know through family, friends, work, church, community activities, etc. Another group may be people whom you don't know but consider potential future clients because of where they live (i.e., a farming area) or their inclusion in a certain demographic (i.e., first-time homebuyers, senior adults, etc.).

When I created my first database, I came up with two categories: Group A and Group B. Group A had the names of people I knew well and who I felt were most likely to contact me to sell or purchase a home. I also believed this group would be the most likely to refer me to their friends, family, and co-workers who needed to buy or purchase a home.

Group B included everyone else who were acquaintances, or I had met at one time or another in the past but didn't interact with on a regular basis. They may have been people I knew through our children's schools or sports leagues or people my wife and I associated with at church or other activities. I also included people in this group who were in my geographic farming areas.

As I grew my contact group, I also refined it. It grew to more than five hundred contacts, and I needed to define it better and remove names from Group A who should have been in Group B and vice versa. I whittled it down to about three hundred fifty names with about twenty of them marked as my "Gatekeepers." This last group was the ones who assisted me in significantly increasing my business.

THE GATEKEEPERS

Twenty or so individuals in my database were my "Gatekeepers." What is a Gatekeeper? A Gatekeeper is a person I identified who could play an active role in helping me grow my business. The Gatekeepers were most likely to refer business to me on a regular basis. They also were individuals I trusted to seek counsel on how to improve the operation of my business.

My Gatekeepers included my accountant, attorney, pastors, barber, dentist, doctors, banker, mortgage lenders, title attorneys, home inspectors, and a few other professionals. They all interacted with people who could be potential referrals for me. Also, I believed since I regularly did business with them they would consider me when someone had a real estate need. They usually received my referrals when someone I knew was in need of their services. This group was the one group of people who contributed the most to my sales numbers through the years.

WHO CAN REFER BUSINESS TO YOU?

Besides defining who your Gatekeepers are going to be, you need to create a list of people you know who could refer someone who may need your services. The following list contains people you might know who could become an excellent source of leads. I am sure you can think of others to add to it!

MY GATEKEEPERS AND REFERRAL PARTNERS

Attorneys

_____

Pest/insect control

_____

Financial advisor

_____

Accountant

_____

Insurance - auto/health/home

_____

Home repairs/improvement

_____

Handyman/carpenter

_____

Plumber/electrician/HVAC/painter

_____

Drywall contractor

_____

Tile person

_____

Roofer

_____

Window installation/cleaning

_____

Flooring installation/cleaning

_____

Landscape/exterior

_____

Landscape design/maintenance arborist/tree trimmer/gardener

_____

Cement/mason

_____

Foundation repair

_____

Deck installer/repair

_____

Fence installer/repair

_____

Pool installation/maintenance

_____

Sprinkler system installation

_____

Snow removal

_____

Garage door repair/installation

_____

Moving company

_____

Security systems

_____

Locksmith

_____

Housewarming/after-the-move housekeeper

_____

Florist

_____

Caterer

_____

Photographer

_____

Appliance repair/rental

_____

Furniture sales/rental

_____

Furniture cleaning/repair

_____

Drapery cleaning

_____

Window covering/cleaning

_____

SYSTEMATIZING YOUR DATABASE

To stay in touch with your contacts on a regular basis, you are going to have to implement a Customer Relationship Manager (CRM) program. A good CRM will remove much of the burden for you in trying to regularly "touch" everyone.

A CRM such as Top Producer, Wise Agent, and Contactually can automatically send out personalized pre-scheduled email drip campaigns, newsletters, market update reports, and more to your database. Most real estate CRM programs are internet-based and billed through a monthly or annual subscription. Costs vary depending on the amount of "add-on" features you include in your subscription. Also, most of the more notable CRMs have transaction and document management sections that can assist you with offer and contract paperwork and post-closing follow-up.

An organized and well thought-out database system will allow you to manage your contacts better, support your customer service, and enable you to be more focused on the people who can either use your services or send you qualified referrals. A real estate agent's business should have a database at the heart of their business operation. Prospects and clients fuel our business. Keep track of them, and it will pay off for you down the road.

CHAPTER 9

Building a Team for Your Business

"Many ideas grow better when transplanted into another mind than the one where they sprang up."

— OLIVER WENDELL HOLMES

Many in our business believe real estate teams are the future of the industry. Real estate teams have grown significantly over the past few years, and more are being formed every day. Teams offer agents the opportunity to be part of a group of real estate professionals who work together in helping buyers and sellers. The synergy a team can create is a result of a team leader who is well organized and motivated to see the team succeed.

Today's team model is one that has licensed and unlicensed members performing a myriad of tasks such as lead generation and follow-up, contract administration, marketing, client management, buyer representation, general administrative support, closing management, post-closing follow-up, etc. Many teams have similar organizational and business structures as a real estate brokerage. A team cannot survive without good leadership, effective systems and processes, and team members who are committed to the mission and vision of the team.

SHOULD I FORM A TEAM?

You should form a real estate team out of necessity and not because you think it will create additional revenue for you. If you're forming a team because you want to increase your production and income, you will probably fail. It is much more difficult to succeed with a team when you see dollar signs instead of focusing more strategically on your business. Many agents launch a team once their production level reaches between forty to fifty transactions annually.

A team model is much more complex than a single-agent model. It requires very specific goals and objectives on the number of transactions needed to generate income to keep the team afloat. Current and projected expenses need to be carefully quantified, so the team's profit and loss statement doesn't consistently show expenses outweighing income. The team leader should be able to track the average cost per transaction, the team's marketing expenses, the cost associated with each lead source, conversion ratios of leads from internet and print advertising, etc.

> *Only form a real estate team out of necessity and not because you think it will create additional revenue for you. If you're forming a team because you want to increase your production and income, you will probably fail.*

Your team should have its own business plan, which needs to include who is on your team and what their responsibilities should be as outlined in each position's written job description. Most large teams have a team leader who is considered the primary rainmaker. Others on the team may include a licensed or unlicensed assistant, a transaction coordinator who handles contract-to-close activities, an office manager, a buyer's agent, a listing coordinator, and a marketing coordinator who may also handle social media.

TEAMS VS. AGENT PARTNERSHIPS

Many agents call themselves a "team" if they have an assistant or they partner with another agent to assist with listings and buyers. That is not a team; it is an agent partnership. True teams are those where all the transactions are managed by the team as a whole and not by individual agents on the team. The team leader is usually the primary designated agent for a seller or buyer. Team structures are more like a brokerage model.

FORMING YOUR TEAM

Based on your business plan, you need to decide how many members will be on your team and what roles they will play.

Your first thought might be to hire a buyer's agent. This is probably not a good idea when launching your team. You need to have the right systems, processes, training, and administrative support in place for any licensee to become a team member. If you don't have the resources and support available for an additional agent, you will be working more hours handling administrative and transaction paperwork duties and soon become very frustrated as your transaction load increases.

HIRE A TRANSACTION COORDINATOR

The first person you should hire for your team is a contract-to-close person or transaction coordinator.

Most transaction coordinators are independent contractors and charge between $300 and $500 per transaction to handle the paperwork. They are familiar with the forms you use in your transactions, are very computer savvy, utilize digital document and signature systems, and are well versed in what residential real estate is all about. You may even be fortunate to find one who holds a real estate license.

Many agents who no longer want to sell or who have decreased production become good transaction coordinators. They know what they are doing.

HIRE AN ADMINISTRATIVE ASSISTANT

Next, consider hiring someone who can serve as your administrative assistant. (See Chapter 10 for a detailed explanation of hiring an administrative assistant.) One of the reasons you start a team is to get the paperwork and other administrative responsibilities off your desk. A good admin person can take on these duties. However, you must be willing to delegate and give up control of the day-to-day office work. You need to be building your business by being out securing new listings, showing houses, and interacting with prospects and clients.

You will need to write a detailed job description for this position, so they clearly understand their responsibilities and their role on your team. A job description can also assist you in what activities and responsibilities you need to assign to someone else. Whether the position is full-time or part-time will depend on your current sales production and what you expect to sell in the months ahead.

Make sure you hire the right person to be your assistant. My best advice? Don't employ someone like you in this role. If you do, you will end up right back where you started — disorganized and frustrated.

Find someone who is a self-starter, willing to take direction, works well with people, highly organized, detail-oriented, and computer literate — especially in Microsoft Office products. Your admin person should be able to "pick up the ball and run with it" when you need them to.

If you find someone who has these qualifications, offer them competitive pay with increases based on production. Remember, there's truth to "you get what you pay for."

HIRE OTHER AGENTS

Once you have a transaction coordinator and administrative assistant in place, you can begin considering adding other agents to your team.

Whom should you hire? It depends on your goals and what selling role *you* will play on the team.

Will you be more of a "general" who oversees "the troops," or will you be out in the trenches selling? If you want to continue to sell full-time, should you focus more on sellers or buyers?

If you are concentrating more on procuring listings than buyers, you might want to hire a seller's agent. If you want your team working with buyers through internet leads or within your sphere of influence, then you should hire a buyer's agent to assist you. As your business grows, you may decide more buyer's agents would make more sense if you are working buyer leads on a daily basis.

As your production increases and you add agents to your team, your role will evolve to more of a mentor or manager for the team. You will always be the "face" of the team, but you will need to define your personal interaction with clients from the initial lead all the way to the closing table.

I know of team leaders who are the first to meet with a client and then introduce them to other agents on the team who will be working with them on a daily basis. Some clients don't like this because they thought they were going to have the team leader with them every step of the way in the transaction, only to find out another agent would be their primary agent.

Everyone should be involved at all times in one way or another, so the client feels the entire team is working for them. Many successful teams operate this way.

SCREENING POTENTIAL TEAM MEMBERS

- Prior to hiring any team member, have them complete a DiSC profile. A DiSC profile is a tool used for assessing a person's behavioral differences. The participant will be asked to complete a series of questions that produce a detailed report about their personality and behavior. (For more information on DiSC, visit www.discprofile.com.)
- They should also complete a criminal background check and drug screening. You need to know if there is any issue that may impact the team and their individual performance.
- Ask an impartial third party to interview them. Consider asking your principal broker to meet with them. The broker will know the right questions to ask and will provide you with honest feedback.
- Try to interview more than one candidate for the position. Interviewing at least two or three individuals will allow you to compare strengths and weaknesses of each one so you can make a more objective hiring decision.

COMPENSATING YOUR TEAM MEMBERS

Whomever you hire, make sure they clearly understand their role on the team, your expectations, and how they can professionally grow under your leadership.

You'll need to decide on specifics and clearly communicate them, such as: Do you want them to work out of your office or at home? How many open houses should they host? Are they expected to attend your brokerage's sales meetings? The most effective way to ensure everyone is clear on expectations is by putting everything down on paper. You need to have a signed agreement between you and them that outlines their duties, responsibilities, and compensation.

Their compensation will be based on the business they bring to the team on their own as well as the leads they convert from prospects to clients utilizing your lead generation system. Be fair, but remember you are the one who is giving them a chance to sell and work regularly with clients. Many team agents are paid on a 50/50 commission split. I have also seen commission splits at

60/40 (team leader keeps 40 percent). Factor in what you are giving them for support and education as well as the amount of time you are personally spending with them to make them a better agent. There is a cost to the services and benefits you will provide them. (Note: Check with other teams in your office or REALTOR® association to determine what other team leaders are paying members of their teams.)

IMPORTANT TEAM MEMBER CLASSIFICATION CONSIDERATIONS

- Develop a competitive compensation structure for both independent contractors and employees on your team.
- Follow IRS guidelines for independent contractors. Be careful how you treat agents who are independent contractors. If you require them to do the following, they may be considered an employee (compensation reported via IRS Form W-2):
  - work specific hours during the day;
  - require them to attend team meetings at certain times;
  - follow your directions on how they perform their job including requiring them to use your software or follow specific procedures;
  - or require them to work open houses, prospect, or complete any tasks you assign them.

If team members are employees, you will need to do the following:
  - You will be required to withhold federal and state income tax, any state or local business or franchise and excise taxes, Social Security and Medicare taxes. (You will need to file all of this information with the IRS per their filing guidelines for employers.)
  - provide them office space or a designated work area
  - pay for worker compensation
  - possibly provide liability or errors and omissions insurance, if applicable
  - provide health insurance, if applicable

Team members who are independent contractors (compensation reported via IRS Form 1099) are not employees; therefore, you are not obligated to provide them with office space, insurance, or any other benefits.

ONCE THE TEAM IS FORMED

Creating a successful team can be challenging. Teams are not for everyone. However, if you develop a realistic business plan with realistic and attainable goals, you can do it. You need to hire the right people, compensate them fairly, and develop them as they grow with your team.

Once your team is formed, you should:

- Hold regular meetings with the team in order to make them feel connected as well as informed on any matters you would like to discuss with them as a group.
- Have some fun time! Take team members out to lunch or dinner individually or as a group.
- Consider providing a year-end bonus to team members if you experience a profitable year.

If team members aren't "making the grade," you need to be willing to let them go and find a qualified replacement. Stay focused and you can have a high-performing team that will allow you to convert more prospects to clients, close more deals, and make more money.

CHAPTER 10

When It Is Time to Hire an Assistant

"Sometimes, asking for help is the most meaningful example of self-reliance."

As a productive real estate agent, you probably spend between ten to twelve hours each day working on and in your business. If you are at a point where you feel your real estate business might not be growing the way it should because your daily tasks are overwhelming you, then it might be time to consider hiring an assistant.

To keep your business moving forward, you need to determine what administrative duties you could delegate to someone else. By doing so, you will have more time to focus on the revenue generating segment of your business, which includes prospecting, interacting with clients and leads, and closing your transactions. Also, an assistant can free up your schedule so you can have more personal and family time.

A good and reliable assistant can handle many tasks for you and your clients. Some of their responsibilities can include posting to your social media sites, assisting in preparing buyer and listing presentations, managing your marketing efforts, and handling your transaction paperwork. If they hold a real estate license, they can do even more for you. Licensed assistants can manage incoming leads, show property for you, host open houses, and complete transaction paperwork.

SHOULD YOU HIRE AN ASSISTANT?

How do you know if it's time to hire an assistant? I recommend you consider hiring an assistant (preferably one who is licensed) when you are closing between two to four deals each month or at least twenty-five consistently over a twelve-month period. Another clue that you need assistance is that you are becomingly increasingly more frustrated and exhausted by trying to keep everything organized and getting your work completed and on time. This type of stress and anxiety can impact how you come across to your clients, peers, and family.

One late afternoon, I walked by the office of one of my top agents, Alex, and noticed he was holding his head in his hands.

"It looks like you're having a tough day," I said.

He said, "Yes, and I am up to my ears in paperwork!"

After we spoke for a few minutes, I encouraged him to consider getting someone to assist him with paperwork and organizing his contract-to-close process. He took me up on my advice and a couple of weeks later had a part-time assistant helping him with listing and contract paperwork. Alex's stress level was reduced, and he seemed so much happier to turn the paperwork duties over to someone else.

If you are unsure if you need an assistant, begin tracking all of your daily activities for the next month. You may be surprised at the amount of work you are currently doing. From the list you create, you should be able to determine what activities an assistant could oversee. These activities should be incorporated into the assistant's job description. Another benefit of this exercise is seeing what in your business you might be able to streamline or eliminate.

PREPARING TO HIRE AN ASSISTANT

Before hiring an assistant, make sure your real estate business is in order. Review the following to determine if the time is right to bring an assistant on board:

- You must know the financial situation of your business concerning its profit and loss. Can your business plan and budget support another person right now? If it can, you need to establish the salary or hourly rate you will pay the assistant. If you are not sure what the compensation should be, ask other agents in your firm who employ assistants.

- Create a written job description outlining the duties and re-sponsibilities of the assistant. Without a detailed job description, you will not effectively assimilate an assistant into your business and ensure he or she is doing what you need for them to do each day.
- Be willing to delegate some of your daily duties and respon-sibilities to someone else. This can be difficult for someone who likes to be in control — especially Type-A personalities. If you cannot let go of some of the work you are doing now, it might not be the right time for you to hire someone.
- Set aside time in your schedule each day during the first month or two to train an assistant. You cannot "throw them in the deep end and expect them to swim." You will need to plan an organized training schedule, so you know what to cover with them each day. A properly trained assistant makes for a happy and long-term employee!
- Your lead generation and customer relationship management systems should be in place, so you can quickly explain how it works and transfer the responsibility over to your assistant.
- You must be proficient in all the forms and documents you use in your business. This includes listing and sales contract paper-work and brokerage forms. You need to be able to explain all the forms you use in your transactions and why they are used.
- Be aware of what an unlicensed assistant can and cannot do. Most state real estate commissions have a specific list of the "dos and don'ts" for an assistant who does not hold a real estate license. I suggest you hire an assistant who is already licensed or someone who will be licensed soon after they begin working for you.
- You must be willing to terminate the assistant if they do not work out. Firing employees has been the hardest thing I've done as a manager. Don't let someone stay on board if they are not doing what you need them to do for you. Send them on their way and find a replacement.

The decision to hire or not hire an assistant is up to you. How-ever, as you work with more prospects and clients and close more transactions, you will discover you cannot get to everything you need to accomplish during the day. An assistant can be the best thing you can do for your business so that you can take it to the next level.

CHAPTER 11

Manage Your Money So You Don't Go Broke

"A slack hand causes poverty, but the hand of the diligent makes rich."

PROVERBS 10:4

Remember when you had a full-time job with a consistent paycheck and benefits? Oh yes, those were the days! Well, those days are over. You are now your own boss, and your family is dependent on *you* to feed, clothe, and shelter them. Knowing what you need to earn and how you are going to pay the bills is critical to your survival as an agent.

Selling real estate can be either "feast" or "famine." Depending on the market and other conditions, our wallets are full of money, or they are full of dust. Finding the middle ground of sustainability is hard for most agents. Real estate agents are notorious for not properly handling their finances. Successful agents know how to manage their income and control their expenses. Sound financial management is not that difficult if you have a budget and stick to it.

Before I received my real estate license, I knew I needed money to survive the first six months in the business and a budget to manage my income and expenses. I quickly learned a budget for my business was a critical component of my business plan. Budgeting supported my need to remain focused and on track as I was selling real estate.

I include budget worksheets at the end of this chapter if you need a template to help you create your own budget.

TIPS FOR REAL ESTATE AGENT BUDGETING

In order to properly manage your business finances, you must oversee your personal expenses. The following tips can assist you in preparing your personal and business budgets.

Reduce your debt. You need to develop a debt-reduction plan as soon as possible. Debt is what stands in the way of us having money we can spend on the things we need and want. You should develop a plan that will reduce your debt over a specific period of time.

Outside of your mortgage, where is your debt? Automobile and student loans, medical and hospital bills, as well as other consumer debt such as credit cards and revolving charge accounts make up a large amount of most families' debt service.

What debt do you pay off first? I encourage you to pay off your highest-rate debt first. For example, paying $500 toward a $2,500 credit card bill with an interest rate of 19 percent will save you much more than paying off a $750 bill at 5 percent. Another option is debt consolidation. You might consider taking out a home equity line of credit (HELOC) or a second mortgage on your property to reduce your debt. Interest rates for these loan products are much lower than what is charged by the major credit card companies.

Build up your personal reserves. At any given time, you should have at least six months of cash reserves set aside in the event your sales drop due to a downturn in the economy.

Build up your personal reserves. At any given time, you should have at least six months of cash reserves set aside in the event your sales drop due to a downturn in the economy. This money can assist you in paying your bills and providing food and other needs for your family.

Set aside a business reserve. Like personal cash reserves, you need a reserve for your business. You never know when a computer might break down or a laser printer needs to be replaced. It makes good business sense having the money on hand and not using a high-interest credit card to pay the expense.

Ask your bank or credit union for a line of credit for your business. If your personal credit is good to excellent, you will probably qualify for a small business line of credit. As you grow your business, you may need to make investments in equipment, office space, and team members. A business line of credit also provides you with a cushion, so you are not feeling additional pressure between commission checks. These credit lines may be secured or unsecured. Unsecured lines of credit will allow you to draw money, but they will have a smaller cash limit than secured lines. If the credit line is secured, you will need to be able to provide the necessary collateral for the line to be approved by your bank.

Divide your commission check so you can pay taxes and business expenses. When I receive a commission check from the sale of a home, I do not deposit the entire amount in my checking account. I always put approximately 30 percent aside to pay my quarterly estimated federal income taxes and 15 percent back in to my business. The remaining 55 percent goes to cover my personal expenses.

Never deposit money in only one account, as you are more likely to spend it on personal necessities and not for expenses that will occur in your real estate practice. I have two accounts at my bank that I deposit commission monies. The first one is my business checking account to cover taxes and business expenses, and the other one is my personal checking account that I use for expenses outside of my business.

Use your money to provide you with the best return on investment. Selling real estate is an expensive proposition. You need to make smart decisions when spending money on your business. Most agents do not know what lead system or marketing tool will work for their business, so they overspend trying to find that "one thing" that will make their business successful. An agent must use some discernment when it comes to spending money. Ask high-producing agents what and where they are spending their money. They can provide you with some invaluable advice on what to do and what not to do when it comes to operating your business.

Sometimes the lowest price does not provide the best return on your investment. Don't purchase the cheapest laptop at the local discount warehouse store because you probably will need to replace it after a couple of years. It will be worth spending more for a computer that can meet your needs for several years. Also consider the "little things" you spend your money on such as printer paper, signage, photography, cell phone, customer relationship systems, closing gifts, etc. Make smart decisions that will help lower the long-term costs of your business. Remember, "You get what you pay for."

Set aside money for continuing education. I believe an agent can grow their business by choosing the right "tools" for their "toolbox." A large number of tools involve knowledge. As a real estate instructor and a continuing education course curriculum author, I am a big proponent of professional development for agents. When we learn new skills, techniques, and ideas, it not only benefits our clients, but it also contributes to the bottom line. The more you know, the more you can make.

For example, those who take classes on making effective listing presentations will be better positioned to procure more listings than someone who doesn't. An agent who is knowledgeable on how to sell real estate in the midst of a couple getting a divorce will be more likely to catch the eye of divorce attorneys and accounting firms.

Getting a National Association of REALTORS® designation or certification may or may not put more money in your pocket, but it will provide you with the latest information on how to best work with buyers and sellers in today's competitive real estate market. People like to work with professionals who know what they are doing.

Invest in your education, training, and professional development.

MONEY MANAGEMENT TIPS

I suggest you find some creative ways to cut spending, so you can keep money in your pocket. Don't go out and buy the latest luxury SUV unless you have plenty of money to pay for it. High automobile loan or lease payments can drain you of money you need to pay other expenses. Consider washing your own car instead of going to the local car wash. Cut out the local dry cleaner and iron your own shirts. Eat in more than you eat out. It is amazing how much money you can save when you consider reigning in the "little" expenses.

Also, there are numerous discount programs available for REALTORS®. Go to the National Association of REALTORS® website and take advantage of the REALTOR® Benefits Program. NAR has developed unique discounts and offers from a wide array of companies. Discounts are available on technology, cell phones, transaction management, travel, education, and marketing companies, to name a few. In addition, check with your local REALTOR® association to see which local businesses have discounts available for real estate professionals.

Where is your money going? How much are you spending in certain areas of your budget? Can you make any changes? You need to ask these questions and track your expenses so that you know where every penny you earn is being spent. Consider cutting back in some areas if you do not see the results you want. Good business people always stay on top of their expenses.

In the fall of each year, begin the budgeting process for both your business and personal expenses. If you want to make $100,000 next year based on what you think you will need to live on, then you need to develop an income plan to achieve your goal.

MY 12-MONTH REAL ESTATE BUSINESS BUDGET

INCOME

Sales commissions	_____	Rental fees	_____
Referral fees	_____	Broker price opinion fees	_____

EXPENSES

Auto Expenses

Auto monthly payments	_____	Wash and detailing	_____
Insurance	_____	Parking	_____
Gas	_____	Emission testing and license renewal	_____
Maintenance	_____		

Office Expenses

Monthly brokerage fee	_____	Printing	_____
Internet service provider	_____	Advertising (online and print)	_____
Internet hosting for personal website	_____	Office rental (per IRS guidelines)	_____
Computer/computer supplies	_____	Office equipment	_____
Dues and subscriptions	_____	Depreciation on office equipment	_____
Continuing education	_____	Broadcast email provider	_____
Entertainment — meals	_____	Customer relationship program	_____
Closing gifts	_____	Online subscriptions	_____
Office supplies	_____	E and O insurance (renewal)	_____
Postage and freight (USPS, FedEx, UPS)	_____	Legal expenses	_____
Telephone (office and fax)	_____	Mobile internet connectivity	_____
Telephone (cellular)	_____		
Professional fees	_____		
Marketing materials	_____		

Travel Expenses (REALTOR® conferences, events, and continuing education)

Airfare	_____	Misc. travel expenses	_____
Rental auto	_____	Meals in travel	_____
Hotel charges	_____	Airport parking	_____

MY 12-MONTH PERSONAL HOUSEHOLD BUDGET

Giving

Tithing   _____

Offerings   _____

Charities   _____

Specific needs — consider
creating a giving fund   _____

Food

Groceries   _____

—Restaurants   _____

—Pet food/treats   _____

Property Expenses

Mortgage   _____

Rent   _____

Property taxes   _____

Household repairs   _____

Homeowners
Association dues   _____

Utilities

Electricity   _____

Water   _____

Gas/heating   _____

Trash disposal   _____

Telephone   _____

Cable TV   _____

Internet service   _____

Clothing

Children's clothing   _____

Adult's clothing   _____

Transportation

Fuel   _____

Tires   _____

Oil changes   _____

Maintenance   _____

Parking fees   _____

Repairs   _____

DMV fees   _____

Vehicle replacement   _____

Medical

Primary care   _____

Dental care   _____

Specialty care —
orthodontist, eye doctor,
chiropractor, etc.   _____

Prescription medications   _____

Medical devices   _____

Insurance

Health insurance   _____

Homeowners insurance   _____

Renters insurance   _____

Auto insurance   _____

Life insurance   _____

Disability insurance   _____

Identity theft protection   _____

Long-term care insurance   _____

Household Items/Supplies

Toiletries   _____

Laundry detergent   _____

Dishwasher detergent   _____

Cleaning supplies   _____

Tools   _____

MY 12-MONTH PERSONAL HOUSEHOLD BUDGET (continued)

Personal

Gym memberships   _____

Hair cuts   _____

Salon services   _____

Cosmetics   _____

Babysitter   _____

Child support   _____

Alimony   _____

Subscriptions   _____

Debt Reduction

Mortgage   _____

Credit card   _____

Personal loan   _____

Student loan   _____

Retirement

Financial planning   _____

Investing   _____

Education

Private school (elementary and secondary)   _____

Children's college   _____

Your college   _____

School supplies   _____

Books   _____

Conferences   _____

Savings

Emergency fund   _____

"Peaks and Valleys" fund — for people with variable incomes   _____

Other savings   _____

Gifts

Birthday   _____

Anniversary   _____

Wedding   _____

Christmas   _____

Special occasion   _____

Fun money   _____

Entertainment

Games   _____

Dining out   _____

Spontaneous giving   _____

Vacations   _____

Subscriptions (Netflix, Hulu, etc.)   _____

CHAPTER 12

Stepping Outside Your Expertise: Commercial Real Estate and Property Management

"You've got to be very careful if you don't know where you are going, because you might not get there."

There's something especially attractive about property management and commercial real estate to residential agents. Over the years, I've fielded all sorts of questions about opportunities to lease a warehouse, office, or shopping center. At other times, agents would ask about managing single-family and multi-family properties. In both scenarios, when I asked if they had any experience working in the respective areas of real estate, almost every time the answer was "no." Stepping outside of your real estate discipline to practice on the commercial or property management side of what we do can be rewarding, but also full of several challenges.

Commercial real estate is so much different than residential due to varying pricing structures, complex legal documentation, letters of intent, etc. Property management requires an agent to be skilled in creating management agreements, leasing documents, maintenance plans, vendor selection, etc. It is challenging to use your residential real estate skills and apply them to the commercial or property management side of the real estate industry.

COMMERCIAL REAL ESTATE

In most states, a real estate license allows an agent to practice in multiple disciplines within the real estate industry. Before jumping into a commercial real estate opportunity, however, a residential agent needs to be aware of the following:

1. Are you well versed in all that is involved in selling and leasing commercial real estate? Do you understand the various types of commercial real estate, especially leasing commercial properties?

2. Have you ever leased or sold a commercial property? If so, what type was it, and what issues did you face in the transaction?

3. Do you have the correct documents and forms to use in a commercial real estate transaction? In residential real estate, on most occasions, we use a Purchase and Sale Agreement that creates a contract. In the commercial world, Letters of Intent are used to initiate the sale or lease of commercial property. Also, attorneys who are experienced in working with commercial transactions usually draw up the contracts.

4. Do you understand commercial leases? Are you in tune with the current lease pricing in the local market? Residential leases are pretty straightforward in the way they are quantified — with a tenant depositing a monthly lease amount. Commercial leases are quoted on either a net or gross price. Some leases may be quoted on a per square foot basis. Do you know what net, double-net, and triple-net leases mean? What about a bondable lease or a ground lease? Commercial agents understand the pricing structure of commercial real estate leases.

5. Are you aware commercial transactions take much longer than residential transactions? Can you be willing to wait an extended period of time before you get paid?

If you want to try your hand at commercial real estate, consider partnering with an experienced commercial agent. A seasoned commercial agent can mentor a residential agent and help them learn the ins and outs of the commercial side of real estate. They also can recommend continuing education courses that can assist the agent in understanding the complexities of the commercial world.

Most commercial agents have their Certified Commercial Investment Member (CCIM) designation from the CCIM Institute. The CCIM designation requires experience and knowledge in the commercial real estate industry. There are local chapters of CCIM members where commercial agents can network with one another and learn about opportunities to grow their businesses. For more information go to www.ccim.com.

PROPERTY MANAGEMENT

Before providing property management services, you must be aware of what lies ahead for you. Property management is considerably different from residential real estate transactions. Overseeing properties on a regular basis requires a great deal of time and effort.

A couple of questions you must ask yourself before entering property management includes: Is this something I want to do on a part-time or full-time basis? Is the return on investment worth my time, energy, and financial resources? Maybe yes, maybe no. It depends on you and the goals you established for this component of your business.

Many times, the owner of the property is relying on you, the property manager, to ensure his investment is protected, costs are kept within budget, the tenants are paying their bills, and maintenance items are resolved quickly, etc. You will need systems in place to track income and expenses for each property.

Before adding property management to your business mix and revenue stream, you must first consult your principal broker, and you must be aware of any state landlord and tenant regulations you and your property owner will need to follow. Some of these laws are complex and can impact how you manage rental property.

Also, taking several courses and seminars on property management should be a top priority if you plan on becoming a property manager. Classes are offered through real estate schools, local REALTOR® associations, or professional associations such as The Institute of Real Estate Management, an affiliate of the National Association of REALTORS®. More information is available at www.irem.org.

You should also consult with your Errors and Omissions insurance provider to make sure you have the proper insurance coverage for property management or whether an additional rider will be required.

A CONSIDERATION

Before you venture into areas outside of your expertise, be aware that you could be without legal coverage should a commercial client sue you, or a regulatory complaint is filed against you. Your errors and omissions insurance carrier may reject your request for legal assistance and insurance coverage to defend you in the courtroom or at your state's real estate commission hearing. Why? They may not cover the claim because you were working outside of your licensing expertise and did not have the knowledge or experience to manage the transaction and the client in the way an experienced commercial agent or property manager does on an ongoing basis.

If you venture into these two areas, you should consider finding a qualified commercial real estate agent or property manager and ask for a referral fee. If you have your mind set to handle a commercial transaction or manage a property, partner with an agent who will be willing to mentor you through each step of the process. This is one way you can move toward success in these other areas of the real estate industry.

CHAPTER 13

Let's Keep It Civil: Managing Your Social Media Posts

"A fool takes no pleasure in understanding,
but only in expressing his opinion."

– PROVERBS 18:2

Since the creation of Facebook in 2004 and Twitter in 2006, social media has grown exponentially with millions of people posting stories, pictures, videos, advertisements, and other media online. For most of us, checking our social media accounts is part of the daily routine, and the use of social media platforms continues to grow.

Social media plays a big role in real estate agents' marketing and advertising efforts. It has become a primary advertising tool for listings, as well as for promoting an agent's business. Social media sites such as Facebook and Twitter offer private pages for agents to post about issues they are facing in the local real estate market, as well as request recommendations for home inspectors, structural engineers, handymen, and other service providers. Social media has replaced the water cooler, picture album, and office bulletin boards of years past.

I scroll through my social media accounts every day. I try not to spend too much time on them as I discovered early on they are "time suckers" taking me away from more meaningful and productive activities. I participate in social media sites used for personal and family postings and several professional sites used to acquire and disseminate information from other real estate professionals and industry leaders. Sometimes I find the viewing enjoyable and entertaining and other times troubling.

There is no question that all aspects of social media are part of our everyday lives — so much so that people's daily routines and experiences are being played out on social media sites like never before. This is all well and good, but some degree of caution should be exercised before we put something out there for all to see.

Some of the threads I regularly see on these sites are from a wide variety of people, including close friends, acquaintances, and fellow agents, as well as complete strangers. Many of the comments contain strong opinions on social, political, and ideological issues that may be viewed by some as inappropriate and insulting and may possibly harm long-standing relationships. On a regular basis, I read threads full of arguments and heated discussions that go on and on with insults and insinuations that genuinely "cross the line." Some of these come from my fellow real estate agents.

As a real estate professional, keep your social media posts neutral and non-controversial. Always assume your clients and fellow agents are reading your posts and viewing your videos.

You need to keep in mind that your personal posts can be seen by many people, including your current and past clients, prospects, and friends who might refer future business to you. If one of your posts appears to be on a controversial subject with a disagreeing or differing point of view from your client, it could easily backfire and cause damage to your relationship with the client and possibly do damage to your business.

Also, there are others out in cyberspace reading your posts or viewing your videos. Poor judgment may also hinder your real estate career. As a managing broker, I review social media accounts before and after hiring agents. I have great concern when I see something that is incongruent with the values of our company. If a current agent is posting inappropriately, I will have a serious discussion with them and, at times, take corrective action or release their real estate license from the firm. And, I am not alone. Almost all employers in every industry now review social media before deciding to hire an employee.

I know we all have opinions and want to share those opinions with others. However, remember who is looking at your posts. Our businesses depend on getting referrals from those we know — and many of these folks are on social media. Once it is out there, it's out there. Yes, you can take your post down, but remember anyone can take a screenshot of what you posted. The old saying, "closing the stable door after the horse has bolted," applies here.

As a real estate professional, keep your posts neutral and non-controversial. Always assume your clients and fellow agents are reading your posts and viewing your videos. If you create a fire on social media with opinions and conversations that are contentious, you might find yourself trying to fix the damage that could be irreparable.

SECTION **TWO**

Client Management

CHAPTER 14

Which Client is Behind Door Number One?

"I love mankind ... it's people I can't stand!!"

— CHARLES M. SCHULZ

I joked with one of my office managers that if it weren't for the people and paperwork, I probably would like my job. Of course, I was kidding. I do like my job! But there are days when clients can drive you over the edge.

It might be the phone call from a client shouting on the other end because an agent just showed their house to a buyer but forgot to close the back door, allowing the owner's cat to escape. Or, maybe your patience has worn thin with the client who can't make up their mind about making an offer on a property because they lack the confidence needed to move forward. What about the seller client who obnoxiously tells you exactly what to do to get their home sold?

Client behaviors and the issues they can cause for agents, brokers, and others in a real estate transaction are becoming more significant and challenging to manage. For agents and their brokers, it is essential to know the personality of clients and prospects. You must know with whom you are dealing and how to interact and communicate with them correctly, so your relationship is not negatively impacted because of something you say or do. Numerous types of personalities become our clients. They often require us to become chameleons, so we can effectively work with them and see them through to the end of the transaction.

SIX TYPES OF CHALLENGING CLIENTS

Several years ago, I wrote a course called Managing Transaction Behavior. I wanted to provide a class for agents to take so they could better understand client behavior and how to work with individuals who are difficult and problematic. In developing the course, I identified six types of challenging clients an agent may face in their business. The six categories have personality traits ranging from quiet and reserved to loud and explosive. At some point in your real estate career, you will more than likely have to work with one or more of these client personality groups.

The following is a brief overview of each personality type and ideas on how you can best work with them.

	Primary Character Traits	Defining Phrase	How to Work with This Client
Nick Know-It-All	Egotistical, dominates conversations	"I know more than you do about everything."	Take a curious attitude and ask a lot of questions.
Yolanda Yes, Of Course	People-pleaser, slow decision maker	"That's fine with me."	Provide a safe environment for sharing information.
Ned No Way	Discouraging, pessimistic, dismissive	"I don't like it."	Use the pen and paper approach to focus on the positives.
Nancy Nothing	Quiet, no feedback	"I don't know."	Offer statements to force an answer.
Paul Pit Bully	Pushy, ruthless, loud, rants	"Did you hear me? I demand ..."	Give sixty seconds to vent, then interrupt and repeat three statements you heard.
Thelma Thermo-Nuclear	Angry, explosive, possibly mentally or emotionally unstable	"$%@*#!!!" (insert expletives)	Don't offer any time to vent; interrupt and reassure you will work it out.

1. NICK KNOW-IT-ALL

He knows everything. At least, he thinks he does.

This type of client will come across as knowing everything about anything and will be the dominant voice in any conversation.

HOW TO WORK WITH THIS CLIENT GROUP:

- You can provide the Nicks with your expert counsel and professional experience, but they will always want you to know they know more than you do. These clients' know-it-all attitudes bring their egos front and center.
- Ask a lot of questions about what they say and how they say it. The key words are "a lot" because you will find they will quickly "hit bottom" as they will have nothing else to throw at you. They do not have the depth of knowledge you possess as a real estate professional.
- Take a "curious attitude" and ask more specific questions until they start making big generalizations. Eventually, they will realize they don't know as much as they thought they did.

USE CAUTION WITH THIS GROUP:

Be careful in how you handle the "know-it-all" client. You must be careful not to step on their ego. Their ego is enormous, and if they feel you are trying to deflate it, they will quickly turn away from you. You want to derail bad ideas, but you do not want to embarrass them.

2. YOLANDA YES, OF COURSE

Highly agreeable but slow to deliver.

Yolandas tend to be highly agreeable to everything, but slow to make up their minds on a decision that they must make. They have a people-pleasing tendency that may hinder their ability to provide you with honest, valuable feedback to move forward in a transaction.

HOW TO WORK WITH THIS CLIENT GROUP:

- To handle this group the right way, make it safe for them to be honest with you. They need to feel they can trust you.
- There will be no relationship consequence if they say something contradictory to you or about something or someone.

It will be important you provide a safe environment for them, so they perceive you as being sensitive. For example, you might want to say to them, "If the houses we look at this afternoon are not a good fit for you, Mr. or Ms. Jones, it is OK to tell me."

3. NED NO WAY

He'll probably find something wrong with every property you show him!

Talk about glass-half-empty types! The Neds always tend to be discouraging and pessimistic. As buyers, they will probably not be happy with any home you present to them. As sellers, they may dismiss any idea you give to them to market their house.

HOW TO WORK WITH THIS CLIENT GROUP:
- You need to break them out of their negativity. They will always lean to the negative side of things. Try to steer them toward the positive.
- I have found the best way to work with them is to use what I call the "pen and paper approach." To get them to make a smart decision, use a pen and paper and list the positives and negatives of whatever subject you are addressing at the time. They may be contemplating a home they are thinking about purchasing or a specific marketing plan you are presenting to them to get a buyer to make an offer on their house. Always begin with the negative points first when creating the list. Then, refocus their attention on the positives so they will be better able to make a decision that is more objective.

4. NANCY NOTHING

She tells you nothing and provides no feedback, verbal or non-verbal.

Nancys will stay quiet, and they will drive you crazy with their silence. Their first response to any question you ask them is often "I don't know." At times, you will feel like you need a crowbar to get anything out of them. If you are a conversational person, you may become frustrated with this group.

HOW TO WORK WITH THIS CLIENT GROUP:
- Try to determine how they feel about a particular situation and offer statements to force an answer out of them.

- Also, like the Neds, use the pen and paper approach with the Nancys. You will likely need to guess the "pluses and minuses" on the lists you create rather than relying on them to tell you. For example, you might want to say to them, "This home has the open floor plan with the kitchen and living room. I'm guessing that's a positive for you, right?"

5. PAUL PIT BULLY

Paul is pushy, ruthless, and loud. He rants when he is upset.

I decided to name the Pauls Pit Bullies because their characteristics are similar to a pit bull dog. Pit bulls are loud barkers, and they never stop making noise when they are upset or want something. These clients are always going to be pushy, ruthless, and loud.

HOW TO WORK WITH THIS CLIENT GROUP:

- They will go off on a rant when something upsets them.
- They demand immediate action. They will be impatient waiting for you to give them an answer. If they call you on the phone and leave you a voicemail, I am confident their message will have an upsetting tone because you were not available to take their call.
- I would encourage you to give them sixty seconds to vent — no more, no less. After the sixty-second tirade, interrupt your client and highlight some of their points to show you were listening and reassure them that you're on the same side. For example, "Mr. Smith, we both care about getting the most for your property. I heard you say ...." Then, repeat three of the statements you heard. Why three? Because after three statements they will feel you are hearing what they are saying.

6. THELMA THERMO-NUCLEAR

You feel like you should go underground for shelter!

Thelmas are the most difficult of the six client groups. Like a nuclear explosion, all "you-know-what" breaks loose! You will want to find shelter immediately. They have unprovoked rages that seem disproportionate to the issue at hand. Their rants can be about anything, anyone, or everything.

HOW TO WORK WITH THIS CLIENT GROUP:
- You cannot give Thelmas any time to vent. They will feed on negative energy, and it will only provide them with more fuel to make them angrier.
- You will need to immediately raise your voice to interrupt them, using their name. For example, "Mrs. Baker, I care. You don't have to feel this way. We're going to work this out."

Don't tell them to calm down, as you will only make them more furious. Instead, you should step back and take a deep breath, then interrupt them, so it breaks their venting. Continue the conversation in your normal tone and use a statement like, "Let's take a moment and talk about it."

USE CAUTION WITH THIS GROUP:
It is rare, but sometimes a client will become abusive. A Thelma could be mentally or emotionally unstable and may place you at either professional or personal risk. Please consult your broker if you feel physically threatened or abused in any way. Contact 911 immediately if you fear imminent danger.

TIPS TO USE WITH EVERY CLIENT GROUP

With all six of these groups you must listen to determine their needs, wants, and concerns. It also might take some creative solutions to make them happy and get them to a decision or other significant point in their real estate transaction. With all of them, you should:
- Listen to them. Listening should be your biggest priority in any conversation with them.
- Find out what are their concerns, fears, hopes, etc.
- Give them the opportunity to express their emotions.
- Educate them on the market and the current market conditions by sharing specific information on houses that are active, pending, and closed.
- Ensure they clearly understand the real estate transaction process — from initial offer to the closing.
- Remember that you are a professional, and you know what you are doing. Your clients rely on you for your expertise.
- Develop a creative solution to address an issue with your client.
- Ask for assistance from others who are experts in a particular area or skill.

- Not be afraid to try something different to get the result you and your client want.
- Be empathetic to their needs. Try to put yourself in their shoes.
- Try to relate to a client and set your preferences aside.

Being armed with the knowledge of the different types of clients will equip you to serve them well. Understanding how best to navigate obstacles to better communicate with the Nicks, Yolandas, Neds, Nancys, Pauls, and Thelmas of the world is yet another key contributing factor to your real estate success.

KEEP YOUR EMOTIONS IN CHECK

It's not always easy working with difficult clients, other agents and brokers, and other professionals whom you'll encounter in this industry. We must always, however, watch that our emotions don't compromise the job we are to do: protect the interests of our clients.

We have a responsibility to ensure their real estate transaction moves forward in a way that results in a successful closing. However, when we inject our emotions into an issue, we can cause more harm than good. The tone of our voice and the words we use can inflict damage that might be hard to repair. It is imperative we maintain our professionalism during any situation.

Remember, your responsibility is to steward the process for your client so at the end of the day, everyone is happy — the client closes on their home, and you get paid.

Don't let your personal opinions get in the way. Always remind yourself that you are the professional third party who subscribes to the ideals and standards of conduct outlined in the National Association of REALTORS® Code of Ethics and Standards of Practice.

By doing so, you will be assured the interest of your client — and your reputation — will be protected.

Don't become your own worst enemy.

CHAPTER 15

Setting Client Expectations

"Things we do not expect, happen more
frequently than we wish"

— PLAUTUS

If you are frustrated with your buyer or seller clients, it might be your fault.

One of the most significant issues real estate agents face in their transactions is the disconnect between them and their clients. Communicating expectations is central to an effective agent/client relationship. The lack of good and clear communication with an agent has always been the number one complaint consumers have as it relates to their home-buying or home-selling experience.

One issue in this communication gap involves "unexpected" issues, situations, or events popping up in the listing period or during the transaction. The client may face something they should have known might occur along the way. The agent probably did not explain the possible "what ifs" or "could happens" during the listing presentation with the seller or at the initial meeting with the buyer. Agents frequently do not take the time to discuss the expectations the client has of not only them, but also of the entire buying or selling process. The difficulties agents experience with their clients can be significantly reduced if there is a discussion on expectations before the listing or transaction commences.

ELIMINATE THE UNEXPECTED

Erin was a good agent. I never received any complaints from her clients or agents who worked with her during the years. One afternoon, she called me to share her anger toward a buyer client who was under contract on a new home. The client called the on-site agent directly to amend the contract to change the closing costs paid by the seller because their lender had sent a new loan estimate. Erin found out about the contract amendment when the builder's agent emailed it to her for her files.

She was upset and frustrated because her client did not contact her directly to handle the change to the contract. After all, she was their agent. I asked Erin if she clearly explained the various steps in the transaction to the client and the importance of her involvement in every phase. She responded with, "Well, I *thought* I did."

Erin's response was typical of other agents in similar situations.

COMMON SITUATIONS AGENTS FACE WITH BUYERS AND SELLERS

Buyers	Sellers
• Buyer views potential properties without your knowledge or participation.	• Seller shows their property to someone without you knowing anything about who they are or when they are to see it.
• Buyer decides to make an offer to purchase on a property without your knowledge and negotiates the terms and conditions without your involvement.	• Seller negotiates with a buyer on the sale of their home without you being present during the negotiations.
• Buyer elects to contract on a new construction home without your knowledge.	• Seller does not disclose any adverse facts concerning their home.
• Buyer meets with a FSBO (For Sale by Owner) directly, makes an offer, and negotiates the terms and conditions of the offer.	• Seller is unwilling to prepare the home for sale and does not declutter, clean, make repairs, paint, etc.
• Buyer assumes they are able to work with any agent they encounter as they think all agents are working for the Seller.	• Seller impedes your efforts to show the property to prospective buyers by not being flexible with their schedule.
• Buyer regrets their decision to purchase, but they do not let you know as they are concerned you will be mad at them.	• Seller does not disclose any liens on the property or liens against them (i.e., IRS).
• Buyer does not understand the complexity of the buying process.	• Seller does not understand the complexity of the selling process.
• Buyers are unable to properly communicate.	• Sellers are unable to properly communicate.

ESTABLISHING EXPECTATIONS

Many of the frustrations agents have when a client does something "behind their back" come from a failure to walk the client through each step of the transaction process and discuss what may happen during buying or selling a property. Clear, specific communication can eliminate unwelcomed surprises for both the agent and the client.

HOW TO MANAGE YOUR BUYER'S EXPECTATIONS

Working with buyers takes a lot of hard work. However, the job can be more tolerable and enjoyable if you know what you are facing and possess the confidence to handle any situation that comes your way. Revise your business plan to incorporate some of the following ideas. Stay focused and do what needs to be done to make the buyer representation side of your business successful. Trust me, it will pay off in the end.

1. **Be ready to sell yourself.** Before you make the first contact with a buyer, make sure you have the confidence to do what needs to be done to assist them in buying a property. *You must understand that you must sell yourself before you can sell your client!* You cannot go into a relationship with any self-doubt. The prospect will sense this and be less likely to want to work with you. You must know that you can get the job done with excellence, integrity, and professionalism. Remember, you are the professional, and they need to understand it. Ask yourself: Would you buy from you?

2. **Embrace your buyer representation value proposition.** In other words, what will you "bring to the table" in the relationship with the buyer? Ask yourself: Why should they use you? What sets you apart from the competition? What are the benefits you provide to them? Know all the key selling points of the buyer representation side of your business and how to communicate those to the client.

3. **Do not put a buyer in your car until you have had a face-to-face meeting with them.** By meeting with the buyer — preferably in your office — before looking at properties, you will eliminate any misunderstandings, build rapport, and begin to establish trust between you and the buyer. Carefully discuss how you

operate your buyer representation business, how you will work with them, the buying process, and what takes place every step of the way. Set realistic expectations up front so there are no surprises or issues that could harm the relationship. It will be important that the buyer's goals and objectives are written down, so they can refer to them when looking at properties and after a contract on a home has been bound. Staying focused on their goals will be vital. You do not want them to get off track.

4. **Explain to the buyer that you earn your living selling real estate.** They need to know you are a business owner, and you operate under a business plan with buyer representation as a segment of your real estate practice. (If you don't have a business plan, develop one *now*! This is an absolute must! See Chapter 2 where I walk you through creating a real estate business plan.) Also, explain how you are compensated at closing and how the listing broker usually pays your commission. I would also encourage you to explain what *agency* (the legal term for the agent/client relationship) is and how it benefits the buyer before, during, and after the transaction.

5. **Make sure they clearly understand the current real estate market** and the possibility of facing multiple offer situations if it is a "seller's market." They might have to go through several offers on properties before one actually "sticks." Have the latest data available to show them how the market is performing.

6. **They must understand how much they can afford** and be willing to be pre-approved for a loan by a reliable lender. You need to discontinue working with them if they are not willing to contact a lender to get pre-approved.

7. **Provide the buyer with a buyer packet** containing tips on purchasing a home, information on how to obtain a mortgage, local community and school information, contract and disclosure forms they will sign, etc. You might want to consider sending this packet before the initial conference with them if you have some time between setting the appointment for the meeting and the actual meeting.

8. **Real estate is emotional.** Buyer clients must take the emotion out of the buying process including the offer stage and the contract-to-close period of the transaction. You, as their real estate agent, can help them remain objective and view the entire

transaction from a bigger picture point of view. Also, explain to the buyer what "buyer remorse" is and how to be proactive to ensure this does not happen to them. (See Chapter 35 on handling buyer remorse.)

9. **They must know how sellers and their agents operate.** In other words, they need to understand the psychology of sellers. Sellers do not want low-ball offers, nor do they want "tire-kickers" looking at their home.

10. **Get a buyer representation agreement signed sooner rather than later.** (See Chapter 31 on how to get the buyer representation agreement signed.) This protects the client and provides a way for you to get paid at closing if the seller is not offering a selling commission.

11. **Tell the buyer you are going to provide them with a hassle-free, drama-free buying experience.** You will run interference for them in order to protect them from any obstacles they might face.

Be patient and stay calm. Buyers can drive you crazy, and at times, you will want to drive them out into the country and leave them on a dirt road in the middle of nowhere. Don't do that. Your principal broker will get a phone call.

HOW TO MANAGE YOUR SELLER'S EXPECTATIONS

It's not just the buyers who drive us crazy. Sellers, too, have their own way of getting under our skin. All agents have stories about wanting to be put out of our misery already because working with our sellers was a total disaster. In those situations, you probably realized if you knew what you were getting yourself into at the "get-go," the results would have been entirely different.

When working with sellers, I find the following helpful:

Set realistic expectations with both buyers and sellers by giving detailed explanations, asking the right questions, and listening to their answers. In doing so, you will better meet their needs, helping to ensure a good experience resulting in a successful closing and future referrals from them.

1. **Determine what their particular expectations are and how you can best meet those expectations.** Or, if needed, compromise on a "common ground" on which both of you can work. By doing

so, your job will be easier and less stressful, plus, there will be fewer surprises along the way. And, wouldn't that be nice?

2. **Explain the real estate market to establish pricing that sells.** Sellers must understand the reality of the real estate market and what homes in their neighborhood or the general vicinity have sold for over the past few months. There is no question we have experienced several years of appreciation in home prices; however, don't let the seller talk you in to a price just because the neighbor's house down the street went for "X" amount. You need to carefully research the comparable sales in the area and provide the seller with a realistic price range where the property will probably sell. Remember, if the price is not right, you will not have a marketable listing.

3. **Stop that crying, Mr. Seller!** Like buyers, sellers have to take the emotion out of the home-selling process. Once they decide to list their home, their property becomes a house, which means it is a commodity in the market and is competing with hundreds, if not thousands, of other properties. Removing the emotion is difficult for the homeowner who decides to sell their home. Many sellers have a hard time "detaching" themselves from the place where they raised their children or created special family memories. One way to alleviate the emotion is to have them focus on their next home and why they are selling their current one.

I have found most sellers will have three significant emotional "trigger" points in the selling process. The first one comes when offers are received and reviewed. If a low-ball offer comes in, many times, a seller will feel insulted and become angry and adversarial toward the buyer.

The second trigger point occurs during the inspection and resolution periods because they find themselves negotiating repairs and other items in the transaction to get the deal to close. They learn about defects or adverse facts for the first time and may become emotional.

The third and final emotional period for them is the actual closing and moving. They are exhausted, want their life to settle down, and want to stop living out of boxes. Be aware of their reactions and behavior, so you can properly navigate them through each of these stages in selling their home. If you don't, the entire transaction may implode, and your hard work will be for naught.

4. **Some sellers believe they know *everything* about selling a home.** This could include everything from pricing the home, seeing the value in professional staging, paying the amount of commission you and the selling agent should earn, whether they should or should not be present during showings, etc. Find out if they have done any research, and be prepared to support or refute anything they say or present to you. You are the professional, and you need to be able to explain why you think their ideas may or may not be good ones. You must gain their trust!

5. **Explain to them the importance of preparing their home for sale.** This one is significant. I have toured homes during a listing appointment, and it is amazing the poor condition the home is in because of outdated furniture, carpet, decorating, paint, etc. A home that is not properly staged will not stand out in the crowd and may be overlooked by qualified buyers. Professional staging will allow your listing to sell quicker and probably at a higher price. Also, don't forget about the exterior curb appeal. A well-maintained lawn, nicely trimmed bushes, and weed-free flower beds provide an excellent presentation when a prospective buyer steps out of their car and walks up the sidewalk to see the house.

6. **Finally, tell them you are there for them, *not* for yourself.** As their agent, you are their advocate, negotiator, counselor, and intermediary. You are shepherding them through the entire selling process. If they see you are not focused on their needs, they will be less likely to listen to you when you need them to do — or *not* to do — something that can impact the sale of the home. Remember, the money will follow if you are taking care of your client!

It is essential you understand working with sellers can be challenging and stressful. Even in a seller's market, it can still be problematic. You will find yourself very frustrated if you are not adequately prepared with a good "game plan" identifying the client's expectations when you list their home.

Setting realistic expectations by asking the right questions will better meet their needs and allow you to have a good experience resulting in a successful closing and future referrals from them.

CHAPTER 16

Your Client and You – A Partnership Relationship

"Alone we can do so little; together we can do so much."

I always believe the relationship that exists between my clients and me is a partnership. We are working together in finding their new home or selling the one in which they currently live. The partnership is founded on mutual trust, honesty, respect, loyalty, and commitment. These five basic principles should be at the foundation of your real estate business and always stay at the forefront of the client/agent relationship.

Early in my real estate career, I learned a few hard lessons from situations where clients behaved in a way that was incongruent with the expectations of the relationship I had with them. One buyer, whom I felt connected to, decided to go behind my back and use another agent to purchase a home. On another occasion, a seller received an offer from a buyer without notifying me and asking me to be present during the negotiations. The house sold, and I was left out of the transaction. I believe I could have prevented both situations from occurring if I had clearly explained the importance of the "partnership" aspect of the client/agent relationship.

> *The partnership between agent and client is founded on mutual trust, honesty, respect, loyalty, and commitment.*

I finally reached a point where I decided I needed to do a better job of communicating my relationship expectations to my clients. I had to be more open and honest with buyers and sellers on how I managed my business and how I saw the relationship between them and me. I decided at the initial buyer conference or seller listing presentation I would explain the various expectations of the partnership created by an agency relationship. I reviewed how I earn a living, my business philosophy, and what I asked of them as we worked together. I soon discovered clients became more dependent on me for assistance, rarely viewed a home without me being present, and always told other agents they were working with me as their exclusive buyer representative or listing agent.

EXPLAINING HOW I OPERATE MY REAL ESTATE BUSINESS

You earn your living selling real estate, and your real estate practice operates as a small business. Your business does not provide you with a regular wage or salary as you are paid a commission at the time your client's home closes. We are one of the few business professions that receive pay at the *end* of the process, even though you must pay all of your business expenses in advance. The commission you earn reimburses you for your time and expenses.

It's important your client truly understands how your business works. For clients who are not familiar with real estate or commissioned sales, they may believe you draw a monthly salary from the company name on the yard sign. Take time to educate your client on this important point.

AN EXAMPLE OF A REAL ESTATE BUSINESS PHILOSOPHY

To provide you, my client with friendly, professional, knowledgeable, and "stress-free" real estate seller representation. While we are marketing your home, **my time is yours**. I strive to provide a level of service that will make you proud to say that I am your REALTOR®!

You'll also want to communicate your business philosophy with your client at the beginning of your relationship with them. It should be based on your particular beliefs and principles that you work toward every day and may be reflected in your mission or vision statement. It is the operational blueprint of your real estate practice. Your business philosophy explains your overall goals and purpose.

WHAT YOU NEED TO ASK OF YOUR CLIENT

Since you will be working for your client and your client only, you should ask them to agree to the following:

- To work with you as their exclusive real estate agent. Remind them you and they will sign a listing agreement or buyer representation agreement designating you as their agent. This agreement ensures they are properly represented in a real estate transaction and afforded all the protection under the agency laws in your state.
- *(For Sellers)* To contact you immediately if another real estate agent or prospective buyer approaches them with an interest in their property (i.e., the agent wants to tour their home or make an offer to purchase).
  (For Buyers) To contact you about information on any property that the buyer client sees or that is brought to their attention, including "for sale by owners" and "builder direct/ new construction" properties.
- *(For Sellers)* To be cooperative in allowing their home to be shown during the listing period. All showings will be scheduled ahead of time under the terms the seller agrees to in the listing agreement.
  (For Buyers) If the buyer visits open houses, they should tell the host they are working with you. In addition, if any agent offers information on homes that may be of interest to the buyer, please ask the agent to pass the information on to you.
- *(For Sellers)* To disclose any adverse fact they are aware of that would impact the value of the property, its structural integrity, or the health of those who occupy it.
- *(For Sellers)* To disclose anything that would impact your ability to effectively market their home (i.e. title defects, IRS or other government liens on the property, current litigation in which you are involved, family disputes, etc.).
- The client should not negotiate with anyone about purchasing or selling the client's home without you present.
- The client should speak with you the moment a concern arises. You are available to answer any of their questions.

For buyers, I developed a one-page form titled "Home-Buying Partnership Acknowledgment" explaining the buyer representation side of my business, my business philosophy, and the expectations

I have of the customer/client. It is a simple but straightforward document that I always include in my buyer packets and in my presentation during our initial meeting. I ask the buyer to sign it acknowledging their understanding of the contents of the document.

I've included it here for your use as you establish new partnerships with your buyer clients. Also, you will find one to use when working with sellers.

HOME-BUYING PARTNERSHIP ACKNOWLEDGMENT

I earn my living selling real estate. As a professional REALTOR® I operate a small business and receive no wage or salary as I am paid a commission at the time your home closes. All expenses are paid solely by me in advance. The commission reimburses me for my time and expenses.

My business philosophy is:

To provide you, my clients, with friendly, professional, knowledgeable, and "stress-free" real estate buyer representation. While you are looking for a home, my time is yours. I strive to provide a level of service that will make you proud to say "I am your REALTOR®!"

In return, I ask you to agree to the following:

- **To work with me as your exclusive REALTOR®** (You and I will sign a Buyer Representation Agreement to ensure you are properly represented in a real estate transaction and afforded all the protection under the buyer agency laws of the state.)
- **Immediately seek pre-approval from a home lender if you have not received a pre-approval for a home mortgage.**
- **To contact me about information on any property** that you see or that is brought to your attention, including "for sale by owners" and "new construction — builder" properties.
- If you visit open houses, tell the host you are working with me.
- If any agent offers information on homes that may be of interest to you, please ask them to pass the information on to me.
- **Do not negotiate without my presence.**
- **Speak with me the moment a concern arises.** Let me answer your questions.
- The highest compliment you can give me is to recommend my services to your family, friends, and associates.

Thank you ahead of time for allowing me to help you with the purchase of your new home!

Client   Date

Client   Date

Agent   Date

NOTE: This form does not replace a Buyer Representation Agreement and does not establish an agency relationship between you and me. We will sign a Buyer Representation Agreement to legally solidify our relationship, so I can properly represent you in your real estate transaction.

HOME-SELLING PARTNERSHIP ACKNOWLEDGMENT

I earn my living selling real estate. As a professional REALTOR® I operate a small business and receive no wage or salary as I am paid a commission at the time your home closes. All expenses are paid solely by me in advance. The commission reimburses me for my time and expenses.

My business philosophy is:

To provide you, my clients, with friendly, professional, knowledgeable, and "stress-free" real estate seller representation. While you are selling your home, my time is yours. I strive to provide a level of service that will make you proud to say "I am your REALTOR®!"

In return, I ask you to agree to the following:

- **To work with me as your exclusive REALTOR®** (You and I will sign an Exclusive Right to Sell Listing Agreement designating me as your agent. This agreement will ensure you are properly represented in a real estate transaction and afforded all the protection under the seller agency laws of the state.)

- To **contact me immediately** if another real estate agent or prospective buyer approaches you with an interest in your property (i.e., wants to tour your home or make an offer to purchase)

- To be **cooperative in allowing your home to be shown** during the listing period. All showings will be scheduled ahead of time under the terms you agree to when we sign the listing paperwork.

- To **disclose any adverse fact** you are aware of that would impact the value of the property, its structural integrity, or the health of those who occupy it

- To **disclose anything that would impact my ability to effectively market your home** (i.e., title defects, IRS or other government liens on the property, current litigation in which you are involved, family disputes, etc.)

- **PLEASE DO NOT NEGOTIATE WITH ANYONE ABOUT PURCHASING YOUR HOME** without my presence.

- **Speak with me the moment a concern arises.** Let me answer your questions.

- The highest compliment you can give me is to recommend my services to your family, friends and associates.

Thank you ahead of time for allowing me to help you with the sale of your home!

_____   _____
Client   Date

_____   _____
Client   Date

_____   _____
Agent   Date

NOTE: This form does not replace a formal listing agreement and does not establish an agency relationship between you and me. We will sign an Exclusive Right to Sell Listing Agreement to legally solidify our relationship, so I can properly represent you in your real estate transaction.

CHAPTER 17

These People Are Driving Me Nuts! Ideas to Improve Client Relationships

"Let your speech always be gracious, seasoned with salt, so that you may know how you ought to answer each person."

— COLOSSIANS 4:6

Managing the relationship with a client can become challenging at times. Most sellers and buyers are stressed to the max because they are embarking on a significant benchmark in life: the sale or purchase of a home. Our role in a relationship with a client is crucial. We have a responsibility to shepherd the deal and the parties involved in the transaction in a way that results in a positive outcome — a successful closing. An agent must possess the tools that can always keep everything in forward motion and reduce as much trauma and drama as possible for the client.

Relationships, in general, have very interesting dynamics. Some are easy, and some are very, very hard. The same is true with our relationships with our clients. I discovered early on in my career that no two clients are alike. To manage any client relationship, you need to know how to navigate the relationship in a way that eventually brings you to the closing table. Here are some ideas to consider as you manage your clients in selling or purchasing a home.

MANAGING CLIENT RELATIONSHIPS

When a client nears the end of their adventure in real estate, they may not ultimately see the outcome they initially expected when the journey began. Buyer clients can experience disappointment and discouragement as they look for a new home to purchase.

The market in the Nashville area during the past few years has been a "seller's market" and very challenging for buyers. We have seen homes come on the Multiple Listing Service, and within hours multiple offers are in the inbox of the listing agent's email account. Some listings will see as many as ten to twenty offers with very few contingencies or stipulations. At times, it can turn into a circus. Because of this selling environment, buyers must be open to the real possibility of not getting the house they want and be willing to consider other options.

Advise clients to consider multiple outcomes. I call this the "What-Ifs." For example, an agent should be prepared to ask their buyer, "What if the seller rejects our offer?" or "What if we can't find the home of your dreams in the area in which you want to live?"

For sellers, ask questions such as, "What if we don't receive an offer within the first fifteen days; will you be willing to lower the price?" or "What if the buyer wants to move in before closing; are you willing to consider temporary housing?" Agents need to discuss alternatives with the client when the original objectives cannot be met.

Be an agent who understands rather than an agent who is right. My wife reminds me on occasion that I am not always right. She's correct; I am not always right. I would like to be, but I'm not. When working with sellers and buyers, we envision a path from the contract signing to the closing table that will work for both them and us. We have the experience and expertise to make this happen, right? We know what is best for them, correct?

Unfortunately, it never completely works that way. No two clients are the same, and no two transactions are the same. We must be open-minded, flexible, and understanding to their specific wants and needs and adapt to assisting in a way that results in the best outcome for them, *not* us. Remember, there is never only one way, and our approach is not always the right way.

Never take it personally. A professional real estate agent always maintains a well-defined boundary between the "professional" and the "personal." In other words, it's not about you. It is about the client. If any drama occurs along the way in a transaction, you need to step out of it and maintain a neutral, objective position, so you can help to resolve the issue. An agent's personal opinions can do more harm than good and may alienate your client or the cooperating agent on the other side of the deal. The bottom line is this: Keep your feelings to yourself and maintain your professionalism at all times.

Look at it from their perspective. The saying, "Put yourself in their shoes," is so true in client management. They all have different needs and perspectives. It can be hard for us to see things from their standpoint.

You may think they would be happier in a particular part of town, but they might have to be in a location close to an elderly parent who needs their assistance on a regular basis. Or, the buyer may be qualified for a $300,000 home, but only wants to spend $200,000. He is trying to save money. You know you can find him a home in his price range but doing so might be difficult. You must see the situation from his perspective, however, and do everything you can to find the home that meets his budget. That is why we are paid to do what we do. We are there for our clients, not for us.

Always build rapport. One of the first steps in the selling process is building rapport, which offers harmony, concern, and understanding between you and your client.

Rapport is built on respect, trust, and loyalty and allows each party in the relationship to feel they can openly communicate. Rapport is vital in real estate and must be established early in the relationship so that you are able to work together effectively.

Help clients to "step out of their box." I remember I had out-of-town buyer clients who had their heart set on a particular part of Nashville where they wanted to find a home. They loved the neighborhoods, parks, schools, and churches in this section of the city. The wife said it would be the perfect place.

Unfortunately, after looking at several houses in the area, we could not find the right home at a price they could afford. I explained to them there were other parts of Nashville that had the same qualities and conveniences as where they wanted to be — and there were plenty of houses available in their price range. I showed them several homes and was successful in finding one that would work for them. It was close to a city park and an elementary school for their children and a relatively easy commute to work.

After we closed, they told me they were so glad they were willing to be open-minded to consider other options. A good agent will always try to assist a client to be more objective in finding a property that best meets their needs.

Be aware of your triggers. We must keep our personal feelings to ourselves and outside of the transaction. Therefore, we must be aware of what can "set us off" and be careful how we react to a situation. Words can be dangerous, and what comes out of our mouth could exasperate the problem or issue at hand. Trust me, it is very easy to do.

Several years ago, I submitted an offer for a buyer client to a listing agent on a home in Franklin, Tennessee. After the offer was received, the listing agent called me and said it was a ridiculously low offer, and my clients must be stupid to send something so outlandish. My reaction to her comments was not pretty, and I fired back without any hesitation.

Long story short, we got the deal done, but the relationship with the listing agent was tenuous and adversarial all the way to the closing table. Watch your triggers. Your behavior can negatively impact your client and their objectives to purchase or sell a home.

Take responsibility. Whether a particular situation in a transaction was your fault or not, the way to diffuse it is to take responsibility and then offer multiple solutions. When something goes wrong, don't spend the time pointing fingers or arguing over who is to blame. Develop a solution that will keep the transaction moving forward. If it was your fault, own up to it. However, don't give up. You must continue to work in the best interest of your client to get the transaction closed.

Use the thirty-thousand-feet view. During the years, my agents and clients would hear me say, "Let's look at it from a thirty-thousand-feet perspective." There is always the bigger picture.

When clients are "stuck in the weeds" and struggling, help them understand the importance of the big picture. Remind them that you are there to help find the best outcome. The initial inspection, offers and counteroffers, the home inspection, and the final walk-through are stages in a transaction where an agent must sometimes counsel the client to focus on the bigger picture. This can motivate them to better deal with the situation at hand and reach a decision or resolution faster.

TIPS FOR CREATING AND MAINTAINING A STRONG CLIENT RELATIONSHIP

1. **Build a relationship that goes beyond agent and client.** People want to work with those they like, trust, and respect. Creating a healthy personal connection goes a long way in establishing a healthy business relationship. Get to know the client, their family situation, how they like to spend their free time, their hobbies, their motivations, their interests, etc.

2. **Regularly communicate with the client** and address any and all problems immediately! A lack of communication is the number one complaint consumers have with real estate agents. If you take a proactive approach to communicating, instead of a reactive one, it will build trust with the client. They will rely on your professional expertise in assisting them with their real estate needs. Answer their calls, texts, and emails promptly.

3. **Ask the right questions.** Even before listing a property or taking a buyer out to view properties, seek to learn more about the client's expectations. Some questions to ask include: "Do you think the real estate market is working in your best interest or against you? What do you think your home is worth? What are you looking for in a house? In what area of town do you see yourself living?"

4. **Agree on strategy, objectives, and timelines.** Until you and your client agree on tactics, goals, and schedules, you are always at risk of them not understanding what success is and how it should be measured. Create a document that outlines details, budget, and metrics. This document will alleviate any confusion over expectations and hopefully eliminate an awkward conversation.

5. **Be a counselor.** When you offer clients advice, direction, input, and business counsel, you are supporting your unique value proposition. This style of open dialogue helps to establish respect necessary to ensure better client and transaction management. Clients need your point of view and do not want a "yes" person who will act as a clone of them.

6. **Be a good listener.** Listening is one of the most underused tools in managing client expectations. Many clients are unsure of what they are trying to accomplish or not very good at articulating it. You must have excellent listening skills and

intuition to identify critical messages communicated. One of the best ways to compensate for a client who communicates poorly is to repeat what you have heard and ask them to confirm the accuracy of critical points, which will ultimately impact expectations.

7. **Always keep the interests of your clients first in your mind.** One of the primary reasons clients want us to represent them is so we can protect their interests. Remember your fiduciary duties as their agent.

8. **Establish boundaries in the relationship.** Make sure you know when and where to speak into the relationship and don't overstep boundaries. Do not interject your opinion unless it will produce a positive result for the client. Make sure the personal relationship does not impact the business relationship. Remember, you are working with the client to support your business and you and your family.

9. **Protect the client's privacy** and provide them with a sense of security. You need to practice discretion when representing a client, especially if they are well known in the public's eye. Make sure you convey your firm's privacy policies as well as security measures you and your broker have in place when you are out in the field with the client.

Client management is one of the most challenging aspects of an agent's job. It requires skill and hard work. Keeping a healthy relationship with a buyer or seller is probably the most crucial aspect of what we do as real estate professionals. If it needs improvement, work hard to strengthen it. You will be glad you did.

CHAPTER 18

Protect Your Compensation

"When you start seeing your worth, you'll find it harder to stay around people who don't."

I recently searched Google asking the question, "Are real estate agents overpaid?" The search results were eye-opening. Most of the comments I read were negative. Here are some of the ones I read that did not contain inappropriate language:

- "Real estate agents are the most overpaid, useless professionals on the planet. ... "
- "Is there anyone in this country more overpaid than real estate agents? ... "
- "Six percent commission has always been too high, and especially in these challenging times."
- "Real estate agents are a rip-off."
- "No real estate agent is worth that kind of money."
- "Why can't we solve the real estate agent 6 percent rip-off?"

After reading these, it became apparent to me that we, as an industry, have done a terrible job of conveying our true worth to the consumer. Many believe we don't work very hard for the money we charge a client to assist them in selling or purchasing a home. From the consumer's point of view, we stick a sign in the front yard, do some paperwork along the way, and get paid a ridiculous amount of money at closing.

CHANGING THE PUBLIC'S PERCEPTION
ABOUT REAL ESTATE AGENTS

From a bigger perspective (the thirty-thousand-feet view, as I like to call it), we are not the only industry suffering from a "professional rip-off" consumer mentality. Doctors, attorneys, accountants, CEOs, and others are right there with us when it comes to the idea that service providers and business executives charge too much for what we do.

We can overcome the negative public perception concerning the value we bring to a real estate transaction, though. Here's how.

To be successful in this industry, you have to believe in two things: yourself and the services you provide a buyer or seller. Don't expect the consumer to accept the fee you charge if you cannot show them you are worth every penny of it. We do a tremendous amount of work to get a real estate transaction from the offer stage to the closing table. If you don't convey to the client what you do behind the scenes to get the transaction closed, you will always be fighting to keep your commission.

HOW TO OVERCOME THE CLIENT
MEDDLING WITH YOUR COMPENSATION

If you've not experienced it yet, you will have a prospective seller or buyer client ask, "Is your commission negotiable?" When a prospective client asks me if I am willing to negotiate my commission, I always respond with, "Of course. How much more are you willing to pay?" Seriously, I do this every time a client confronts me about my compensation. Some laugh; some do not.

I do not lower my commission. No matter what the client's response is, I always stand my ground on the amount of commission I charge in a transaction. Of course, there are exceptions.

SPECIAL CIRCUMSTANCES IMPACTING
COMMISSION

If a seller client is a friend, and they allow me to represent them in the purchase of their next home, I might lower the commission slightly since I will benefit from two concurrent real estate transactions. The key word is "might." It depends on the client's financial circumstances, personal situation, and our relationship. Most of the time, when a seller client asks me to consider a lower commission, they are in the midst of a financial crisis and need every penny they can get at closing to service their debt.

Once, a single mother with four small children asked me to help her sell her house because her ex-husband stopped paying child support and alimony (he eventually ended up in prison on drug charges), and the mortgage company was about to initiate foreclosure proceedings. Her job did not pay her enough to cover the monthly mortgage payment. To assist her, I elected to waive my listing commission, so she would have more money at closing to move on to the next chapter in her life. Outside of selling a property for my church, this was the only time I did not charge a fee.

IF YOU REPRESENT THE SELLER, DO NOT LOWER YOUR FEES IF THE BUYER IS UNREPRESENTED

What should you do if a buyer wants to make an offer on your listing and they don't have an agent? Do *not* lower your commission if the property comes under contract with an unrepresented buyer. Also, you should not reduce your fee if you decide to be a transaction broker/facilitator in the transaction. In both circumstances, you will find yourself doing more work since the buyer is not represented. See Chapter 26 for more information on protecting your commission when an unrepresented buyer comes to your listing.

PROTECT YOUR COMMISSION

Early on in my real estate sales career, I learned a great way to show a client what goes into the traditional 6 percent commission we charge sellers to list and sell their home.* It is called the "The Six Dollar Bill" technique. (Note: This exercise only works in traditional brokerage models where you are sharing the gross commission with your broker through a split. This technique is more challenging in a 100 percent commission brokerage, but it can work.)

THE SIX DOLLAR BILL TECHNIQUE

When you make your listing presentation, and the client asks you to lower your commission, pull six one-dollar bills from your

---

* *Disclaimer: This is an example. Remember, all real estate commissions are negotiable.*

wallet or purse and lay them out in front of the seller. Explain to them each dollar represents 1 percent of your commission (based on a 6 percent commission). The breakdown of each is as follows:

TRADITIONAL BROKERAGE AGENTS
- The first three dollars go to the cooperating broker.
- The fourth dollar bill has to go to your broker.
- The fifth dollar bill has to be put in your business to cover operating expenses.
- The sixth dollar bill is used to provide for your family.

100 PERCENT BROKERAGE AGENTS
- The first three dollars must go to the cooperating broker.
- The fourth dollar bill has to be to the Internal Revenue Service (IRS) for taxes.
- The fifth dollar bill has to be put in your business to cover operating expenses.
- The sixth dollar bill is used to provide for your family.

Point out the dollar bills you have no control over, which is most of them. The one you can control is the one that supports your family. If you remove that one, there will be nothing left for you. Your family may starve.

This exercise is easy to do and explains how the compensation is divided. It is probably the most effective one to institute because clients will see how the money is distributed, and they will be more than likely to concede to why you charge what you charge.

DEFENDING YOUR PAYCHECK

Almost every real estate licensee in the United States is an independent contractor. As an independent contractor, you are paid on a commission basis and must report your income to the IRS on a 1099 form. Your commission is your paycheck. Your commission checks may be frequent if you are a high producer or infrequent if you sell just a few properties annually or work as a part-time agent. In any case, the money you receive goes to operating your business and maintaining a desired standard of living.

When you are faced with the "Will you lower your commission?" conversation, you need to be armed with the necessary weapons to counter the client's request. The following three strategies can assist you in keeping your hard-earned money in your pocket:

1. If the client says, the "other agent" will charge less commission, tell the client, "If he is willing to charge less commission, how do you expect him to get the most money for you when he is negotiating with the cooperating agent?" Tell them they will get what they pay for.

2. If the client says he or she needs as much money as possible at closing, explain to them you are skilled at finding a buyer. Would they cut their salary in order to allow their boss to make more money? They will say "no." With this example, you need to use your value proposition as a tool in comparing lowering your fee to them taking less in their paycheck.

3. Say "no" to the client. Sometimes you need to tell the client your commission is non-negotiable and stand your ground. Some clients will respect you for doing so and be willing to move forward with you. Others will not. Remember, you must show your value to them *before* you say "no."

WHEN A BUYER ASKS YOU TO LOWER YOUR COMMISSION

Occasionally, a buyer will want you to lower your sales commission for them to get a better deal on a property. When this situation occurs, be ready to stand your ground with the buyer. Explain to them the selling commission, which is paid by the listing broker, goes towards operating your business and feeding your family. Use a similar approach as the Six Dollar Bill technique, but use three one dollar bills to show where the typical 3 percent selling commission goes.

TRADITIONAL BROKERAGE AGENTS
- The first one dollar bill goes to your broker.
- The second one dollar bill goes towards operating your business and paying the IRS for taxes.
- The third one dollar bill is used to provide for your family.

100 PERCENT BROKERAGE AGENTS
- The first one dollar bill goes to operating your business.
- The second one dollar bill goes to the IRS for taxes.
- The third one dollar bill is used to provide for your family.

The bottom line on broker compensation is we are paid what we are paid because of what we do for the client. In fact, I believe we should charge more to navigate our clients through the crazy and unpredictable real estate market we've experienced over the last few years. Real estate transactions are becoming more complicated, and the risk for the client and the agent continues to increase. We will not survive if we do not have the means to operate our businesses in a professional manner that allows us to meet the needs of today's sellers and buyers.

A BONUS TOOL FOR DEMONSTRATING YOUR VALUE TO YOUR CLIENT

On July 25, 2006, Pat Vredevoogd-Combs, a past president of the National Association of REALTORS® testified before Congress at a hearing of the House Financial Services Subcommittee on Housing and Community Opportunity. In the document she provided the committee containing her testimony, she included an attachment titled "Actions, Research Steps, Procedures, Processes and Review Stages in a Real Estate Transaction." In this attachment are possible actions, research steps, procedures, processes, and review stages that a REALTOR® may provide in a typical, successful residential real estate transaction.

You should incorporate this list into your listing and buyer presentations as you demonstrate your value proposition to the client.

THE CRITICAL ROLE OF THE REALTOR® IN THE RESIDENTIAL REAL ESTATE TRANSACTION

By Pat Vredevoogd-Combs

SELLER(S)' REPRESENTATION

PRE-LISTING ACTIVITIES

1. Contact property owner(s) and make appointment with seller(s) for listing presentation.

2. Send seller(s) confirmation of listing appointment and call to confirm.

3. Review pre-appointment questions.

4. Research appropriate sampling of currently listed comparable properties (i.e., appropriate by property type, price range, and location).

5. Research trends and sales activity for an appropriate period (past three to six months is recommended) from MLS and public records databases.

6. Research "average days on market" for the property type, price range, and location.

7. Download and review property tax roll information.

8. Research property's public record information for ownership and deed type.

9. Research property's public record information for lot size and dimensions.

10. Research and verify legal description.

11. Research property's land use coding and deed restrictions.

12. Research property's current use and zoning.

13. Ascertain need for lead-based paint disclosure.

14. Prepare market analysis to establish broker opinion of value.

15. Prepare listing-presentation package with above materials.

16. Perform exterior "curb-appeal assessment" of subject property.

17. Verify public-school zoning and discuss with the seller(s) the impact of school districts on market value determination.

18. Review listing-appointment checklist to verify that all steps and actions have been completed.

LISTING-APPOINTMENT PRESENTATION ACTIVITIES

19. Review broker's and company's credentials and accomplishments in the market with seller(s).

20. Present company's profile and position of "niche" in the marketplace.

21. Give seller(s) an overview and projections of current market conditions.

22. Present market analysis results to seller(s), including sold comparables, current listings, and expired.

23. Offer pricing strategy based on professional judgment and interpretation of current market conditions.

24. Discuss goals with seller(s) to market effectively.

25. Explain marketing power and benefits of the MLS.

26. Explain the different marketing options and their effectiveness.

27. Explain work the brokerage does

"behind the scenes" and the broker's availability on weekends.

28. Explain brokerages role in taking calls to screen for qualified buyers and to protect seller(s) from curiosity seekers.

29. Present and discuss strategic master marketing plan.

30. Review results of curb-appeal assessment with seller(s) and provide suggestions to improve sale-ability.

31. Research and verify city sewer/septic tank systems. Verify when property's septic system was last pumped or inspected.

32. Well water: Confirm well status, depth, and output from third-party well report.

33. Natural gas: Research/verify the availability of natural gas and supplier's name and phone number.

34. Verify security system, current term of service, and determine if it's owned or leased.

35. Verify if seller(s) has transferable termite bond — obtain a copy of the terms and conditions of bond that may be available to buyer(s).

36. Discuss home-warranty program with homeowner.

37. Verify if property has rental units involved.

38. Make copies of all leases for retention in listing file.

39. Verify all rents and all deposits.

40. Assess interior décor and suggest changes.

41. Prepare net sheet for seller(s).

42. Review accuracy of current title information with sellers. (If possible, obtain copies of seller(s)' deed, owner's title insurance policy, and most-recent survey.)

43. Verify names of owner(s) as they appear in county's public property records.

44. Verify with seller(s) if there are any outstanding or expired construction permits or if any changes have been made to the property since the seller(s) purchased the property.

45. Obtain copy of current Title Insurance Policy.

46. Complete listing contract and addenda (using names of seller(s) as they appear on deed or title policy). Obtain seller(s)' signature(s) on the listing agreement and return a signed copy of the listing contract to the seller(s). (If property is jointly owned, all owners should sign listing agreement.)

47. Review with seller(s) the standard closing costs and pro-rations typical to the HUD statements.

48. Obtain seller(s)' permission to use a lock box.

49. Measure interior room sizes.

50. Confirm lot size via owner's copy of certified survey, if available.

51. Note any and all unrecorded property lines, agreements, and easements that are known to the seller if they are not otherwise noted.

52. Obtain house plans, if applicable and available.

53. Review house plans and make a copy.

POST-LISTING ACTIVITIES

54. Compile and assemble formal file on property.

55. Obtain copy of subdivision plat/complex layout.

56. Verify with seller(s) if there are any outstanding or expired construction permits or if any changes have

been made to the property since the seller(s) purchased the property.

57. Obtain copy of current title insurance policy.

58. Provide seller(s) with a copy of a blank sales contract to review in preparation of their receipt of an offer.

59. Inform tenants of listing and discuss how showings will be handled.

60. Arrange for installation of yard sign.

61. Have seller(s) complete the seller(s)' disclosure form.

LISTING ACTIVITIES

62. Order plat map for retention in property's listing file.

63. Prepare showing instructions for buyer(s)' broker and agree on showing-time window with seller(s).

64. Install electronic lock box and program the lock box with agreed-upon showing-time windows.

65. Obtain current mortgage loan(s) information: companies and loan account numbers.

66. Verify current loan information with lender(s).

67. Identify homeowner association manager, if applicable.

68. Verify homeowner association fees and pending or unpaid assessments with homeowner association manager.

69. Research electricity availability and supplier's name and phone number.

70. Prepare detailed list of property amenities and assess market impact.

71. Prepare detailed list of property's "inclusions and conveyances with sale."

72. Compile list of completed repairs and maintenance items.

73. Explain benefits of homeowner warranty to seller(s).

74. Assist sellers with completion and submission of homeowner-warranty application.

75. Place homeowner warranty in property file for conveyance at time of sale.

76. Make extra key for lockbox.

77. Place a copy of the seller(s)' completed disclosure form in the property file.

78. Arrange for interior and exterior photos to be taken for MLS listing.

79. Arrange for creation of a virtual tour if one will be used in marketing the property.

80. Complete a new-listing checklist.

81. Enter listing into office records and/or create listing file.

MLS-RELATED ACTIVITIES

82. Prepare "MLS profile sheet." (Listing broker is responsible for "quality control" and accuracy of listing data).

83. Enter property data from profile sheet into MLS listing database.

84. Proofread MLS database listing for accuracy, including proper placement in mapping function.

85. Take additional photos of the property to upload into MLS and for use in flyers.

86. Provide seller(s) with a copy of the MLS profile sheet data form.

87. Add property to company's active listings list.

MARKETING AND SHOWING ACTIVITIES

88. Create print and Internet ads with seller(s)' input and approval.

89. Provide "special feature" cards for marketing, if applicable.

90. Submit ads to company's participating Internet real estate sites.

91. Reprint/supply brochures promptly as needed.

92. Create QR codes.

93. Prepare mailing and contact list.

94. Generate mail-merge letters to contact list.

95. Order "just listed" labels and reports.

96. Prepare flyers.

97. Prepare property marketing brochure for seller(s)' review.

98. Order an appropriate quantity of marketing brochures or flyers.

99. E-mail marketing material to brokers and agents with marketing material.

100. Upload listing to company and broker's Internet site, if applicable.

101. Mail out "just listed" notice to all neighborhood residents.

102. Inform Network Referral Program of listing.

103. Coordinate showings with owners, tenants, and other REALTORS®. Return all calls promptly (weekends included).

104. Provide showing time comments and feedback to seller(s) and recommend changes according to potential buyer comments.

105. Review comparable MLS listings and new trends regularly to verify property remains competitive in price, terms, conditions, and availability.

106. Provide marketing data to buyers coming through international relocation networks.

107. Provide marketing data to buyers coming from referral network.

108. Convey price changes promptly to all Internet groups.

109. Request feedback from buyers' brokers after showings.

110. Review weekly market study reports.

111. Discuss feedback from showing sales associates with seller(s) to determine if changes will accelerate the sale.

112. Call seller(s) weekly to discuss marketing and pricing.

113. Promptly enter price changes in MLS listing database.

OFFER AND CONTRACT ACTIVITIES

114. Verify proper licensure of buyer's broker and salesperson.

115. Obtain a signed and dated verification that escrow deposit was delivered to escrow agency.

116. Receive and review all offer to purchase contracts submitted by buyers or buyers' brokers.

117. Evaluate offer(s) and prepare a "net sheet" on each offer, for the seller(s) to make comparisons.

118. Review offers with seller(s) and review merits and weaknesses of each component of each offer.

119. Contact buyers' broker to review buyer(s)' qualifications and discuss offer.

120. Provide seller(s)' disclosure to buyer(s)' broker or buyer upon request (prior to offer if possible).

121. Confirm buyer(s) is pre-approved by contacting lender.

122. Obtain a copy of the buyer(s)' pre-approval letter from lender.

123. Negotiate all offers and counteroffers on seller(s)' behalf.

124. Prepare and convey any counteroffers, acceptance, or amendments to buyer(s)' broker.

125. When offer to purchase is accepted and signed by seller(s) ("contract"), deliver contract to selling/buyer(s)' broker or if none, to buyer(s).

126. Verify contract is signed by all parties.

127. Provide copies of the contract and all addenda to closing attorney and the title company.

128. Record and promptly deposit buyer(s)' earnest money with escrow agent.

129. Disseminate "under-contract showing restrictions" as seller(s) requests.

130. Deliver copies of signed contract to seller(s).

131. Provide copies of contract to lender.

132. Inform seller(s) how to handle additional offers to purchase submitted between effective date of contract and closing.

133. Change status in MLS to "sale pending".

134. Update listing file to show "sale pending".

LOAN-PROCESS ACTIVITIES

135. Contact buyer(s)' lender weekly to verify processing is on track.

136. Follow buyer(s)' loan processing through to the underwriter.

137. Relay final approval of buyer(s)' loan application to seller(s).

HOME-INSPECTION ACTIVITIES

138. Coordinate buyer(s)' professional home and termite (WDO) inspections with seller(s).

139. If property is vacant, arrange for power and water to be turned on.

140. Review home inspector's report and WDO report with seller(s) and discuss issues and options, if needed.

141. Enter home inspection WDO inspection completion into listing file.

142. Verify seller(s)' compliance with home inspection report and WDO report repair requirements.

143. Recommend or assist seller(s) with identifying trustworthy contractors to perform any required repairs.

144. Obtain copies of repair bills showing seller(s) has made required repairs.

145. Coordinate entry into the property and buyer's review of completed repairs, if needed.

APPRAISAL ACTIVITIES

146. Make arrangements for appraiser to enter property.

147. Follow-up on appraisal.

148. Enter appraisal completion into listing file.

149. Discuss appraisal report with seller(s) and suggest options, if necessary.

CLOSING-PREPARATION ACTIVITIES

150. Distribute signed contracts to all involved parties (buyer, seller(s), title company, lender, seller(s)/buyer(s) broker, closing agent) and provide contact information as needed.

151. Coordinate closing process with buyer(s)' broker and lender.

152. Update closing forms and files.

153. Confirm location, date, and time where closing will be held and notify all parties.

154. Confirm with closing agent that all title problems have been resolved.

155. Confirm that the seller has the proper Power of Attorney or trust documents, as required.

156. Work with buyer(s)' broker in scheduling and conducting buyer(s)' final walk-through prior to closing.

157. Confirm with closing agent that all tax, HOA, utility, and other

applicable pro-rations have been resolved.

158. Request final closing figures from closing agent.

159. Review closing figures on HUD statement with seller(s) to verify accuracy of preparation.

160. Forward verified closing figures to buyer(s)' broker and confirm buyer(s)' broker has received and reviewed closing figures.

161. Confirm buyer(s) and Buyer(s)' broker has received title insurance commitment.

162. Provide homeowners warranty for availability at closing.

163. Recommend courtesy closing agent for absentee seller(s), as needed.

164. Review closing documents with seller(s) and their counsel.

165. Provide earnest money deposit check from escrow account to closing agent. If closing agent is holding escrow funds, make sure it appears on the final HUD.

166. Coordinate this closing with seller(s)' next purchase and resolve any timing problems, if applicable.

167. Confirm seller(s)' net proceeds check at closing.

AFTER-CLOSING ACTIVITIES

168. Provide REALTOR® referral information for seller(s)' relocation destination, if applicable.

169. Change MLS status to "sold." Enter sale date, price, selling broker, and listing broker's ID numbers, etc.

170. Close out listing in company files.

171. Follow up with seller(s).

BUYER(S)' REPRESENTATION

BUYER(S)-PRESENTATION ACTIVITIES

172. Respond to prospective buyer(s) inquiries.

173. Interview the buyer(s) prospect and obtain buyer(s) personal information and explain the homebuying process.

174. Determine if REALTOR® has a conflicting brokerage relationship or other conflict of interest with the buyer(s).

175. Discuss the pre-approval financial process with the buyer(s).

176. Suggest at least three mortgage lenders to assist buyer(s) in becoming pre-approved.

177. Determine through discovery the buyer(s)' preferences in a home as well as the location, price, size, type of home, special needs, and ADA accommodations etc.

PRE-CONTRACT ACTIVITIES

178. Obtain and review pre-approval letter from lender.

179. Search the MLS for properties that meet the buyer(s)' criteria.

180. Make appointments with seller(s) or seller(s)' listing broker to show the properties selected by thebuyer(s).

181. Show the buyer(s) their selected properties.

OFFER AND CONTRACT ACTIVITIES

182. Obtain a "good faith estimate" from the buyer(s)' lender for the target purchase price and review with buyer(s).

183. Meet with buyer(s) to preview offer, contract form, addenda, and miscellaneous forms.

184. Complete offer to purchase and all addenda.

185. Provide seller(s)' disclosure forms to buyer(s).

186. Submit offer to purchase signed by buyer(s) to seller(s)' broker.

187. Provide credit report information to seller(s) if property will be seller-financed.

188. Provide buyer(s) a copy of all forms used in making the offer.

189. Negotiate all offers on buyer(s)' behalf.

190. Prepare and convey any counteroffers, acceptance, or amendments to seller(s)' broker.

191. Verify final offer is signed by all parties ("contract"), and that all necessary documents are attached.

192. Deliver fully signed and initialed contract to buyer.

193. Distribute signed contracts to all involved parties (buyer(s), seller(s), title company, lender, seller(s)/buyer(s) broker and closing agent) and provide contact information as needed.

194. Record and promptly deposit buyer(s)' earnest money in escrow account or deliver to closing agent and obtain a receipt.

195. Provide receipt of escrow deposit to seller(s)' broker.

196. Place copies of signed contract in office file.

197. Inform buyer(s) of additional offers to purchase that are submitted between effective date of contract and closing.

198. Update listing file to show "sale pending."

HOME AND TERMITE INSPECTION ACTIVITIES

199. Provide buyer(s) with at least three home inspection companies and three WDO inspection companies from which to select.

200. Coordinate buyer(s)' professional home and WDO inspection with seller(s)' broker.

201. Review home and WDO inspection reports with buyer.

202. Enter completion of home and WDO inspection reports into the listing file.

203. Order septic system, well, or mold inspections, if applicable.

204. Receive and review septic system, well, or mold reports with buyer(s) and note any possible impact on sale.

205. Provide copy of septic system, well and mold inspection reports, if any, to lender and seller(s).

206. Verify seller(s)' compliance with all inspection repair requirements.

TRACKING THE LOAN-PROCESS ACTIVITIES

207. Coordinate with lender on discount points being locked in with dates.

208. Confirm verifications of deposit and buyer(s)' employment have been returned.

209. Contact lender weekly to verify processing is on track.

210. Follow loan processing through to the underwriter.

211. Relay final approval of buyer(s)' loan application to seller(s).

APPRAISAL ACTIVITIES

212. Schedule appraisal with seller(s) or seller(s)' broker.

213. Inform buyer(s) of options if appraisal report is different than the contract/purchase price.

214. Provide comparable sales used in market pricing to appraiser.

215. Follow-up on appraisal until completed.

216. Enter completion into the listing file.

CLOSING-PREPARATION ACTIVITIES

217. Coordinate closing process with seller(s)' broker, lender, and closing agent.

218. Update closing forms and files.

219. Verify all parties have all forms and information needed to close the sale.

220. Assist in obtaining power of attorney or trust documents, as required.

221. Work with seller(s)' broker in scheduling and conducting buyer(s)' final walk-through prior to closing.

222. Confirm buyer(s) has received title insurance commitment.

223. Confirm location, date, and time where closing will be held and notify all parties.

224. Confirm with closing agent that all tax, HOA, utility, and other applicable pro-rations have been resolved.

225. Request final closing figures from closing agent.

226. Review and verify closing figures on HUD statement with buyer(s).

227. Forward verified closing figures to seller(s)' broker and confirm seller(s)' broker has received and reviewed closing figures.

228. Verify that seller(s)' broker has provided homeowners warranty, if purchased, at closing.

229. Forward closing documents to absentee buyer(s) as requested, if applicable.

230. Provide earnest money deposit check from escrow account to closing agent. If closing agent is holding escrow funds make sure it appears on the final HUD.

231. Confirm collected funds from buyer(s) are available for closing.

232. Explain filing for homestead exemption.

233. Verify transfer of all keys (house, mailbox, and HOA/community), garage- door openers, HOA/security/ gate access codes, pool equipment, and appliance manuals.

234. Close out listing.

AFTER-CLOSING ACTIVITIES

235. Assist with filing claims with homeowner's warranty company, if requested.

236. Respond to any follow-up calls and provide any additional information required from office files.

237. Follow up with buyer(s).

In addition to the above activities/services which may be performed by a REALTOR® during a real estate transaction, today's real estate market requires REALTORS® to offer additional assistance when the transaction involves short sales, foreclosures, or bank-owned properties.

Also, during the marketing process, homeowners may be in need of property-management services which REALTORS® also perform. Whether you are buying, selling, or in need of a property manager, we encourage you to discuss with your REALTOR® in detail what additional services may be necessary for you to accomplish your objective.

CHAPTER 19

When to Fire Your Client

"Goodbye always makes my throat hurt."

– CHARLIE BROWN

Holding on to a client who is not the right fit for your real estate business is one of the worst things you can do as a real estate professional. You invested time, money, and energy on them, but they are negatively impacting you and your business. However, if you don't fire them, you will lose additional time and money, as well as the energy that can be better spent on other clients or prospects.

Trust me, there will come a time in your real estate career when you will have to end an agency relationship with a client. It is a hard decision to make, but successful agents know when it is time to say goodbye.

NINE TELLTALE SIGNS IT'S TIME TO FIRE YOUR CLIENT

A successful working relationship is built on trust, loyalty, and honesty. When even one of those elements is broken, the relationship is in jeopardy. Watch for these signs that your agent-client relationship is in trouble.

1. THE CLIENT LIES TO YOU

An agency relationship implies an assured level of trust between you and your client. Trust is broken when the client lies to you. Why do they lie? The most obvious reason is that they want to keep something hidden from you.

A client may not want you to know information regarding

their financial condition, an adverse fact regarding their home, an impending divorce, the real reason why they didn't show up for an appointment, etc. Another reason people lie is to be in control. When a person lies, they are in complete control of the story or situation. Their narrative is one they can manage when avoiding the truth. The truth, in fact, will be a threat to them because they will not be in control.

I feel very betrayed when someone is lying to me. Lying is one of my "cardinal sins," and some of my past relationships with clients, friends, and family have significantly changed or ended due to lies. Relationships are hard to repair when trust is broken.

2. THE CLIENT IS PHYSICALLY OR EMOTIONALLY ABUSIVE

It is rare, but sometimes a client will become abusive. As a principal broker, I walked several agents through situations where the client was verbally abusing them or others on their team. Abuse can come in many forms, including throwing a tantrum, calling you names, storming around shouting, or otherwise acting threateningly.

Other types of abusive behavior can include bullying you or making disparaging remarks about your gender, race, or appearance, even if it is to someone else involved before, during, or after the transaction. To me, if a client shows any sign of abuse, I am finished with them.

It seems to be a "no-brainer" for an agent to walk away from an abusive client relationship. However, some agents put up with it because they don't dare fire the client who might turn on them. They also might be willing to put up with abuse, so they can get their commission when the transaction closes.

Your principal broker or team leader can assist you in terminating your agency agreement with an abusive client. If you feel the person may become violent towards you, call the police immediately.

3. THE CLIENT MAKES UNREASONABLE DEMANDS

Some clients can be demanding. However, some clients can cross the line and become downright unreasonable with their demands. What is considered unreasonable? Anything out of proportion or out of the ordinary.

For example, a client calls or texts you at midnight to discuss potential properties to view, or a buyer client wants you to negotiate the commission of both agents in the transaction so that they can get the house at a lower price. If a client asks this of you, fire them on the spot! Tampering with our compensation is entirely out of bounds in my book. We work too hard for the money.

4. A CLIENT IS RELUCTANT TO MEET WITH A LENDER TO DISCUSS FINANCING

If a client or prospect is unwilling to meet with a lender to get pre-approved for a loan, don't move forward with helping them find a home. This is a *major* red flag! The client is more than likely hiding something that can impact their ability to obtain financing for a home.

5. THE CLIENT KEEPS CHANGING HIS OR HER MIND

Nothing is more frustrating than a client changing his or her mind either before the offer is submitted or after the seller has accepted the offer. Several years ago, I had a client, Barbara, who was excited to find a new home and agreed to sign an exclusive buyer representation agreement with me. She was a single woman with no children. Barbara was very friendly and appeared to know what she wanted in a home.

We looked at several houses and found one that met her needs. We returned to my office and wrote up an offer on the property. When I completed all the paperwork, I faxed the offer to the listing agent. (Yes, I used a fax machine; it was before sending offers via email was common practice.) Three hours later, Barbara called me and told me to withdraw the offer. She said she thought about it more and decided it was not the "right" one for her.

About two weeks later, we made another offer on a home that she said was "the one." She called me about six hours after I sent that offer to the listing agent and told me she changed her mind. I was frustrated, but I shook it off. I continued to show Barbara properties.

We finally found a house that was, in my opinion, *the* home for her. It had everything she wanted and needed in a home. We wrote an offer and sent it to the listing agent. Guess what? She pulled the offer. Yes, two hours after I submitted it.

My patience finally ran out on this client. I called Barbara and said I was not the agent for her. I fired her by terminating her buyer representation agreement with me. I never looked back, and I am, to this day, glad I sent Barbara on her way. That experience taught me a very valuable lesson.

A client who keeps changing their mind is not committed to purchasing or selling a home. They do not have the self-confidence needed to make important decisions — especially big ones such as buying a home. This type of client will take a tremendous amount of your time and resources, and you will reach a point of total frustration.

6. THEY DON'T TAKE YOUR ADVICE BUT BLAME YOU WHEN THINGS GO WRONG

One of the reasons a buyer or seller utilizes the services of an agent is because we have the experience and expertise clients need to navigate through the complexities of a real estate transaction. Clients seek our advice so that they can make wise and informed decisions.

Unfortunately, when they don't listen to our counsel, they can find themselves frustrated, angry, and bewildered. When this occurs, they usually point the finger at their agent. If they are not willing to benefit from your professional wisdom and insight, you might need to let them go.

7. THE CLIENT WANTS TO DEBATE HOW MUCH YOU SHOULD GET PAID

What are you worth? If you counted all the hours per week you spend in and on your real estate business, would you know your hourly rate? I think you would be surprised at how low your rate is, based on the amount of time and effort you spend taking care of your clients.

A pet peeve of mine is when clients — especially sellers — start fiddling with my compensation. Clients always expect to save money in a transaction if they can lower the agent's commission. But, the opposite happens. It costs them more. The work we do — the marketing, negotiating, management, and handholding — from the first appointment to the closing table offers value. When our compensation is cut, though, we can find ourselves less motivated to "go the distance" for them.

I know I am worth every penny I charge a client. You are, too!

8. THE CLIENT PITS YOU AGAINST YOUR COMPETITION

Several times when I would give a listing presentation, the seller would bring up the competition and what they would charge to list their home. I felt the client was backing me into a corner when they mentioned a competitor's name and the lower commission they would charge.

When this happened, I presented my value proposition with confidence, espousing the unique benefits that my brokerage and I brought to the table for the seller. Yes, they can pay less, but are they prepared to give up my willingness to fully negotiate for them and forfeit a large part of the marketing needed to sell their home? I believe in the old adage, "You get what you pay for!"

9. YOUR CLIENT WANTS YOU TO DO SOMETHING THAT COULD JEOPARDIZE YOUR LICENSE OR SEND YOU TO COURT

Some buyers and sellers will cross the line of illegality when they feel it will benefit them both personally and financially. These kinds of people may look respectable and charming on the outside, but their behavior and actions in a transaction can have a negative impact on you and your brokerage if they are not playing by the rules.

Under Tennessee state law, real estate licensees must follow all lawful instructions of their client. Our state laws are consistent with real estate rules and regulations throughout the country. If a client asks you to do something that is illegal or puts your license at risk, fire them immediately! It is not worth losing your license and spending thousands of dollars on attorney fees when a client is dishonest and unethical. Don't walk away from them; *run* away from them!

Terminating an agency relationship should only be done after careful consideration and discussion with your principal broker. If you find yourself in a "no-win" position with a prospect or client and there is little to no hope of getting a deal done, then it is time to fire them.

SECTION THREE

Selling Properties

CHAPTER 20

The Home-Selling Process

*"If it's dressed right, priced right, and ready
to go, it will sell!"*

— UNKNOWN

My wife and I sold our first home in Louisville, Kentucky, back in 1989 after living in it for almost two years. It was a great house, but our second child was born, and we needed a larger home that would give us more space for our growing family. We decided to use the agent who represented us in the purchase of our home. Looking back, we probably should have interviewed a couple of other agents who knew how to market and sell a property.

Our agent was a fantastic buyer's representative (a side note: back then, buyer's agents were sub-agents for sellers) but not a very good listing agent. It was our first time to list a home, and we did not know what to ask or expect from her. She did not do a listing presentation or provide us with how the selling process worked. Her listing appointment, if I can call it that, consisted of a quick five-minute meeting in our kitchen where she had us sign two forms to list the house and put it on the MLS.

Before she left, she opened her car trunk and put a "For Sale" sign in our front yard. After she drove out of our driveway, she stopped in the middle of the street in front of our house and snapped a quick photograph of our home. That was it.

The market was a good one at the time, even with interest rates in the low teens. Our home sold in about two weeks. We closed a few weeks later and moved to our next house. And yes, our agent was our buyer's representative on that property.

I share this story because we didn't know anything about the home-selling process. During the years, working with other real estate agents to market our homes, we learned more about what happens to sell a house. But it wasn't until I was licensed that I truly understood everything that needs to take place in listing a property, getting it under contract, and seeing it through to closing.

Several years ago, I created a flow chart for a presentation I was giving to our company agents on listing properties. I've included the chart in this chapter. It visually notes each stage of the selling process. My agents find it is an excellent talking-point guide to use in listing presentations. The following is a brief narrative you can refer to when discussing each step of the process.

STAGES IN THE HOME-SELLING PROCESS

Good listing agents are good communicators. They are able to present to the seller how they will sell their property for the highest amount of money in the least amount of time. In addition, they make sure the seller knows what to expect at every step of the home-selling process. The more you can inform them, the more likely their expectations of you will be clear. A seller who knows all that goes into marketing a home will be less likely to be surprised when issues arise.

The text below follows the included flow chart. Use it in your listing presentations.

THE DECISION TO SELL THEIR HOME

This is the first step in the home-selling process. They should be able to answers questions such as:
- Why do you want to sell your home?
- What is your timeframe for moving?
- How much money do you want to receive at the closing table?

PROFESSIONAL CONSULTATION WITH YOU, THEIR REAL ESTATE PROFESSIONAL

This step in the selling process is critical in how you present your marketing plan and strategy to sell the property. At this stage, you will need to:
- Discuss your professional experience and expertise
- Review market research with the seller

- Explain recent sales in the area compared to the seller's home
- Assist them in determining the list price
- Present your marketing plan

IMPORTANCE OF PRE-LISTING ACTIVITIES

In order to maximize the return on investment the seller made in their home, they need to consider doing everything they can to have a successful sale. If the property is "dressed right, priced right, and ready to go," it will sell!
- Preparing/staging the home
- Pre-listing appraisal
- Pre-listing inspection

FORMALIZING THE PARTNERSHIP

The next step is to enter into an agency relationship as their designated agent so you can represent their interests and negotiate for them. They will sign a listing agreement and all the necessary disclosures to get the home on the market.

IMPLEMENT PROPERTY MARKETING PLAN

NETWORKING
- MLS agent network
- Broker open houses
- Personalized marketing to your sphere of influence

PUBLIC
- The "For Sale" sign — the number one marketing tool!
- Open houses
- Marketing and advertising materials (brochures, flyers, postcards, etc.)

ONLINE
- Multiple listing service
- National websites such as Zillow, Trulia, Realtor.com, and other syndicated sites
- Social media sites

COORDINATE SHOWINGS TO PROSPECTIVE BUYERS AND AGENTS

Explain how you will coordinate all showings and carefully screen serious buyers only.

PRESENTATION OF OFFERS TO PURCHASE

Tell the seller you will advise them on how to respond to an offer that is best for them.

NEGOTIATING OFFERS AND COUNTEROFFERS

Explain to the seller how you will work with the buyer's agent to negotiate the terms and conditions of the contract acceptable to them. Point out the common contingencies in an offer including inspection, financing, appraisal, sale of home, etc.

ACCEPTANCE OF OFFER AND BINDING THE CONTRACT

At this point the offer becomes a contract, and the parties are now legally bound to perform on the agreement.

CONTRACT ADMINISTRATION

Explain the contract-to-close process thoroughly and how you will work with the title company, inspectors, appraisers, the buyer's agent/closing coordinator, etc. to ensure everything is coming together.

PREPARING FOR CLOSING

Prepare the seller for closing and what needs to take place:
- Transfer of utilities
- Mortgage payoff
- Submission of any final documentation to the title company
- Final inspection/walk-through
- Coordinate keys, garage door remotes, gate codes, etc.

CLOSING AND POSSESSION

Explain the paperwork the seller will sign at the closing table to transfer title to the buyer and receive the proceeds from the sale of their home.

THE HOME-SELLING PROCESS

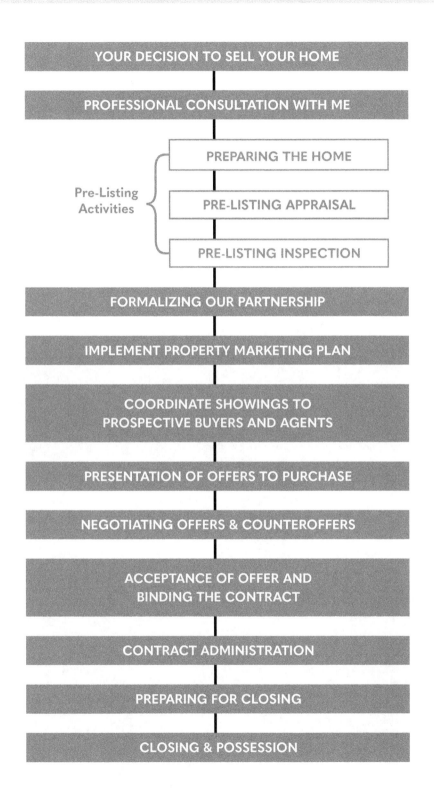

YOUR DECISION TO SELL YOUR HOME

PROFESSIONAL CONSULTATION WITH ME

Pre-Listing
Activities

PREPARING THE HOME

PRE-LISTING APPRAISAL

PRE-LISTING INSPECTION

FORMALIZING OUR PARTNERSHIP

IMPLEMENT PROPERTY MARKETING PLAN

COORDINATE SHOWINGS TO
PROSPECTIVE BUYERS AND AGENTS

PRESENTATION OF OFFERS TO PURCHASE

NEGOTIATING OFFERS & COUNTEROFFERS

ACCEPTANCE OF OFFER AND
BINDING THE CONTRACT

CONTRACT ADMINISTRATION

PREPARING FOR CLOSING

CLOSING & POSSESSION

CHAPTER 21

Prepare to Meet the Seller

*"In preparing for battle I have always
found that plans are useless, but planning
is indispensable."*

- DWIGHT D. EISENHOWER

When I was selling real estate full-time, the majority of my business came from sellers. Sellers were much easier to work with, had a much more successful closing rate, and most of the time, a cooperating agent would bring me a buyer. I closed a lot of real estate with seller clients. The old saying, "Those who list — last!" held true for me.

Joel was a successful agent with a strong track record and numerous sales awards under his belt. Most of Joel's past business had come from buyers. One couple to whom he'd sold a home a few years prior contacted Joel about listing that house for sale for them. Because it was only the second listing opportunity in his career, Joel realized quickly that he had some prep work to do.

I helped him get ready for his meeting with the seller. I started with asking a few basic questions: Are you ready for the meeting? Have you prepared a listing presentation? Are you convinced you can get the listing because they are a past client? I told Joel that unless he could answer all of the questions in the affirmative, he may not get the listing. I worked with Joel on creating an effective listing presentation that demonstrated his value proposition to the seller and communicated that he could get the most money for their home in a quick period of time.

Here are five key points to help you prepare for your next listing presentation. (I feel confident that they're effective; Joel used these same tips and got the listing!)

1. **Prepare a list of questions to ask the seller.** It is easy to sit down with a homeowner and tell them all about you, your brokerage, and the marketing and advertising you will do to sell their home. However, no two sellers are alike. If you are not prepared when you meet with them, you will come across as inexperienced and unprofessional.

   You should ask questions such as the following:
   - Why do you want to sell?
   - When do you want to sell?
   - How much do you believe your home is worth?
   - Why did you purchase this home?
   - What do you like about your street and neighborhood?
   - What do you like about your home?
   - What do you dislike about your home?
   - What outstanding mortgages and home equity loans are on the property?
   - Are there any liens on the property?
   - Where are you moving?
   - Do you need assistance in finding your new home?

   These are just a few of the questions you can ask to engage the seller, determine their motivation to sell, and get the information you need for the listing. Trust me, there are many more questions you can and will need to ask, but this will provide you with a beginning framework to customize your marketing plan for the home.

2. **Prepare a strong comparative market analysis (CMA) to establish a list price that will get the property *sold*!** Home sellers rely on the expertise of a real estate professional to provide them with pertinent sales information on similar homes in their area. You will want to show them sales prices and days on the market for properties that closed in the last six to twelve months and those that have come under contract within the last thirty to forty-five days.

   I believe the concept of developing a "forensic" Comparable Market Analysis (CMA) is important. An agent needs to really "drill down" in the MLS and county tax records to find the most comparable properties that have sold in the area, so the list price is justified when a prospective buyer comes forward to make an offer to purchase. This process takes time, but it is worth it.

Adjustments will need to be made when preparing the CMA so that square footage, number of bedrooms, features, lot size, etc., can be equalized in the comparisons. An interior and "curb appeal" assessment should also be conducted so you can determine if any improvements should be made to present the property in the best possible way.

You are not the one who sets the list price! An agent should never — and, I mean *never* — be the one who decides on the list price! The seller is the ultimate decision maker when it comes to pricing their home to sell. Our responsibility is to provide the seller with a range of pricing where the property probably would sell if listed today.

Trust me, sellers appreciate the research an agent does in helping them price their home. It reduces surprises for them at the offer stage, in negotiations, and at the time of the buyer's appraisal.

3. **Review tax information on the property.** I am shocked at how many agents do not take the time to review all the information contained in the county property tax records. These records include vital information on the owner's name, the legal description of the property, lot size, acreage, mortgages, loans and other liens, quit claim deeds, date of construction, flood zones, etc. All of this data is vital for an agent to know and can reduce problems at the time of listing or during the contract-to-close period. Let me give you an example.

    A few years back, when I was an active principal broker, one of my agents telephoned me in a panic. He represented the seller of a property in the Nashville area. His transaction was about five days from closing. When he called, he just received an angry phone call from a woman living in another state who told him he had no right to sell her home in Nashville. He was confused at her accusation and asked who she was and why she was calling.

    She turned out to be the mother of the seller who had signed the listing agreement with our agent. The daughter never told our agent her mother had an ownership interest in the property. After asking a few questions of the agent, I determined he never reviewed the tax record to confirm who owned the home. The tax file showed two people owned the property: the daughter and the mother. Long story short, the closing did not take place because the mother refused to sell the house. As a result, our agent had to write a check to the buyers for several thousands of dollars to reimburse them for all the monies spent on the loan, appraisal, inspections, temporary housing, etc. It was a costly lesson to learn, and it could have been avoided if the agent had done the necessary research of the property's tax record and verified ownership. Ouch!

4. **Prepare a professional listing presentation.** The listing presentation should contain the information noted in items one through three, but it should also include specific details on how you are going to be successful at selling the home. The seller wants to know how fast you will sell their house and how much money you will put in their pocket at the closing table. Your presentation should emphasize your value proposition and demonstrate your ability to get the job done. It needs to contain information on your comprehensive marketing tools including the use of internet sites, social media platforms, public and broker open houses, brokerage networking, traditional advertising, etc. An excellent listing presentation outlining the benefits of working with you and your company in meeting the seller's goals will more likely result in the seller signing a listing agreement with you.

5. **Check your confidence level before ringing the seller's doorbell.** Before going to a listing presentation, you must ask yourself, "Do I believe I am the best person to sell this particular home?"

Well... are you?

If you don't have the confidence to do everything needed to market the property, put it under contract, and get the seller to the closing table, then you might as well walk away.

Obtaining a listing in today's competitive real estate market can be very challenging. Having more knowledge than your competition before you arrive for the listing presentation will enable you to be better prepared and offer a more customized plan to the seller. And, with the right confidence, you are more likely to walk away with a signed listing agreement in your hand.

CHAPTER 22

How to Do an Effective Listing Presentation

"Be so good they can't ignore you."

Congratulations on getting the listing appointment! The seller is allowing *you* to meet with them and discuss how you can market their home. They are giving you an opportunity to find them a buyer. Are you prepared for your meeting? Do you have a property marketing plan to present to the seller on how you will sell their home? If not, the following eleven tips can be a framework for you to use when you meet with them.

1. **Tour the property.** As you enter the house, put everything down and ask them to give you a room-by-room tour of the home. By doing so, it shows the seller you have a real interest in their home, the layout, distinctive features, and any upgrades the homeowners made since they purchased it.

   You will also need to ask them to show you the exterior of the property including any unattached buildings, swimming pool cabanas, or tool sheds. As the seller shows you around, ask them what they liked about the home and what they didn't like about it. Touring the property is a great time to begin building rapport and trust with the homeowner and will provide you with information as you give your listing presentation.

2. **Go to the kitchen table.** After you finish the tour, ask the seller if you can meet at the kitchen table. Why the kitchen table?

   I have found the kitchen is a much more relaxed area

than a living room or den. It is the one room in the house that is always conducive to conversation, and it also reflects the personality of the home and the owners. The kitchen table provides a physical space for your presentation materials and listing paperwork.

If for some reason the kitchen is not available, the dining room is a great second option for the presentation.

3. **Begin with an overview of the current real estate market conditions.** As you start your presentation, summarize the current real estate market. Don't overwhelm them with too much data, but you will need to give them a reasonable assessment of market conditions and the impact the local market will have on the sale of their home. Information from the Multiple Listing Service or local REALTOR® associations is always a reliable source for how the market is performing compared to previous months and years.

4. **Talk about your company and the benefits the firm brings to the table.** You joined your real estate firm because you believed the company could best support you and your business. The seller needs to know what role the firm will play in your marketing efforts. If you are part of a large brokerage operation you might want to talk about the company's market share, the brand recognition of the firm, the vast network of agents in the company who can provide high exposure, the lead generation from the firm's website that can procure potential buyers, etc. If you're part of a smaller firm, explain the niche the firm has in the market and other successes it has had in competing with the more prominent real estate companies.

Don't spend too much time talking about the firm because the seller is looking for *you* to sell their home — not the firm. Five years after you close on their property, they will probably not remember the brokerage you work for, but they will remember you — their real estate agent.

5. **Review the CMA and discuss pricing strategy.** A comparative market analysis (CMA) can be a useful tool in helping the seller establish a list price for their home. It also can be somewhat perplexing and overwhelming. It is crucial you take the time to review with the seller the comparable properties that have sold during the last six months as well as those that are currently active with and without sales contracts.

When I discuss price with a seller, I use a legal pad and pen to draw a graph (see the example below) illustrating the range of prices for each category: closed, active, and under contract. It is a straightforward, but effective, way to illustrate the range of prices in the CMA so they can make a more realistic and informed decision on a sale price.

Whether you utilize the extensive graphic in a CMA software program or pen and paper, make sure they *see* (through a visual example) where their home should be priced. This is the point in the conversation where the seller will need to face the reality of the market and accept the fact that the data does not lie.

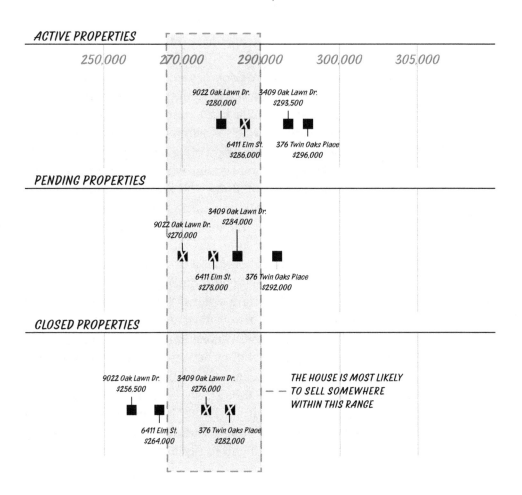

PRICING ANALYSIS FOR 7749 ELM STREET
(X = Most Comparable)

6. **Discuss the seller's goals.** My wife and I have owned numerous homes during our marriage, and we always had two basic questions when selling them: How long will it take, and how much money will we make on the sale? We also had expectations when we put each house on the market. The same is true for your seller. A home has to be priced right to get the top dollar for the home. A high list price will most assuredly extend the listing period and compel buyers to look at more competitively priced properties.

Homeowners may also expect their home to sell quickly — especially when everything around them is selling fast. A quick sale will not happen if a house is not ready. It can sit on the market for quite some time. That is why pricing the home right and making it look its best is critical at the beginning of the listing when most showings will occur.

In addition to getting the list price right, a listing agent needs to be prepared to tell the seller to do interior and exterior work so that the home will look its best for prospective buyers. An excellent interior presentation and curb appeal are critical for getting a buyer to make an offer on the property. It may cost the seller some money to make the needed improvements, but it will be worth it to them in the end.

7. **Prepare the seller for the negotiating process.** Sellers need to be open and prepared to negotiate when they receive an offer. Another round of negotiations will happen when the buyer completes their inspections and presents a list of repair or replacement items for the seller to address before closing. The buyer's inspection and resolution periods are critical points in the transaction, and if it is not shepherded correctly by the agents, the deal could quickly fall apart. There will always be less anxiety for a seller if they know up front what to expect during these two critical stages of the transaction. During this phase of the transaction, many agents feel they are truly earning their money because of the negotiating that happens between the seller and the buyer.

8. **Discuss your role in the listing.** I always tell agents that clients do not understand what we do "behind the green curtain." A real estate professional plays a crucial role in the home-selling process. In fact, it is difficult to explain all of the various jobs

a listing agent does to get a home under contract. Numerous details must be addressed during the contract-to-close period including ensuring the various contingency performance dates in the agreement are met and all transaction paperwork is in order to get the parties to the closing table.

It is important to explain to the seller that you are working exclusively for them. You are their representative, advocate, intermediary, negotiator, counselor, and "go-to" person from the beginning of the listing to the end of the transaction. You must be the one who is screening potential buyers who are qualified to purchase the home. You are the one who will meet the appraiser, inspector, contractors, and others the buyer will use during their due-diligence period. You will work with the title attorney and closing company to make sure the closing goes as smoothly as possible. And you are the one they can turn to at any time to answer their questions, alleviate any of their concerns, or handle any issue that may arise. You are there for them!

9. **Present a strategic and comprehensive master marketing plan.** More times than not, a seller will ask a listing agent how they are going to sell the home. You need to prepare a marketing plan that is both strategic and comprehensive. My marketing plans are customized for each property, but all of them have the same essential components.

The style and location of the house will dictate what kind of buyer will most likely look at it. High-end, multimillion-dollar homes have smaller buyer pools, so your marketing needs to focus on the wealthier buyer. Plan on spending more on professional photography and videography, advertising, print materials, and open houses.

More traditional properties will utilize a broader approach in how they are marketed to their particular group of buyers. I have found traditional forms of advertising (i.e., websites, social media, print materials, networking, open houses, etc.) are quite effective. Whether you're selling a $2 million mansion or a $250,000 ranch-style home, you must develop a marketing plan that will work.

My particular property marketing plans are chronologically based and front-loaded with extensive, "out-of-the-gate" activities taking place within the first fourteen days of the listing period. I utilize numerous marketing and advertising platforms to expose the property to as many people as possible once the house hits the market. It is uploaded on the internet to sites such as Realtor.com, Zillow, Trulia, Yahoo, Homes.com, etc. I also use social media platforms such as Facebook, Twitter, Instagram, LinkedIn, and others to spread the word about my listing. Mailings, networking, and other traditional forms of advertising support my efforts. Trust me, marketing a home will keep you busy!

No matter what your marketing plan looks like, make sure it is written down, and the seller receives a copy. Remember, it is challenging to take a road trip without a map and directions, and the same holds true for how a house is sold. Put the plan on paper and stick with it! Be prepared to make revisions to the plan if you experience a low showing count or current market conditions change.

10. **Discuss your agency relationship.** It is important you discuss your agency relationship with the seller. The relationship between a real estate client and the licensed professional representing the client is what agency is all about.

Most brokerages have a policy stating listing agents must be "designated agents." Through a designated agency listing agreement, the managing broker designates one agent as the exclusive agent for the seller. Designated agency allows the broker to avoid problems arising from what I call "standard agency," where everyone in the firm is considered an agent to the seller.

Furthermore, you may elect to default to a neutral non-agency position if an unrepresented buyer is interested in purchasing the property. If this is the case, you can work with both the seller and the buyer as a "facilitator" or "transaction broker" to close the transaction for both parties. (In my state, Tennessee, state law binds the actions of facilitators, but they do not have a specific fiduciary relationship with the seller or the buyer.) I would encourage you to provide prospects and clients a handout on the various agency and non-agency relationships in a transaction. Speak with your principal broker on your firm's agency policy if you have any questions or need clarification.

11. **Review the listing agreement and other disclosures.** You have

demonstrated to the seller how you are going to market their home and procure a buyer. Now, you need to do the "fun stuff" — the paperwork. Carefully review the listing agreement with the seller and explain the various components of the agreement. A listing agreement is a temporary "employment" contract obligating the brokerage, the designated agent, and the seller to specific terms and conditions. The seller needs to understand what they agree to before they sign the agreement.

Go over the other disclosures and forms and answer any questions they might have concerning these documents. The seller needs to understand they are signing enforceable legal documents allowing you and your firm to sell their home. Make sure you provide them with a copy of every document they sign for their records.

With the ease and prevalence of digital signatures, you may want to email the documents to your client via your document-signing platform. However, inform the seller they should not sign any document digitally until they have thoroughly read each one. I would suggest if you want the seller to sign the paperwork digitally you review each form with them at your listing presentation.

(Note: I have created a digital signature disclosure you can use to ensure they understand the digital signing process and the importance of reading the documents before signing. See Chapter 42.)

PROPERTY CONDITION DISCLOSURE

Explain the importance of the property condition disclosure, the requirement for them to answer each question truthfully, and the need for them to disclose any known adverse facts relating to the property. If the seller wants to sell the property without any representations and warranties, they may provide a disclaimer stating the house is to be purchased in an "as is" condition.

You should never complete any of these forms for your client. Only the seller *fully completes* any disclosure/disclaimer on the property condition. Additionally, you should never advise what should be disclosed and what should not be disclosed on the forms. These are legal questions, and answering them may be considered the practice of law. If a seller has a question concerning what should be disclosed, they should speak with an attorney.

Your listing presentation can be the deciding factor for whether or not you get the listing. Preparation, confidence, and accurate market information will determine your success in getting the seller to sign a listing agreement with you.

When you do get the listing, be prepared for the work ahead of you. It is not an easy task to sell a home. However, if you commit the time and effort and invest in the resources to market the house the right way, it *will* sell.

CHAPTER 23

Where Are the Offers?
The Danger of Overpricing a Listing

"Next to doing the right thing, the most important thing is to let people know you are doing the right thing."

— JOHN D. ROCKEFELLER

I tell agents getting a listing is relatively easy. Selling the listing takes work.

That work begins with pricing the property accurately. Our first job as a listing agent with the seller is to partner together in establishing the right price before putting the property on the market.

Every agent should know that a new property listing should be correctly priced before the ink on the listing agreement has time to dry. A brand-new listing always appears on MLS on the "hot listings" page or at the top of the active property list. Newer listings usually sell for a higher price than properties listed on the market for a more extended period. As the weeks pass, potential buyers begin to wonder why it hasn't already sold. So, what should you do to prevent a very long listing period? Could the list price be to blame for the property's failure to sell quickly?

HOW TO PRICE PROPERTY

The list price a seller puts on his or her home must be carefully considered before placing it on the open market. A high price will cause the listing to remain on the market too long and become stagnant. A below market price will lead to a rapid sale, and the seller will lose money. A competitive pricing strategy will result in a marketable listing that's more likely to lead to an offer, a bound contract, and a successful closing with both the buyer and seller meeting their real estate objectives.

Review the following key points with your seller client when deciding how to price their property.

- **The seller must understand the real value of their home is determined by what a buyer is willing to pay for it in today's real estate market.** Market price is determined by what other comparable properties have sold for during a specified period — usually the most recent six months. Pricing the home above the market price will undoubtedly ensure an extended listing period.

A high price will cause the listing to remain on the market too long and become stagnant.

A below market price will lead to a rapid sale, and the seller will lose money.

A competitive pricing strategy will result in a marketable listing that's more likely to lead to an offer, a bound contract, and a successful closing with both the buyer and seller meeting their real estate objectives.

- **An impartial evaluation of market activity is the most effective way to estimate a property's selling price.** A comparative market analysis (CMA) is a great tool to present to a seller so they can see similar, nearby properties that recently sold. The CMA can also show homes that are currently active on the market, as well as those under contract or those that recently failed to close.

- **The longer a property remains on the market, the lower the price must be for it to sell.** Statistics show that when a property is not correctly priced from the start, it nearly always ultimately sells for far less. As a result, the seller will lose a considerable amount of time and money.

- **When discussing pricing with a seller, a listing agent must convey the three elements impacting the sale of a home: price, condition, and location.** Of these three, the seller can control price and condition. Condition can have a bearing on what a buyer will offer for it. The agent needs to ensure the seller does everything possible to present the home in a condition that will allow it to compete with similar properties for sale.

- **Another critical point in pricing revolves around the seller wanting a certain amount of cash from the sale of their home.** What the seller wants to receive at the closing table doesn't affect the home's market value. The market does not care what they need! This fact is painful for some sellers to accept because they may be counting on money from the sale of the home to go toward the purchase of their dream home. If they cannot grasp this reality, then the listing you worked hard to get will not be a marketable one, and your efforts to sell it will be for naught.

- **Many times, agents will find themselves competing against other agents for the listing.** When I was actively selling homes, I remember numerous sellers saying they spoke to another agent who said the listing price should be at "X." What a competing listing agent says about what the price should be doesn't affect its value. Unfortunately, some agents will tell sellers what they want to hear regarding value, only to then badger them later to keep reducing the price so they can sell the property. Good listing agents advise clients to price it right from the start and convince sellers the right price is the best price.

Your primary responsibility as a listing agent is to find that one "ready, willing, and able" buyer to purchase your client's home. If the property is not priced right from the beginning, the seller — and you — will find yourselves waiting a long time for a buyer to submit an offer to purchase. An essential part of your fiduciary responsibility to your client is to provide your seller with guidance in determining a price that will sell their home.

Pricing it right from the beginning benefits the seller by giving them more money in their pocket and closing on the property in a timely manner. Poor pricing will do the opposite and not only delay the sale of the home, but it will also, most assuredly, impact your relationship with the seller. Sellers begin losing confidence in their listing agent when their home remains on the market for a long period of time.

CHAPTER 24

You Have the Listing.
Now What?

"Getting it right takes a lot of
getting it wrong."

Once the "For Sale" sign is in the front yard, you need to move forward with your property marketing plan. There is not one minute to waste in exposing the property to the world to procure that one ready, willing, and able buyer!

MARKETING YOUR NEW LISTING

One of the very first items to check off your list is to gather specific information about the house, starting with a prior appraisal on the home. Ask your seller to provide you with a previous professional appraisal if one is available.

Why do you want an appraisal? An appraisal will contain a professional measurement of the house as well as other relevant property information. If an appraisal is not available, you should call an appraiser to measure the home. Remember, you will need accurate square footage information before you enter the listing into your Multiple Listing Service (MLS).

DISCOVER TITLE ISSUES NOW,
RATHER THAN LATER

I always ask my title attorney to order a preliminary title search to see if any issues need to be addressed or disclosed by the seller before accepting an offer. The search will reveal any liens on the property or back taxes owed by the seller. The cost for a title search is minimal and well worth it to avoid any surprises down the road in the transaction.

In addition to determining whether or not the property has a clear title, ask the seller for a copy of their title insurance policy. In most states, title insurance companies will offer a discount to sellers if they are paying the buyer's title insurance at closing. This discount usually only applies to sellers who have lived in their home ten years or less.

You will also need city and property tax information and a survey noting the property's boundaries, easements, etc. A plat map of the subdivision can also be useful in knowing more about the location of streets and lot layouts in the neighborhood. All of this information is available at the county courthouse or online through courthouse record providers.

DISCUSS SHOWING INSTRUCTIONS

It's also important to discuss showing instructions with your seller. They need to understand their home will be shown to many people at different times of the day. Explain the importance of being flexible in allowing prospective buyers and their agents to tour their home.

Ask them for how much notice they would like to receive for appointments as well as "blackout" times when the house is not open for showings. Let them know you will be monitoring each showing and asking for feedback from agents who show the home.

REVIEW HOMEOWNER ASSOCIATION INFORMATION

Many neighborhoods and condominium developments have homeowner associations (HOAs) that are managed by professional property management companies. Ask the seller to give you a copy of the HOA bylaws or Covenants, Conditions, and Restrictions (CC&R) that contain the rules and regulations of the neighborhood. Carefully read all the documentation so you understand any restrictions for properties in the neighborhood that might exist.

Contact the management company if you have any questions or need additional information on what is in the CC&R or neighborhood bylaws. (Note: The HOA or their management company should disclose to you or the seller any required transfer fees, present or future assessments, and financial statements for the association.)

GATHER THE COST OF UTILITIES

A prospective buyer will want to know the costs for the home's utilities including electricity, water, sewer, garbage pickup, cable TV, etc. Ask the seller to write down the names of each utility provider and provide you with copies of the last twelve months of bills from each utility company. From this information, you can determine an average monthly cost for each service. I make this data readily available for buyers and their agents by including it in my in-house property brochure or online in the MLS.

FIND OUT WHAT REMAINS WITH THE PROPERTY

Ask the seller what items will convey with the property. Examples include tool sheds and outer buildings, hot tubs, security systems, water softeners, etc. You will need information for each including the service providers and any warranties that may remain in effect.

POSTING TO THE MLS

After you secure the lockbox on or near the front door and install your signage, you will be ready to upload the listing in your MLS. Before the listing goes "active" on the MLS, you need to ensure the information you provide your MLS system is correct and up to date. Be careful not to put any information on the MLS that might be construed as a misrepresentation.

Send a copy of the MLS information page to your seller to review it for accuracy. Our MLS in the Nashville area allows agents to upload documents a buyer's agent will need to make an offer to purchase. If your MLS enables this feature, make sure the materials you upload are correct, complete, and do not contain any confidential information the seller would not want disclosed.

PROMOTING FEATURES AND AMENITIES

Before you design and implement any marketing materials for your listing, you need to gather information on the specific features and amenities of the home, neighborhood, and community. Try to accentuate the top features in more detail with distinct benefits to the homeowner.

Order professional photography and videography so the house will stand out in the various advertising and marketing mediums you utilize. Many photographers offer incredible aerial photography and high-definition videos showing the "bigger picture" of the property and its surroundings.

One of the most effective marketing pieces I use for property listings is a one-page black and white flyer titled, "What Made Your House a Home?" I ask the seller to answer three questions by handwriting their answers after each question. I then put their completed questionnaire in an acrylic display stand near the other marketing materials so that potential buyers can read it as they look at the home.

WHAT MADE YOUR HOUSE A HOME?

You have enjoyed living in your present home! There are many reasons about it that you have liked and appreciated. Possibly some of the same amenities will appeal to the new buyer. Can you assist us in our marketing by listing below some of the reasons why your home was comfortable, practical, useful, and enjoyable?

1. Can you name four reasons why you purchased this property?

2. What four features do you enjoy most about your home?

3. What four features do you like about the neighborhood and location?

I believe a listing will have a much better chance of being seen by a buyer when a listing agent can provide them with the correct property information and marketing materials accurately representing the home and what it can offer a new owner. It takes a lot of work, but as with everything else in selling real estate, it will provide you with the results both you and the seller want.

A 23-WEEK MARKETING ACTION PLAN

All listing agents need to have a written plan outlining specific marketing "action items" that will take place during the listing period. The following Marketing Action Plan spans activities for marketing your seller's home for twenty-three weeks.

23-WEEK MARKETING ACTION PLAN

PRE-LISTING ACTIVITIES

- ☐ Prospect with potential homeowners
- ☐ Set up an appointment for marketing/ listing presentation
- ☐ Research MLS to build CMA (competitive market analysis) and statistics
- ☐ Create listing packet
- ☐ Build draft flyer with picture of the home
- ☐ Present marketing presentation
- ☐ Start Marketing Action Plan

WEEK #1

- ☐ Obtain complete Property Disclosure Statement
- ☐ Input house details into MLS system
- ☐ Review MLS computer printout for accuracy with the homeowner
- ☐ Get digital pictures of home
- ☐ Build ads for the local paper, etc.
- ☐ Build photo home flyer
- ☐ Upload the property to your website
- ☐ Discuss home inspection
- ☐ Set up office tour for area real estate agents
- ☐ Build and review complete Marketing Action Plan (this document)
- ☐ Ask for copies of utility bills to create an operations sheet
- ☐ Review homeowners' needs for new home, relocation, moving assistance, etc.
- ☐ Provide homeowners with a copy of *450 Ideas to Sell Your House Faster* or other materials on how to prepare a home for sale.
  (You may download a copy of this at DoYouHaveAMinuteBook.com.)
- ☐ Ensure that sellers know that your main job is marketing
- ☐ Get copies of warranty deed and any old surveys or appraisals
- ☐ Place seller's Property Disclosure Statement, lead-based paint forms, etc. inside the house and on MLS, if possible
- ☐ Follow up with all agents who left business cards at the listing to get feedback to give to the seller
- ☐ Initial social media advertising on Facebook, Twitter, LinkedIn, Instagram, and other sites.

WEEK #2

- ☐ Review photo home flyer with owners (provide copies for them to give out)
- ☐ Physically take fact sheets to other competitor realtors in your area
- ☐ Build printout of utility cost averages for home
- ☐ Discuss showing comments (from prospective buyers) and any decisions made to date
- ☐ Provide a copy of local ad when running in the paper
- ☐ Ask homeowners if they have any additional questions
- ☐ Provide homeowners with information from office agent tour
- ☐ Prepare postcard mail-out to "feeder neighborhoods" on your new listing
- ☐ Follow-up with all agents who left business cards at the listing to get feedback to give to the seller
- ☐ Update social media advertising

WEEK #3

- [ ] Review any showing comments and decisions made to date
- [ ] Discuss "mortgage verification" information with homeowner; discuss any other liens
- [ ] Do a net sheet with the seller and go over seller closing costs for your area
- [ ] Review ad that ran the past week with homeowners
- [ ] Download and review MLS Hot Sheet statistics with homeowners (CMA Update)
- [ ] Mail fact sheet to the top real estate agents from other companies in your area
- [ ] Follow up with all agents who left business cards at the listing to get feedback to give to the seller
- [ ] Update social media advertising

WEEK #4

- [ ] Review any showing comments and decisions made to date
- [ ] Open discussion with homeowners about new CMA: decision point
- [ ] Update internet/MLS if necessary
- [ ] Set up a time to show homeowners new homes or discuss relocation needs
- [ ] Set up Open House for public flyers (Open House only if needed)
- [ ] Provide homeowners with a list of items they will need to complete before the Open House
- [ ] Mail or email Open House flyers (Open House only if needed)
- [ ] Email seller with any news, either good or bad
- [ ] Follow up with all agents who left business cards at the listing to get feedback to give to the seller
- [ ] Update social media advertising

WEEK #5

- [ ] Hold Open House on Sunday, 2:00 pm – 4:00 pm (Open House only if needed)
- [ ] Give Open House feedback to homeowners
- [ ] Review any showing comments and decisions made to date
- [ ] Review for pricing adjustments
- [ ] Review for condition adjustments
- [ ] Send photo flyer to agents, noting any change in listing (price, terms, conditions)
- [ ] Try an Open House for real estate agents
- [ ] Follow up with all agents who left business cards at the listing to get feedback to give to the seller
- [ ] Update social media advertising

WEEK #6

- [ ] Review any showing comments and decisions made to date
- [ ] Provide homeowner with copies of ads
- [ ] Review suggestions from agents to date
- [ ] Get a new agent to help with a Sunday Open House
- [ ] Email seller with any news, either good or bad
- [ ] Follow up with all agents who left business cards at the listing to get feedback to give to the seller
- [ ] Update social media advertising

WEEK #7

- [ ] MLS Hot Sheet Information
- [ ] Appraisal needed?
- [ ] Do another CMA update
- [ ] Review any showing comments and decisions made to date
- [ ] Review ad copy and make any needed changes
- [ ] Follow up with all agents who left business cards at the listing to get feedback to give to the seller
- [ ] Update social media advertising

WEEK #8

- [ ] Visit competitive homes to see how they compete with the homeowners' house
- [ ] Make any changes necessary after checking the competition
- [ ] Review any showing comments and decisions made to date
- [ ] Provide homeowner with copies of ads
- [ ] Review MLS stats for the area and provide an update to the homeowner
- [ ] Send a photo flyer to agents again noting additional changes in listing
- [ ] Get a new agent to help with a Sunday Open House
- [ ] Email seller with any news, either good or bad
- [ ] Follow up with all agents who left business cards at the listing to get feedback to give to the Seller
- [ ] Update social media advertising

WEEK #9

- [ ] Try an Open House for agents again (Open House only if needed)
- [ ] Create new CMA
- [ ] Update sellers with any showing comments
- [ ] Review house again — critically — and discuss any changes needed
- [ ] Work with homeowners to create a new ad and get placed
- [ ] Consider a "bonus" on listing (i.e., increased commission, seller to pay additional closing costs, washer/ dryer, refrigerator, landscaping or carpet allowances, etc.)
- [ ] Email seller with any news, either good or bad
- [ ] Follow up with all agents who left business cards at the listing to get feedback to give to the seller
- [ ] Update social media advertising

WEEK #10

- [ ] Update your office agents and ask for help!
- [ ] Prepare new MLS Hot Sheet to review activity in the area around the house
- [ ] Change remarks in MLS
- [ ] Review any showing comments and decisions made to date
- [ ] Review appraisal as soon as completed
- [ ] Discuss any changes in listings as per the appraisal
- [ ] Change MLS/website information due to above
- [ ] Get a new agent to help with a Sunday Open House (Open House only if needed)
- [ ] Email seller with any news, either good or bad
- [ ] Follow up with all agents who left business cards at the listing to get feedback to give to the seller
- [ ] Update social media advertising

WEEK #11

- ☐ Discuss showing reports
- ☐ Prepare new photo flyer — provide copies to seller to give to friends and work colleagues
- ☐ Prepare a list of all houses in a $20,000 spread on the market in the general area of the property to emphasize the amount of competition
- ☐ Discuss real estate trends and economic trends in the area
- ☐ Make any changes in the listing that are brought about due to above
- ☐ Email seller with any news, either good or bad
- ☐ Follow up with all agents who left business cards at the listing to get feedback to give to the seller
- ☐ Update social media advertising

WEEK #12

- ☐ Price adjustment again, especially if none has been made
- ☐ Review information to use to push the property inside brokerage
- ☐ Update office agents per above
- ☐ Review any showing comments and decisions made to date
- ☐ Review ad copy and change ad
- ☐ Email seller with any news, either good or bad
- ☐ Follow up with all agents who left business cards at the listing to get feedback to give to the Seller
- ☐ Update social media advertising

WEEKS #13-22

- ☐ Review any showing comments and decisions made to date
- ☐ Do weekly CMA
- ☐ Review ads and comments
- ☐ Email seller with any news, either good or bad
- ☐ Follow up with all agents who left business cards at the listing to get feedback to give to the seller
- ☐ Update social media advertising

WEEK #23

- ☐ Extend listing if still wanted and if price adjustment can be made to sell the property

CHAPTER 25

Fair Housing Language:
The Good, The Bad, and
The Ugly

"Housing is absolutely essential to human flourishing. Without stable shelter, it all falls apart."

— MATTHEW DESMOND, SOCIOLOGIST

Real estate licensees need to pay close attention to the language used in any advertising and marketing materials. This includes what is written in the "remarks" section of the Multiple Listing Service (MLS), on websites, and on social media platforms.

The U.S. Department of Housing and Urban Development (HUD) and the U.S. Justice Department monitor language in real estate advertising to ensure there are no fair housing violations as noted in the Fair Housing Act of 1968 and subsequent amendments added with the passage of the Fair Housing Amendments Act of 1988. Along with federal guidelines for fair housing, individual states have laws to protect the public from discrimination in the sale and rental of real estate.

Discrimination is a serious matter, and agents need to be well versed in federal and state fair housing regulations. HUD utilizes "testers" on a regular basis to see if real estate agents are saying or doing anything that might be considered discriminatory. HUD testers are trained to disguise themselves as prospective buyer and seller clients. It is difficult to distinguish them from an actual buyer or seller.

In my second year of selling real estate, I am pretty sure I had a HUD tester contact me about a property I listed in south Nashville. Some of his questions concerned a large Hispanic population in the area around my listing. I think he was testing me to see if I would steer him away from that area because of the particular ethnic demographic profile. I can't be certain he was from HUD, but based on the conversation I had with him, I am pretty sure he was one of their testers.

Violating federal and state fair housing laws is serious. The first offense of a federal fair housing violation carries substantial civil penalties imposed by the U.S. Federal Court system. Additional violations are much more substantial and, in certain cases, may carry a prison sentence.

The Fair Housing Act prohibits certain categories of discrimination in housing. This federal law prohibits publishing advertisements indicating "any preference, limitation or discrimination based on" the protected categories "with respect to the sale or rental of a dwelling" [42 U.S.C. § 3604(c)]. The protected categories include:

1. race
2. color
3. religion
4. sex
5. disability or handicap
6. familial status
7. national origin

FAIR HOUSING WORD AND PHRASE LIST

This word and phrase list was adopted from various HUD publications, multiple REALTOR® Associations, and publishing organizations. It should be used as a guideline to assist you in complying with state and federal fair housing laws. It is not all-inclusive and does not contain every word or phrase that could violate any local, state, or federal statute. Each word must be considered in context.

As a general rule, describe the property, not the people who may live in the property. Contact your principal broker if you have any questions as to which words to use in your property advertising, marketing materials, and MLS listings.

UNACCEPTABLE
The following words or phrases are UNACCEPTABLE.

Able bodied	Congregation	Homosexuals, no
Active adult community*	Couple(s)	Hungarian
Adult living*	Couple only	Impaired, no
Adult park*	Crippled	Independent living
Adults only*	Deaf	Indian
African, no	Disabled	Integrated
Agile	Drinkers, no	Irish
AIDS, no	Employed, must be	Italian
Alcoholics, no	Empty nesters*	Jewish
American Indians, no	English only	Kids, no
Asian	Ethnic references	Latino, no
Bachelor pad	Families, no	LDS Temple
Bisexuals, no	Gays	Lesbians, no
Blacks, no	Golden-agers only	Married
Blind, no	Grandma's house	Mature complex*
Catholic	Group home(s), no	Mature couple(s)*
Caucasian	Handicap parking, no	Mature individual(s)*
Chicano, no	Handicapped, not for	Mature person(s)*
Children, no	Healthy only	Membership approval required
Chinese	Hindu	
Christian	Hispanic	Mentally handicapped
Colored	HIV, no	Mentally ill
		Mexican

Mexican-American

Migrant workers, no

Military, no

Mormon Temple

Mosque

Muslim

Nationality

Nanny's room

Negro

Newlyweds

Number of children

One child

Oriental

Parish

Philippine or Philippinos, no

Physically fit

Play area, no

Preferred community

Polish

Puerto Rican

Religious references

Restricted

Retarded

Shrine

Single person

Singles only

Social Security
Insurance, no

Spanish speaking, no

Stake Center

Supplemental Security
Income (SSI), no

Synagogue, near

Tenant (description of)

Traditional neighborhood

Transgenders, no

Unemployed, no

Ward House

Wheelchairs, no

White

White(s) only

**Reference to ANY of
the protected classes:**

Race, Religion, Familial
Status, Sex, National Origin,
Color or Handicapped

USE CAUTION

The following list is comprised of words or phrases that
should be used with great CAUTION.

Active

Bachelor

Board approval required

Close to _____

College students, no

Curfew

Desirable neighborhood

Domestic quarters

Exclusive

Executive Female(s) only**

Female roommate**

55 and older community*

Gender specific

Gentleman's farm

Grandma's house

Golden agers*

Handyman's dream

Housing for older
persons/seniors*

Ideal for... (should not
describe people)

Landmark reference

Male(s) only**

Male roommate**

Man (men) only**

Mature

Near _____

Number of persons

Older person(s)*

One person

Perfect for ... (should not
describe people)

Pets, no

Prestigious

Private

Quality neighborhood

Retirees*

Retirement home*

Safe neighborhood

School name or district

Seasonal worker(s), no

Section 8, no

Secure

Senior adult community*

Senior citizen(s)*

Senior discount*

Senior housing*

Senior(s)*

Sex or gender**

Single woman/man** Straight only Walking distance of, within
62 and older community* Students, no Winter/summer visitors*
Smoker(s), no Temple, near Woman (women) only**
Snowbirds* Tranquil setting
Sophisticated Two people

ACCEPTABLE

The following list includes words or phrases that are ACCEPTABLE.

Assistance animal(s) Guest house Private setting
Assistance animal(s) only Handicap accessible Public transportation, near
Bedrooms (number of) In-law apartment Quality construction
Bus, near Kids welcome Quiet
Church, near Luxury townhouses Quiet neighborhood
Convalescent home Membership available Responsible
Convenient to Mother-in-law apartment Section 8 accepted/
Credit check required (or suite) welcome
Den Neighborhood name Security provided
Drinking, no Nice Single family home
Drug users, no Non-smokers Smoking, no
Drugs, no Number of sleeping areas Spanish-speaking
Equal Housing Nursery Square feet
  Opportunity Nursing home Starter home
Families welcome Pets limited to Student(s)
Family room   assistance animals Townhouse
Family, great for Play area Traditional style
First-time buyer Privacy Verifiable income
Fixer-upper Private driveway View of _____
Gated community Private entrance With view
Golf course, near Private property

Permitted to be used only when complex or development qualifies as housing for older persons

**Permitted to be used only when describing shared living areas or dwelling units used exclusively as dormitory facilities by educational institutions. All cautionary words are unacceptable if utilized in a context that states an unlawful preference or limitation. Furthermore, all cautionary words are "red flags" to fair housing enforcement agencies. Use of these words may serve to invite further investigation and/or testing.*

CHAPTER 26

Working with Unrepresented Buyers

"We don't have to be smarter than the rest.
We have to be more disciplined than the rest."

During the past several years, the *Profile of Home Buyers and Sellers*, published annually by the National Association of REALTORS® (NAR), has consistently reported 10 to 13 percent of home buyers did not have professional representation when purchasing a home. Included in these numbers are those buyers who worked directly with a new construction on-site agent or builder representative. Unrepresented buyers elect not to work with agents for a variety of reasons, but two of the biggest ones are they feel they can "go it alone" and save money in the transaction.

WORKING WITH UNREPRESENTED BUYERS

I divide unrepresented buyers into two groups. The first group consists of individuals who are relocating to the area from another state. They arrive in town and begin looking at properties on their own. They may or may not want an agent, but if they find a listed property on their own, they are more than likely to remain unrepresented allowing the listing agent to guide them through the transaction.

The second group is the buyers who feel they just don't need an agent to represent them in the transaction. Some people will be naive and will not understand the benefits of having someone who can negotiate and protect their interests. Others are the "smart ones" who think they know everything involved in a real estate transaction and don't need any assistance in purchasing a home. They believe they are intelligent enough to make an offer, negotiate it, traverse the "contract-to-close" period, and close on the property. In addition, these buyers will assume they can get a better deal from the seller if they don't have an agent. They don't see the value in having an agent who can represent them as their buyer representative.

Unfortunately, with both of these groups, the listing agent will always act in the best interest of their seller and do what they can to have the upper hand in negotiating the purchase price and other terms and conditions of the contract benefitting their client. The unrepresented buyer can find themselves on the "short end of the stick" when going up against an experienced agent.

Real estate agents sometimes cringe when they face the possibility of working with buyers who do not have an agent. They really should not feel this way. Real estate laws and regulations in most states protect unrepresented buyers by specifying the fiduciary responsibilities of real estate licensees whether the consumer has representation or not. These duties include practicing real estate with integrity and professionalism, working honestly and in good faith, disclosing adverse facts, and protecting anything they learn that is to be kept confidential. Listing agents need to remember these duties as they encounter an unrepresented buyer interested in purchasing their listing.

HOW TO ASSIST AN UNREPRESENTED BUYER

Many listing agents feel they are limited in the scope of service they can provide an unrepresented buyer. Listing agents can assist the buyer in many ways. These include, but are not limited to:
- Preparing information on comparable properties
- Assisting in completing a Purchase and Sale Agreement to make an offer on the seller's property
- Delivering the buyer's offer to the seller
- Meeting the buyer and their inspectors, appraisers, contractors, etc.
- Providing information to the buyer's lender
- Communicating with the seller during the transaction

COMMUNICATING WITH AN UNREPRESENTED BUYER

When an unrepresented buyer contacts a listing agent about a property they have on the market or visits an open house, the agent must be prepared to communicate with the buyer and assist them if they want to write an offer on the agent's listing. They can find themselves in an uncomfortable situation if they do not handle the communication properly.

Some agents believe they should not talk to an unrepresented buyer at all, or they feel the need to refer them to another agent, so they can be represented. The first reason is silly. The second reason is an excellent idea if they want representation as you can refer them to an agent you know and trust. Plus, you can get a referral fee by sending them to another agent.

Remember, unrepresented buyers are people, too! When I was an active principal broker, agents would call me to let me know they had an unrepresented buyer and didn't know what to do. Some were even in a panic. Every time I received one of these calls I wanted to laugh out loud because the agent was making these folks out to be lepers or second-class citizens. Well, they're not and should be treated with respect and professional courtesy as we do our clients.

SHOWING YOUR LISTING TO AN UNREPRESENTED BUYER

Let's say a prospective buyer walks into an open house at one of your listings one Sunday afternoon. They love the house as it meets all their needs and is convenient to their work, school, and church. They want to write an offer. The first words out of your mouth need to be, "Are you working with an agent?" Per the NAR Code of Ethics and Standards of Practice, Standard of Practice 16-9 under Article 16 states REALTORS® must ask the prospect if they are working with a buyer's agent and have signed an exclusive buyer representation agreement.

If they don't have an agent, don't feel like you can't help them in their desire to purchase your listing. You can. However, you do need to explain to them that you represent the seller. As you proceed in working with these buyers, you must not do anything that would impact the loyalty, obedience, and confidentiality established with your client in the listing agreement.

ASSISTING THEM WITH THEIR OFFER

You can present comparable properties that have sold in the area, so they can be informed on what price to put in their offer. You can provide them with the forms necessary to write an offer. You can even write the offer for them. Just remember you *cannot* give them any advice that would jeopardize the position of your seller.

In the years ahead, technology may increase the number of buyers who purchase a home without an agent. With the advent of internet search engines such as Zillow, Trulia, Realtor.com, and others, buyers obtain property information a real estate agent used to possess exclusively. Unlike a few years ago, they do not need an agent to find potential homes and acquire property information. Furthermore, websites provide an endless amount of information educating the consumer on the real estate transaction process. However, if they use the services of an agent, they probably could purchase the home at a lower price, with better terms, and fewer challenges along the way.

CHAPTER 27

How to Make Open Houses Work for You

"You miss 100 percent of the shots you don't take."

Ask a roomful of agents their opinion on open houses, and you'll get two different opinions. Many believe they are a waste of time, but others find them valuable. So, which is it?

Before I acquired my real estate license, my wife and I sold several homes through real estate agents. On the first couple of homes we sold, we asked the listing agent to hold an open house. We assumed a prospective buyer would tour the home and want to make us an offer.

But that never happened.

Instead, neighbors, Sunday afternoon real estate "hobbyists" (those who go to open houses for entertainment), and "tire-kicking" buyers made up most of the people who showed up at the open houses. After a few failed open house experiences, we decided open houses were just not worth the time and effort for us to vacate the property for three hours allowing strangers to walk through our home.

My personal experience with failed open houses carried into my real estate career. During the first few years as an agent, I was very skeptical of hosting open houses for any of my listings. However, my attitude toward open houses changed.

One day, Carol, an agent at my first brokerage, asked me to host one of her upcoming open houses. She had plans to be out of town and needed someone to cover an open house she scheduled for a listing in Nashville. Reluctantly, I agreed and made plans to be at her listing the following Sunday afternoon. I thought it might be a good way for me to pick up a buyer prospect or two. Carol took care of the advertising for the open house including installing the signage in the front yard and at the entrance of the neighborhood.

On Sunday, I arrived at the house about thirty minutes early, so I could turn on all the lights, unlock doors, arrange the in-house property flyers on the dining room table, and place a registration sheet on a table in the foyer. My wife sent homemade chocolate chip cookies and bottled waters with me so I could offer refreshments for everyone who stopped by the open house.

The first visitors showed up, and I warmly welcomed them in with a smile. It was a young couple with a baby. I asked them if they were working with an agent. They said "no." I asked some additional questions about their home search after they finished their tour of the house. We had a great conversation, and I told them I was more than willing to help them find a home. They took me up on the offer, and we scheduled a meeting at my office the following Tuesday.

More people showed up at the open house as the afternoon progressed. In fact, I had more than thirty people look at the property during the two hours I was at the home. An agent from another firm brought her client to see the property. They liked it and wanted to make an offer. I told them that Carol, who was the listing agent, would be back later that day. She said she would get in touch with her. Well, the two agents talked that evening, the buyer submitted an offer, and the seller accepted it the next morning. The house was under contract.

One open house resulted in more than $21,000 in commission from the sale of properties associated with the buyers I met at it.

Yes, open houses do work!

My entire perspective on open houses changed that Sunday afternoon. Not only did the home sell as a result of the open house, but I also picked up a new buyer client (the young couple with the baby) who contracted on a home a few weeks later. Three years later I listed the home they purchased and represented them in the purchase of a larger house.

That one open house resulted in more than $21,000 in commission from the sale of properties associated with the buyers I met that Sunday afternoon. Yes, open houses do work!

During the years, I sold several listings and picked up numerous buyer clients through open houses. I found it to be worth my time, money, and effort to hold both open houses for the public and the brokers. Statistics from the National Association of REALTORS® support my viewpoint as open houses are one of the top five ways buyers find a real estate agent. With the right planning and organization, you can make an open house successful for you and your clients.

HOSTING A SUCCESSFUL OPEN HOUSE

1. **Successful open houses begin with the right planning and preparation**

    Many agents plan a couple of weeks for an open house. Knowing which day to hold the open house is important. An open house should not be scheduled on a day when a local event such as a football game, golf tournament, or street festival is held. Also, if the day is a holiday, it will be unlikely many people will stop by the property. Also, who will host the open house? Will it be you or another agent? Does the open house conflict with your schedule for working with clients? Planning makes the process much more manageable.

2. **Plan your advertising and promotion for the open house**

    You need to know how to get prospective buyers and their agents to the open house. Consider creating a marketing checklist containing all the specific items necessary to advertise and market the open house effectively. The list should include the following:

    - *Online marketing* — Advertise the open house on all of your social media sites including your business Facebook page, Twitter, Instagram, and LinkedIn. Also, make sure the open house is on your website. I believe internet marketing is vital because many buyers who are looking online are not represented by an agent. This could be an excellent opportunity to gain a new client!

    - *Broadcast emails* — You should send an email to your client and prospect database as well as to your agent network including those in your firm, local REALTOR® association, and Multiple Listing Service. MailChimp, Constant Contact, and My Emma offer free and low-cost marketing packages for agents. *Important note:* The Federal

Trade Commission (FTC) has comprehensive rules concerning how you send mass unsolicited emails to prospects. Go to www.ftc.gov to learn more about being in compliance with the CAN-SPAM Act of 2003.

- *Postcards* — Send postcards to the neighbors and other select contacts in your database informing them of the open house.
- *MLS open house announcement* — Most MLS systems provide an opportunity for you to announce your open house. This is probably the best way to reach agents who might have buyers looking for a home in the area where your listing is located.
- *Signage* — Place an open house sign in the front yard of your listing next to your "For Sale" sign. Balloons or colorful pennant flags work great in bringing attention to the sign. Make sure you have pointer signs at various locations including at the front of the neighborhood and nearby road intersections. Remember to follow all local and homeowner association sign ordinances when installing your signage.

3. **Managing your open house**

Review with your seller the need for the house to be clean and "ready to go" for the open house. Inside the home, all bathroom vanities and sinks should be cleaned, carpets vacuumed, hardwood and tile floors swept, dishes washed and put away, and garbage cans emptied.

Outside, the yard needs to be mowed and trimmed, and all landscaping should be cut back. And don't forget to pick up what the doggie leaves behind in the yard!

If the house is larger than 3,000 square feet, ask another agent to assist you with the open house. Arrive at least thirty minutes before the open house start time to get everything set up. Make sure there are no unpleasant smells in the house. One solution is to ask the seller to bake some cookies right before the open house. Do not light candles or use air fresheners, as this will make a prospective buyer think you are trying to cover up a rancid smell in the house.

Turn on the lights and open the blinds, so the home is bright. Have a registration sheet available for everyone to sign. You might want to utilize an electronic open house registration program that you download to your smartphone or laptop. They are easy to use and can provide additional capabilities such as branded and customizable follow-up emails, single-property websites, feedback forms, etc. (Go to the Apple app store or Google Play to download these apps.)

Provide "item of value" materials to hand out to those who attend the open house. These pieces may include comparable property reports on homes in the immediate area, a brochure with tips on preparing a home for sale, lender information, data on the schools in the area, etc. Make sure all of these items have your name, firm name, and telephone number on them.

Provide refreshments. People love to nibble on treats at open houses. Cookies, lemonade, bottled water, and candy are great options for refreshments to have available in the kitchen or dining area.

Don't just "stand around" or sit on the family room couch during the open house. Walk around and ask questions about what the buyers are looking for in a home and what is their timeframe for purchasing a property. Try to get as much information from the buyers so you can determine whether or not they might be a qualified prospect for you.

Listen for feedback — positive or negative. An open house can provide an opportunity to "hear" what people think of the home and share what they like and don't like about it. The attendees can also tell you their opinion of why the house has not sold. Is it priced too high? Does it need to be staged better? Is the backyard not large enough? Ask, and they will tell.

4. **Be prepared for the "Lookie Loos"**

Not everyone who comes to an open house is a potential buyer. You will have neighbors who are curious about what the house looks like on the inside. Many times, they will be very open in providing you with the latest neighborhood gossip. Passersby will stop in because they have nothing else to do. And then there are the Lookie Loos.

Lookie Loos are, essentially, open house "hobbyists." On any given Sunday they will spend their afternoon visiting open houses because they like looking at other people's houses. They have no intention to buy your listing or any other home on the market. They are just curious.

Be prepared for all three of these types of people to come

through the front door. Greet them politely, as you never know if they know someone who is ready to buy or sell a home.

A WORD ABOUT BROKER OPEN HOUSES

Holding an open house for brokers is another option to show off your listing. I am not a big fan of these open houses.

Most of the time, the agents who show up for these events are those who are not selling very many houses. Productive agents do not have the time to take out of their schedules to view a home during the middle of the day. They are out selling.

Broker open houses are more popular in slower markets when there is less buyer traffic. They are expensive to hold due to food and marketing costs. My advice is to try every other tool in your marketing toolbox before deciding to have a broker open house.

THE LAST WORD ON OPEN HOUSES

Don't do an open house just to do an open house. You should hold an open house only if it benefits the seller to give their home additional exposure in order to procure a buyer. New buyer leads and other contacts for your business should not be the primary reason you hold the open house.

Yes, as I stated previously, open houses are a great way to capture prospective clients, but you are there to present the home to someone who might be interested in purchasing it. If you plan accordingly and are strategic in your marketing efforts for an open house, you will be more likely to find a buyer who might be interested in making an offer. Open houses can work. They worked for me.

CHAPTER 28

Divorce and Real Estate

"My husband and I have never considered divorce. Murder sometimes, but never divorce."

— DR. JOYCE BROTHERS

Over the years, I worked with numerous sellers who were ending their marriages. I never sought these particular listings; they just landed in my lap from friends and neighbors who referred a divorcing husband or wife to me. At the heart of a couple's divorce, along with establishing parental rights, is the disposition of their most significant asset — their house.

Transactions involving divorcing couples can take longer than "traditional" real estate deals due to the legal complexities of what is required in a marriage dissolution suit and the time it takes for the parties to decide on various matters concerning their real property. You must be patient if you take on a divorcing party. You will also need to show compassion toward them as this is probably one of the most, if not *the* most, difficult times in their lives.

Divorce transactions take additional skills and know-how, as no two deals are alike. Each phase of the listing period and the time between contract and close can be time-consuming and exhausting, sometimes due to unexpected drama or one or both of the parties' attorneys delaying the closing.

Several of my divorce clients were amicable toward each other while others were completely separated from one another, non-communicative, and uncooperative. If there is tension between the couple, you may only work with one of the sellers during a divorce. I have found the party who contacts me is the one who wants to get the divorce quickly behind them. Be careful, though, because if there is little to no communication, you may find it difficult to get both to cooperate in signing contract paperwork and providing information to the title attorney so they can close the transaction.

I always try to introduce myself to both the husband's and wife's attorneys, so they are aware I have been asked to list the home by one or both parties. If one party does not want me to list it, then I don't list it. I need both sellers' signatures on the listing agreement unless a quitclaim deed has been duly executed and recorded with the county's register of deeds office. There is no need to go through the time, money, and effort to get a house on the market if you know one of the parties will put up a fight to not list the home.

Many times, the court will order a house to be sold to keep the divorce case moving forward. The entire process goes much smoother if the court orders the parties to list the home as soon as possible. In many of the divorce cases I handled, the court named me as the agent who would list the property. The parties usually would cooperate when the judge told them to do so.

Divorces are extremely emotional. I have yet to be involved in a real estate transaction involving a divorce where the emotions of the husband and wife were not high. You need to be prepared for a tremendous amount of animosity each person will have toward the other. It can reach a point where they hate each other. And, I mean *hate* each other. Their anger can cross boundaries to where restraining orders need to be issued to keep the couple physically apart, so both remain safe.

Many years ago, I handled a transaction involving a very wealthy couple who owned a large home in an affluent neighborhood in Nashville. One of my wife's friends referred the wife to me. I called her to schedule an appointment to visit with her and tour their home.

On the day of my meeting, I received a text from her telling me she just filed a restraining order against her husband. He was harassing her on an ongoing basis to the point the police needed to be summoned to the property on numerous occasions. He was eventually arrested and jailed for violating the restraining order. His attorney represented him during the listing period and in the sale of the home.

Remember, couples are divorcing because they cannot get along and attempting to get them to work with an agent to sell their home can be tricky. It is made much more difficult if one of the parties does not want the divorce. If one person has significant anger toward the other one, they may try to do anything they can to cause a delay in listing the home. The house becomes a pawn in the divorce and is used as leverage by one party to get something from the other.

Try to keep the *process* unemotional. When I meet with one or both divorcing parties needing to sell their home, I always express my desire to keep emotion out of the listing and later in the transaction. Emotion clouds one's reasoning ability and their common sense. If they are genuinely committed to dissolving their marriage, any real estate they own must be sold. The parties have to be as objective as possible as I walk them through the listing period and on to the offer and contract stage.

Meeting with the parties takes proper planning and coordination. If only one of the parties can meet with me during a listing presentation, I will ask if I can contact the other party to schedule a time to give them the same listing presentation. The best scenario is to bring both parties together at the same time so all three of us can agree on how I will manage and market the listing. I try to keep my listing presentations and any other subsequent meetings relatively short (thirty to forty-five minutes) because there is a strong possibility they will begin arguing, and one or both of them will walk away. If one party refuses to meet with me for any reason, I will contact their attorney to schedule a meeting to review what I need from that party to keep everything moving forward.

Setting the list price. In a divorce listing, it is critical everyone agrees on a list price. As with my other seller clients, I always have plenty of data showing what homes, similar to the subject property, have sold for during the past six months. With a good comparable market analysis, you can get them both to agree on a price.

Good communication. During the listing and contract-to-close periods, it is critical you communicate with both parties on a regular basis. Communicate through the attorneys when one party doesn't want to speak with you. Keep everyone in the loop so that they can comply with all requests for paperwork, access to the house for inspections, etc. Also, keep all communication consistent when talking with the husband and wife on separate occasions. What one should know, the other should also know.

Finally and perhaps, most importantly, when working with divorcing sellers, remain impartial at all times. One of the parties

may try to vent to you about the other one doing or not doing something, but you must never take sides. You should never state how
you feel or offer any advice outside of your real estate expertise. If
you do cross that line, it will more than likely come back to bite you,
and you may lose the entire transaction because of your impartial-
ity. Just stay on the sidelines and remain neutral.

CHAPTER 29

Selling a Property Owned by Someone Who Has Died

"In this world nothing can be said to be certain, except death and taxes."

At some point in your real estate career, you will have an opportunity to represent a family or trust who needs to sell the home of a person who has died. I handled several real estate transactions for friends who have either lost a parent or other family member. When working with clients who are heirs or executors of an estate, I always found myself balancing their emotions from the death of the relative with the many details of selling the home.

Selling a home that is part of an estate is very similar to selling any other house; however, some details are unique requiring particular attention to legally transferring the property from the deceased person's estate to a new owner. It also requires the assistance and cooperation of family members and others who might have an interest in the home. Understanding the challenges and complexities of a transaction involving a house previously owned by someone who has passed away is crucial for the agent asked to list the property.

Most of the "death sales" I handled were for sons or daughters who inherited the home from a parent who recently died. Children will have emotional ties to the property because they either grew up in the house or associate it with their late parents. I always had to be extra sensitive to the emotions of a decedent's children as lasting memories can impair their thought process to work through the necessary steps required in listing and closing on an estate home.

I found it was much easier to work with the family when I explained to them I was here not just as the agent they hired to sell the home, but also as someone who has experience in working with families following a death of a loved one. I always empathize with a family by conveying my personal experience when my siblings and I had to handle the sale of my parents' home.

I listed a home of an older gentleman who passed away after a long battle with Alzheimer's disease. He had five children who were estranged from one another, and they were never on the same page as to how and when their father's house should be sold. In this particular situation, it was difficult to sell the home promptly as all the siblings needed to agree. None of them would agree, and I finally had to ask an attorney to get involved to resolve the dispute between the children. The entire ordeal was stressful and took several months, but with the assistance of the attorney, we got it sold.

In most cases, you will encounter one or several family members who are heirs to the deceased person's estate. Some are adult children left with the responsibility to handle the many issues arising from the death of a parent. Others are either relatives who were siblings, grandchildren, nieces, and nephews, or distant family of the late homeowner. No matter who they are, you will need to ask them to designate one person who will work with you.

If you encounter multiple family members involved in the sale of an estate property, encourage them to consider having a power of attorney executed so one of them can work with you to address the details of the transaction. In doing so, the family member who has a power of attorney can have discussions with the other relatives to determine a list price. They also can communicate with the family when offers are received from interested buyers. The appointed "attorney-in-fact," the one who holds a power of attorney, will have the authority to address everything else in the transaction including the closing. You need to work with one person and one person only when listing an estate home.

The following tips can assist you when working with a family or trust to sell the home of a family member who has passed away:

TIPS FOR POST-DEATH
REAL ESTATE TRANSFER

Probate. The first thing you need to know is if the estate needs to go through probate, which is a legal process used to determine how the deceased's estate is correctly distributed to family members (heirs) and any designated beneficiaries. Probate also identifies any outstanding debt owed to creditors so that they can be paid. The sale of a decedent's home usually cannot take place until all the claims of creditors are paid.

Most of the time, real property that needs to be probated is distributed according to the decedent's last will and testament, if there is one, or according to state law if no will exists. The probate laws of the state where the deceased resided determine the division of assets.

I always work with the attorney handling probate for the estate, so I'm certain of what's happening in the probate process. It's not that I do not trust the family, but I need legal reassurance I can put a "For Sale" sign in the yard and not encounter difficulties if I receive an offer from a prospective buyer.

I always request a letter or email from the attorney handling the estate or a copy of an order from the court approving the sale. Probate can take between six and twelve months to complete, and probate laws vary from state to state.

Living trusts. Some individuals will transfer their home into a living trust before their death. Living trusts do not need to go through the probate process. The trust identifies a successor trustee who will manage the trust after the person dies. The "successor trustee," the individual designated to oversee the trust upon the property owner's death, transfers ownership to the beneficiaries named in the trust. Living trusts provide a more straightforward and quicker way for the beneficiaries to sell the property.

OTHER CONSIDERATIONS WHEN SELLING AN
ESTATE PROPERTY

Outstanding bills will need to be paid. Make sure the executor of the estate is paying the ongoing bills related to the utilities and maintenance of the home. The last thing you want to happen is put the house on the market, and all the services are disconnected. I have found this is not an issue in most cases, but it does happen.

Request property documentation. Ask for all the necessary documents for the property. Gathering documentation can be a difficult task for the one who is left to oversee the sale of the home, but they should at least be willing to help you acquire them. You should request a copy of the following items:
- The home's title insurance policy, if available
- A copy of the Covenants, Conditions, & Restrictions (CC&R) the property may be subject to if it is part of a homeowner's association
- Copies of past utility bills
- The most recent mortgage statement if the house had not been paid off before his or her death
- Other documents that might be beneficial in preparing the listing

Change all locks and entry codes. To ensure you and the executor have complete control over who accesses the property, have all the door locks and entry codes changed before listing the house. The late homeowner may have given out house keys to neighbors and other individuals unknown to the estate's beneficiaries. A nosy neighbor who is aware no one is living in the house does not need access to the property for any reason. An empty house invites trouble.

Preparing the home for sale. The executor or family members should remove any personal items belonging to the deceased before listing the house. Personal items include clothing, jewelry, tools, kitchen dishes, towels, etc.

What about the furniture? I've watched families remove furniture and other items in a home after the owner passed away. If there are multiple heirs, it is very likely most of the furniture will be divided up among the family. Sometimes the family will get rid of all the furniture, and other times they will leave a few items because no one wanted them. Empty houses can be more challenging to sell than those that are furnished. The executor should consider staging the home before listing it so it shows its best during the listing period.

If the person who lived in the house was older, it's likely numerous items in and on the property were not maintained over time. The house may need new carpet and a fresh coat of paint. Repairs may need to be made to walls, bathrooms, lighting fixtures, kitchen faucets, garage doors, etc. A pre-listing inspection can identify what items need to be addressed before putting the property on the market. I also suggest having the home professionally deep cleaned. This is critical in how the home is presented. Deep cleaning can rid the house of unwanted smells, cobwebs, and dust.

Disclosing a death in the home. Buyers, or their agent, may ask you if the person who owned the home died in the home. Some people are disturbed knowing a person passed away within the walls of the house. Some states require disclosure of a death on the property. In Tennessee, the disclosure of a death in the home is not required even if the death was a homicide or suicide.

However, if asked by a prospective buyer and the agent is aware of a death in the home, they must truthfully answer the buyer's question. Check your state property disclosure statutes to determine if a death in a home must be disclosed. Again, property disclosure laws vary throughout the country.

Selling a home involved in an estate can be a trying experience for everyone involved in the sale. Memories, both good and bad, may come to the surface for the family. It can be difficult for children to say goodbye to the house in which they grew up. The house was their home for many years.

As a real estate agent who is asked to participate in this process, be sensitive to the family's needs and feelings. You will need to use many of the professional and relational skills you have learned over the years to ensure you get the job done for them.

Buying Properties

CHAPTER 30

The Home-Buying Process

"Don't wait to buy real estate. Buy real estate and wait."

Soon after I received my real estate license, my new managing broker provided me a referral from a phone call he received from a prospective out-of-state buyer. The buyer, his wife, and three children were moving from southern California to Nashville. I was excited to receive the lead and immediately followed up on it. I called the husband and introduced my brokerage and myself to him. I asked him what his timeframe was for moving to the area. He said soon, probably within the next sixty days or so. He recently accepted a position with a large accounting firm and would be working out of their corporate office located in downtown Nashville.

He began giving me all of his "wants and needs" in a house, as well as what he wanted to avoid. I made several notes on a legal pad, but he was talking so fast I could not keep up. He said his family needed a home that would be fairly large and located in an area with good schools and convenient to the interstate. I also caught his preferred square footage range as well as the lot size, but that was about it.

Later that evening, I ran a search in our Multiple Listing Service and sent him about a dozen properties I thought would meet the family's needs. Unfortunately, I received an email from the buyer the next morning saying he and his wife only liked one of the homes I had sent them.

I called him to find out what they didn't like about the others on the search results list. He said they needed a downstairs master bedroom, a three-car garage, and an extra room that could serve as an office for his wife. She was working part-time as an editor with an educational publisher in Los Angeles, and as I referred back to my notes, I did not see anything written down noting those particular features. I was a little embarrassed because I didn't feel like I had all the information from them that I should have had to do a thorough property search.

THE IMPORTANCE OF A BUYER SURVEY

Communication is key between the agent and the client in the home search process. I cannot overstress the importance of acquiring as much information as you can from a buyer prior to starting a search for potential properties. One way to ensure you learn what the buyer wants regarding houses, price, location, schools, etc. is to provide them with a buyer survey.

Soon after the buyer from California closed on a house I found for them, I decided to create a detailed survey for my buyers to complete. The form I developed asks specific information, so I can narrow my search and find homes that best meet their wants and needs. It has always been a very successful tool for narrowing down the properties with what a buyer is looking for in a new home.

The following information is what I include in my buyer survey. Of course, this not exhaustive, but it covers the most important criteria I need to conduct a productive home search for buyer clients.

BUYER SURVEY

Tell me about you and your future home:

1. Name(s)
    Birthday(s)   Anniversary
    Phone Number(s)
    Email(s)

2. Why are you buying a home?

3. What types of homes would you consider? (check all that apply)

    ☐ Single Family   ☐ Condo   ☐ Townhome   ☐ Loft   ☐ Duplex
       Residence

4. What's your preferred style of home? (check all that apply)

    ☐ New   ☐ Historic   ☐ Ranch   ☐ Victorian   ☐ Tudor

    ☐ Cottage   ☐ Bungalow   ☐ Industrial   ☐ Other

5. In terms of location, what are some of the things you really want in your
    neighborhood/surrounding area?

6. What are you expecting from your real estate agent?

7. How important is it to be close to where you work?

    ☐ Very   ☐ Somewhat   ☐ Not very

    Address of workplace:

8. Describe your ideal location:

9. What size home do you want/need?

10. What's your price range and monthly payment comfort level?

11. Have you been pre-approved?   ☐ Yes   ☐ No
    If yes, with whom?

12. Who else will be living in your home?

13. How many bedrooms do you need?   Why?

14. Is a dining room important?　☐ Yes　☐ No　Why?

15. Are there any special features you must have in your home?

16. When will you need/want to move in?

17. Do you currently own a home?　☐ Yes　☐ No
    If so, do you need to sell it before you buy?

18. Are you currently renting?　☐ Yes　☐ No
    If so, when does your lease expire?

19. Are you familiar with today's procedures for buying a home?
    ☐ Yes　☐ No

20. What do you definitely not want in your home?

21. Are you willing to purchase a home that needs work?　☐ Yes　☐ No
    If so, what are you comfortable with renovating/replacing?

22. What is your preferred method of communication?
    ☐ Phone　☐ Text　☐ Email　☐ Fax

23. Do you have children?　☐ Yes　☐ No
    If so, how important is the school district?

24. Do you have any minimum land/acreage requirements?
    ☐ Yes　☐ No　Amount?

25. What other concerns or desires do you have that I've not asked?

26. Rank in order of priority (1=most important | 6=least important)
    ___ Size (the right square footage)　___ Location
    ___ Style (the style to fit you)　___ Timing (a particular move-in date)
    ___ Price (price and payments)　___ Investment consideration

27. Who else will be part of the decision-making process on your home purchase?

During your initial conference with the buyer, you should review the home-buying process in detail with them. Answer any questions they might have and explain to them you will be walking with them every step of the way.

GOING THROUGH THE HOME-BUYING PROCESS

You must adequately explain all the steps of the buying process to the buyer client before their home search commences.

INITIAL INTERVIEW WITH YOU

The process of purchasing their new home begins here. Listen carefully to discover their particular "wants and needs" relating to a home. If they haven't yet completed the Buyer Survey, ask them to do so as soon as possible. During this meeting, you will also be able to establish rapport and set the groundwork for a successful and productive relationship.

PRE-APPROVAL BY A REPUTABLE LENDER

There is no need to take them out to view properties if they are not qualified to purchase a home. Provide a list of reputable lenders (at least three) who have assisted your clients in the past in buying a home.

HOUSE HUNTING

At this stage, you begin searching for their new home. Explain to them how you will search for properties and determine the ones that are the best match for them.

WRITING AN OFFER

Once the right property has been found, an offer to purchase will be drafted. Explain what needs to take place when making an offer including the many forms and disclosures used in the transaction.

EARNEST MONEY

Explain to the buyer what earnest money is and the importance of "being earnest" when making an offer. Depending on the current market conditions, the amount of money submitted with the offer may impact how the seller reacts to the buyer's offer.

NEGOTIATING AN OFFER

Explain the importance of negotiating. Remember to tell the buyer that sellers are looking for the most money in their pocket at closing, and buyers are looking for the least amount of money to bring to the closing table.

MORTGAGE APPLICATION

The application process for a home loan has become reasonably streamlined during the past few years. However, with the onset of additional governmental regulations in the mortgage and banking industries, the information and documentation the lender will request from a loan applicant are somewhat detailed. Prepare the buyer for a comprehensive review of their financial ability to obtain a mortgage.

CREDIT REPORT AND EMPLOYMENT VERIFICATIONS

If the buyer is applying for a loan to purchase the property, the lender will need to run a credit report on them. Explain to them the importance of good credit and that they will not be able to "hide" anything from the lender when it comes to outstanding debts, liens, etc. Let the buyer know the lender will request employment information and payroll information from their current and past employers.

INSPECTIONS AND APPRAISAL

Explain the inspection process and how the inspection contingency contained in the contract is removed. Make sure the buyer understands the contract performance dates noted in the inspection paragraphs and the resolution period following the submittal of repair/replacement proposals. Also, the buyer needs to be aware of how appraisals are done and what the lender requires from an appraiser to determine the value of the property.

LOAN UNDERWRITING

When the lender has gathered all the necessary financial, employment, and appraisal information, the loan underwriter will begin their review to determine whether or not the bank/mortgage company can underwrite the loan.

TITLE COMPANY AND CLOSING PROCESS

Explain the importance of having a competent title company and title attorney close the transaction. The buyer needs to understand what a title search is, as well as the importance of having title insurance on the property after they close.

CLOSING AND POSSESSION

A transaction does not close until (1) the deed to the property has been signed by the seller; and (2) the money has been transferred between the buyer and seller.

There is not a closing until these two things occur. Explain possession and the possible need for temporary occupancy agreements in the event the closing does not take place as expected.

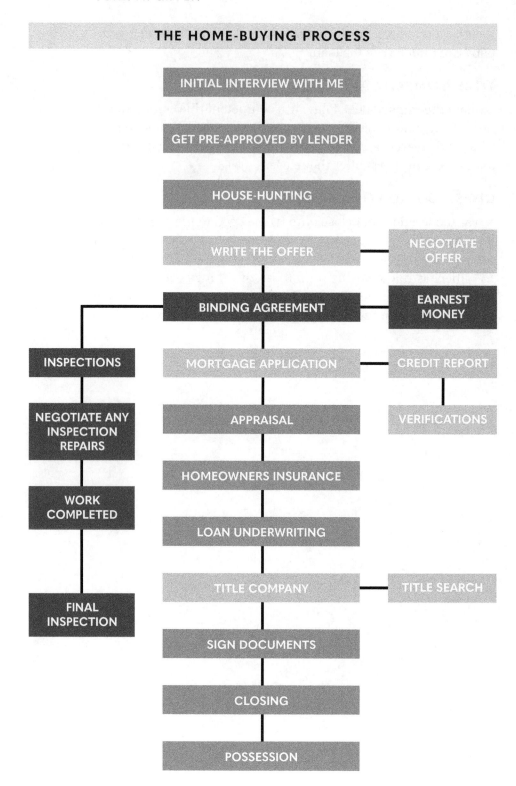

THE HOME-BUYING PROCESS

INITIAL INTERVIEW WITH ME

GET PRE-APPROVED BY LENDER

HOUSE-HUNTING

WRITE THE OFFER — NEGOTIATE OFFER

BINDING AGREEMENT — EARNEST MONEY

INSPECTIONS   MORTGAGE APPLICATION — CREDIT REPORT

NEGOTIATE ANY INSPECTION REPAIRS   APPRAISAL   VERIFICATIONS

WORK COMPLETED   HOMEOWNERS INSURANCE

LOAN UNDERWRITING

FINAL INSPECTION   TITLE COMPANY — TITLE SEARCH

SIGN DOCUMENTS

CLOSING

POSSESSION

CHAPTER 31

Getting the Buyer Representative Agreement Signed by Your Client

"There is only one way ... to get anybody to do anything. And that is by making the other person want to do it."

— DALE CARNEGIE

During the second year of selling real estate, I remember the phone call I made to a new resident at Vanderbilt University Medical Center and his wife. A close friend referred them, and we had been working together for more than six weeks. During this time, we visited numerous homes, and I felt we had established a great rapport with one another. In fact, they told me I was going "above and beyond" for them in finding a house.

When I made the phone call, it had been just a few days since we looked at several properties in their price range in the part of Nashville where they wanted to live. I was hoping we were getting close to finding just the "right one." I called to see if we could schedule time to see a few of the properties they received via my Multiple Listing Service new listing auto-notify system.

The doctor answered the phone and seemed to hesitate as he spoke. When I asked which day would be good to look at properties, he informed me they just signed a contract on a new home under construction in a highly desirable development.

"Why didn't you call me?" I asked, shocked.

He said, "Oh, the agent in the model home took care of everything."

He thanked me for all I had done for them, but said they felt comfortable with the agent they met at the model home. Even though I pressed him a bit further, hoping to figure out some way to redeem the situation, I did not have a signed buyer representation agreement with this couple, and our relationship came to an abrupt end.

Because there was not a buyer representation agreement in place, and I was not the procuring cause for the purchase of their new home, I lost out on a $17,450 commission.

Yes, I remember the exact amount.

I learned an extremely important lesson from that experience: never work with another buyer beyond a day or two unless they signed a buyer representation agreement with me. I made a terrible mistake with the previously mentioned couple by not (1) describing how I work; (2) explaining the importance of buyer representation; and (3) getting them to sign a buyer representation agreement. It never happened again.

One of the biggest mistakes agents make is doing what I did: failing to get a signed buyer representation agreement from their client early in the relationship. Numerous times I have had agents come in my office frustrated because their buyer went behind their back and either used another buyer agent or purchased a home on their own. The time and money spent by an agent working with buyers without a buyer representation agreement can add up quickly. For me, the reality was $17,450.

You can get a buyer representation agreement signed by a buyer if you approach it the right way. It comes down to excellent communication ensuring they know your buyer representation value proposition. A signed buyer rep agreement solidifies the partnership between you and them. It also provides them with protection during the buying process, as you will be in a position to work for them and them only.

Here are eight steps for getting a buyer representation agreement signed by your buyer:

1. **Explain the purpose of a buyer representation agreement**

   A buyer representation agreement is a legal document formalizing the buyer's working relationship with you, outlining what services they are entitled to, and what they should expect from you in return. The agreement is designed to clearly spell out the expectations of both parties as well as emphasize the importance of developing mutual loyalty. It also provides the means for a higher level of service the client will receive from you, their buyer representative.

Like the listing agreement, it is an employment contract. Most buyer representation agreements are lengthy and cover the many legal aspects of the buyer agency relationship. However, it also should be a guide to how you and the client will work together in finding them a property to purchase.

When you ask your client to sign the buyer representation agreement, they should have a good understanding of what the agreement does for them if they sign it. Many consumers believe the form protects only the agent and not them. While it is true the agreement provides a path for how we, acting as buyer representatives, are compensated, it offers more protection for the buyer.

The agreement creates a "client" relationship with the buyer. In real estate, there is a difference between a person who is a "client" and one who is a "customer." All buyers who have not signed an agency agreement with a broker are customers. If an agency agreement is signed with the broker through their designated agent, the buyer is considered a client.

The main difference between the two terms is the fiduciary duty the broker and their agent owe the client. Even though the agent must be honest and ethical with both parties in the transaction, he or she must be loyal to their client's interests and obey all of their lawful instructions. This fiduciary duty is mandated by the terms and conditions of the buyer representation agreement.

2. **Explain "agency" to the buyer**

Under most state laws, if you enter into an agency relationship with a buyer or seller, you must explain to them what "agency" means. Use the following to briefly do this:

"As your Designated Agent, I have been assigned by my Managing Broker as your one and only agent in your purchase transaction, to the exclusion of all other licensees in my company. Even if someone else in my company represents a seller in whose property you are interested, I, as your Designated Agent, will continue to work as an advocate for your best interests. An

agency relationship of this type cannot, by law, be established without a written agency agreement — the Buyer Representation Agreement."

3. **Describe the "Six Standards" of your fiduciary duty**

In your pre-licensing classes, you should have learned the acronym, "OLDCAR." OLDCAR stands for the six specific standards of our fiduciary duty:

Obedience — You must follow your client's lawful and ethical instructions.

Loyalty — You must be loyal to the client's interests and keep their interests ahead of yours.

Disclosure — In most states, the law requires a real estate agent, whether acting in an "agency" capacity or not, to disclose any adverse, or material, facts to their client.

Confidentiality — You must never divulge anything you learn from or about your client, their business, financial or personal activities, or motivations and intentions unless they authorize you to do so. This authorization of disclosure should be in writing.

Accounting — Part of your fiduciary duty is to account for all monies and documentation in a real estate transaction. This includes knowing where earnest money, deposits, and other funds are kept at all times.

Reasonable care and diligence — This standard is based on handling all situations and issues in the transaction with the utmost care and diligence expected from a professional agent. In other words, your actions will not cause any harm to your client.

4. **Convey to the buyer your value proposition based on quality customer service**

In addition to the agent's fiduciary responsibilities, the buyer should expect a higher level of service from their buyer representative. The services you deliver will need to be superior and "above and beyond" what the buyer would expect from an agent. This should be at the heart of your buyer representation value proposition.

One of the foundations of our professional reputation is service. The level and quality of the service you provide a buyer client may require you to work long hours, on weekends,

and on holidays showing homes or visiting new construction developments. It also could involve ensuring the buyer
connects with service providers such as contractors, electricians, plumbers, structural engineers, doctors and dentists,
hair stylists, school personnel, etc. You will do what you need
to do to meet the needs of your client. This is what quality
service is all about.

5. **Tell the buyer they will get more without paying more**

Your client will receive more from you as their buyer
representative without paying more. In almost all real estate
transactions, the seller has agreed to pay the listing broker
a certain amount of compensation to: (1) list and market the
home to procure a buyer; and (2) pay the cooperating selling
broker (you) who represents the buyer. Your compensation is
paid from the funds the seller will receive at the close of the
transaction.

You should also explain to the buyer what happens if the
seller is not willing to pay a cooperating broker commission.
You will need to decide the amount the buyer should pay you
at closing. This varies based on several factors including the
financial condition of the buyer. You need to find out if they
will have the funds at closing to pay your commission. If not,
you will need to make a decision on whether or not to continue in representing the buyer. Explain to the buyer you do not
work for free, and your time and expertise is not free.

6. **To eliminate confusion, explain each part of the buyer representation agreement to the buyer**

Almost all buyer representation agreements are created
so that the terms and conditions do not cause any uncertainty
concerning the duties owed to the client by the agent and the
duties owed to the agent by the client. Signing an agreement is
much easier when both parties know what is required of them.

Take the time to review each section of the agreement and
ask the buyer if they have any questions or need any clarification of any of the wording contained in the form. It is important
you provide a copy of your buyer representation agreement before they sign it, so they have an opportunity to read it carefully,
and if needed, send it to their attorney for review.

Review each section of the buyer representation agreement with your client:

- The parties to the agreement (buyer and broker/ designated agent)
- Property information and source of information
- Price range
- Types of property to be sourced
- Commencement and expiration dates of the agreement
- Broker authorization to represent the buyer
- Broker and agency information
- Special stipulations

7. **Agency relationships are based on mutual consent; we can end it if we don't get along!**

   A buyer representation agreement, like other contracts, needs to specify a beginning and an ending date. Hopefully, the ending date is when the home they are purchasing closes. However, there are times when the agreement terminates before the stated ending date.

   Mutually, the parties agreed to enter into an agreement, and it can be terminated early if both parties consent. You should be willing to terminate the agreement early if the working relationship isn't going well. If things have gone sour, end the relationship. Remember, if someone doesn't want to work with you, you can't force them to do so.

   MY BUYER REPRESENTATION MISSION STATEMENT

   "In essence, as your buyer's representative, I will be working for you, working hard to get you the right home for the best possible price and I will connect you with the right sources for answers to your questions or concerns that may arise during the search process or transaction."

8. **Tell the buyer: "We are forming a partnership."**

   The relationship between a client and an agent should be a partnership. With a formal agency relationship in place, you and your client will work together as partners in finding the buyer's next home.

   When I convey this to my clients, they appreciate the fact I am working both *for* and *with* them. A partnership perspective of the relationship also creates respect, trust, and most importantly, loyalty.

How to Show Properties Without Becoming a Tour Guide

"Buyers decide in the first eight seconds of seeing a home if they're interested in buying it. Get out of your car, walk in their shoes, and see what they see within the first eight seconds."

- BARBARA CORCORAN

I was at the copier in our office on an early Monday morning making copies for a meeting I was about to lead. One of my agents, Paul, walked into the copier room. He looked absolutely exhausted. I asked him how his weekend was, and he responded with, "It was pure Hell!" He said he spent all weekend showing numerous properties, and the buyers did not like any of the houses he showed them. He said he was tired of being their "Uber driver." Apparently, this was not the first time he had shown properties to these clients.

SHOWING PROPERTIES STRATEGICALLY

Showing properties to a buyer is not about just putting them in your car and walking them through available homes listed on the local Multiple Listing Service (MLS). No, it is much more. It involves careful preparation, organization, planning, and follow-up. Before your next appointment to show properties, keep in mind the following so *you* don't end up being someone's glorified chauffeur.

Do your homework. Before you take out your clients, first gather information. Your buyer should first complete a buyer survey (see Chapter 30). If a buyer survey is unavailable, interview them to determine the type of property they are looking for as well as their price range.

After you identify the buyer's criteria, search the MLS and other internet sites containing available properties. Do this the day before you take your clients out to see any listings. If you start searching earlier than one day, homes that were previously active may have already gone under contract.

Map out your home tour. Plan the route you will take to see the properties with your buyer. Not knowing how to get to a showing can be somewhat embarrassing for you and could present an unprofessional impression to your buyer. Before I show properties, I try to either drive the proposed route where the homes are located, or at least find them on Google maps or Waze, so I am familiar with the area.

Prepare a buyer home tour packet. Before seeing the properties, I print out all of the MLS information pages for the homes to be toured, as well as information on the area. Print a copy of the MLS information sheet for you and your client.

Also, I include my "Positive and Negative" checklist form the buyer should complete after seeing a property. This form provides space for them to write any miscellaneous notes concerning the home. It provides a way for the client to remember all the different attributes of the properties included in their tour of homes. If you don't have your checklist, have the buyer carry a notebook with them as you tour homes, so they can make notes on the positive and negative attributes of each house they visit. (You can easily make your own checklist by creating a two-column document with "Positives" and "Negatives" as the column headings. Make sure you leave plenty of room for your clients' notes.)

Gaining access to the home. Almost all property listings have a lockbox placed on the front door, porch, or railing containing a key to the front door. Most agents who are members of the local REALTOR® association or MLS board utilize electronic lockboxes for their listings. These lockboxes are designed to be very secure, and a passcode must be used to unlock it to acquire the key.

If you do not have the electronic passcode assigned to you to open the box, your buyers will show their disappointment pretty quickly and be upset they cannot preview the interior of the home. Make sure you know how to access property lockboxes either through a keycard issued to you or an app on your cell phone. It can be very unprofessional if you cannot open the lockbox.

Entering the home. Don't assume no one's home, even if you ring the doorbell or knock on the door, and no one answers! After gaining access to the house through the lockbox, unlock the door, enter, and announce your presence. I always shout out, "REALTOR®!" so anyone present knows my clients and I are entering the home.

Several times, I've opened a house and announced my presence to discover someone is asleep behind a bedroom door I open. That can be quite embarrassing. Hopefully, when scheduling the appointment, the showing appointment center or listing agent will inform you of anyone who will be present on the property during your showing.

Don't be a salesperson. If there is one time you need to act as real estate *consultant*, not a *salesperson*, it is after you enter the house and begin touring it. I discovered long ago that homes will sell themselves. You do not help the buyer when you come across as aggressive and are the one doing all the talking. As a consultant, you should provide your opinions and offer advice regarding anything the buyers ask you about the home. Be attentive to the comments they make during their walk-through of the property. By listening to the buyer, you will be able to assist them in deciding which home is best for their particular needs.

Navigate the property tour. Buyers will tend to stay in one part of the home that attracts their attention. You don't want to rush them, but encourage them to see the rest of the property. Remind them there are other showing appointments scheduled, and you want to be on time for each one. Also, if you are showing a home to a family, make sure you keep everyone together. The last thing you want to happen is a child running around the house without supervision. It's no fun calling the listing agent to tell them a child broke something in the house during a showing.

Leaving the property. Before you head out the door to your next showing appointment, you need to ensure you have left the current property exactly the way you found it when you entered it. Turn out any lights and close doors that you opened. Return the key to the lockbox and securely close it.

Review the showings and follow-up. Once you and your buyer have seen all the properties on the showing schedule, review each one and eliminate the ones that will not work for the client. This discussion can take place at the last showing, back at the office, or at the local coffee shop.

Answer all of their questions, and if they are not prepared to make an offer on one of the homes you showed them, schedule a time when you can get back together with them to look at additional listings. Tell them you will continue searching properties and forward any promising ones to them for their review.

As a side note, please provide feedback on your showings to the listing agents. It is important for each seller to hear from you and your client on how the home showed, as well as its features and price. Any feedback you give a listing agent should be honest and specific.

AN IMPORTANT NOTE ON SHOWING PROPERTIES IN A SELLER'S MARKET

In a tight seller's market, you need to prepare your clients for the possibility that listings they want to see will get away sooner rather than later. I have seen a listing hit the MLS at 8:00 a.m. and be under contract by noon. A hot market will produce numerous multiple offer scenarios for buyers seeking a home. Some buyers may make two, three, four, or more offers on different properties before a seller will accept one.

Remind your buyer that the effort to find them a home will require patience and diligence. In a low inventory real estate market, the buyer cannot be slow to act if a suitable home is available for them to purchase.

CHAPTER 33

When Your Buyer Wants to Make an Offer

"I'm gonna make him an offer he can't refuse."

- VITO CORLEONE,
FROM *THE GODFATHER*

Author's note: This chapter is based on my experience with real estate offers and subsequent contracts executed in Tennessee. I believe the information noted is relevant in all states. However, please consult with your managing broker or a real estate attorney to ensure you are following your state's guidelines for offers to purchase and sales contracts.

Your buyer is excited to submit an offer to buy the perfect home they believe meets all of their wants and needs.

An offer contains more than just the price the buyer is willing to pay. It must contain contingencies and specific dates for inspections, financing, dates for closing and possession, as well as other special stipulations. As your buyer's representative, you can ensure the terms and conditions of the Purchase and Sale Agreement and subsequent counteroffers will protect their interests.

A real estate transaction is very similar to a marriage. A "marriage" to a home starts with a "proposal" by the buyer — the offer to purchase. If all goes well, the proposal the buyer makes will be accepted, and the legal "marriage" to the property will consummate at the closing table. The one difference in this analogy is that any promise made orally, as in the traditional vows recited at a real wedding, is not enforceable in the sale of real property. In most states, all offers must be in writing to be enforceable.

Once an offer is made to the seller, it can be accepted, rejected, or countered. If an offer is countered, the counteroffer constitutes a rejection of the previous offer. Additionally, a party cannot extend the time limit of a counteroffer, have it rejected, and then attempt to accept the original offer. If a party rejects an offer outright, it needs to be noted in writing, signed, dated, and returned to the offeror.

Writing an offer on a single-family home or a parcel of land requires a level of particular know-how and forethought on your part. You must have all the specifics and details before you write the offer, including the prices of comparable properties in the area, the financing your buyer must obtain to purchase the home, and the timeframe needed to close on the house.

WRITING AN OFFER

How you construct an offer with the various contingencies and stipulations can make all the difference between whether or not the seller will accept, counter, or reject the offer. Be careful on the terminology, dates, and conditions you write in an offer. Remember, ambiguous language can cause significant issues in the transaction and possibly impact your client.

THE WHO AND WHAT OF THE OFFER

Names of the parties. It is important the names of both the buyer and seller are clearly noted in the offer. If any party to the agreement is married or are taking joint ownership of the property, then all names need to be included. Many times, I received offers on my listed properties from cooperating agents with the seller's name missing from the Purchase and Sale Agreement. I felt this was laziness on the agent's part because they didn't want to take the time to review the public tax record or the property condition disclosure containing the seller's name. It is not that difficult to do a little research to find out who owns the property.

Legal descriptions. Almost all purchase agreement forms will contain a section where the legal description of the property is noted. The legal description provides more detailed information on how the property is recorded in the public record. This information can be found in the county tax record or the property's recorded deed of trust located in the county register of deeds office. Make sure all of the following information is written in the offer:

address, subdivision or development name, lot or unit number, and the location of the deed book and page number in the county's register of deeds office. With the advancement of digital record management, many municipalities utilize an instrument number for deed identification. This number is a unique numeric identifier for each recorded property deed.

WHAT SHOULD REMAIN AND WHAT SHOULD GO?

Items to remain with the property. In my contract classes, I call the "items to remain" section of the Purchase and Sale Agreement the "screwed and glued" paragraph. If something is attached to the property, it needs to stay with the new owner. Examples of attached items include draperies, window treatments and accompanying hardware, built-in kitchen appliances, bathroom fixtures and mirrors, built-in bookshelves, security systems, fireplace glass doors, flat-screen television brackets, etc.

I remember several pre-closing inspections when my client and I would walk through the house for the last look and discover a missing bracket to the flat-screen television, missing bathroom mirrors, or vanished crystal chandelier from the dining room. I wish I had a dollar for every time I made a phone call to a cooperating listing agent informing them something was missing from the property. This situation always makes for a little stress at the end of a transaction, but with good communication between the agents, a resolution can usually be reached.

Items to not remain with the property. When a buyer submits an offer, it is important to note which items on or in the property should *not* remain after the deal closes. The most common items include exterior hot tubs, tool sheds, play sets, pool tables, and television satellite antennas. As a buyer's agent, I always double-check a few days before closing to make sure the "do not remain" items listed in the contract are removed by the seller. I always try to be as proactive as possible, so no surprises occur as we look at the house one last time.

Leased items. Besides noting what remains and what doesn't in the offer, you need to specify how to address any item the seller might be leasing. The most common leased items include security systems and propane tanks. Many lease agreements with residential service providers are transferrable to the new owner. Make sure you note in the offer whether or not the buyer will assume any of the leases currently in place on the property.

HOW MUCH SHOULD THE BUYER OFFER FOR THE PROPERTY?

The purchase price. An offer must contain a purchase price to be valid and statutory. Also, the offer price should be realistic and not "out of left field." I have seen too many offers come my way that insulted my sellers. If your buyer makes a "low-ball" offer, the seller is more than likely to reject it. A good comparative market analysis (CMA) noting what has recently sold near the subject property can assist you and your buyer in determining the right price to put in the offer.

Sometimes the CMA will not be helpful if you are buying in a tight and competitive "seller's market." Under these conditions, a buyer is more likely to find themselves having to offer at least the list price or higher to stand out from other submitted offers. A seller's market will contain a low inventory of homes and buyers paying over asking price to get a house. Multiple offers are very common, and some buyers who qualify for FHA, VA, or other conventional financing can find themselves competing with cash buyers and investors who can close quickly. Buyers who have few or no contingencies in their offer may receive more consideration from a seller.

Property condition. The condition of the home can impact the price of the buyer's offer. You and your buyer should take detailed notes when inspecting the home and reviewing the seller's property condition disclosure. In Tennessee, the law states it must be submitted "prior to the acceptance of a real estate purchase contract." Many sellers will make the necessary repairs and upgrades before putting their house on the market. Other sellers will elect not to make repairs or improvements to the property before listing it.

If the home has a certain amount of noticeable wear and tear issues and needs substantial work, your offer should reflect the property's condition. Unfortunately, homes in poor condition in a seller's market may force a buyer to make a decision to take the property "as is" in order not to lose it to competing multiple offers.

As the buyer's agent, you must ensure the buyer clearly understands these disclosure forms, and you should be able to answer any questions they may have concerning them. If a buyer has questions about what is noted on the disclosure forms, they need to contact an attorney who specializes in real estate. Title attorneys can be an excellent resource.

Seller motivation. Ask the listing agent what the seller's "situation" is so you can determine if their motivation is time, money, or both. They may be seeking the highest price to get the desired amount of net proceeds at closing. The seller may also be on a schedule to move to their next location due to a job change or family issue. You never know what their motivation is unless you inquire. The listing agent may not reveal any information to you, but it doesn't hurt to ask.

No matter what the local real estate market looks like, the price you offer should be one that the seller will take seriously. Do your homework correctly, so your buyer has a better chance of having their offer accepted.

EARNEST MONEY DEPOSIT

Earnest money is an integral part of the home-buying process. It not only helps fund the buyer's down payment, but it also communicates to the seller how serious the buyer is in purchasing their home. The amount of earnest money needs to be discussed with the buyer before they start looking at homes.

I would talk about earnest money deposits in the initial buyer interview, so they are prepared when the time comes for them to write the earnest money check. I believe the more earnest money a buyer puts down on a house, the more likely they are to have the seller accept their offer. As your buyer's agent, you need to encourage your client to submit as much earnest money as they possibly can to have a strong offer.

How much earnest money should a buyer present with their offer? There is no right or wrong amount, as it is up to each buyer. However, I always encourage buyer clients to consider at least 1 percent of the purchase price for earnest money. Again, the more they can put down, the stronger the offer.

WILL THIS PURCHASE BE CASH OR CHARGE?

How is your buyer going to pay for the home of their dreams? They have two options: financing or cash.

Financing. If the buyer is going to borrow money to buy the home, the offer must contain a contingency stating the buyer will seek the necessary financing to close the transaction. The seller will want to know what type of loan the buyer is qualified for as well as the amount of their down payment. This information will be included in a lender pre-approval letter you attach to the offer.

Also, most Purchase and Sale agreements have a section for the type of loan and the amount of the buyer's down payment. The majority of Americans purchase their homes with either a conventional fifteen- or thirty-year mortgage. There are numerous loan products available to buyers including low down payment financing options through the Federal Housing Administration (FHA) and Veteran's Administration (VA). FHA only requires a 3.5 percent down payment, whereas the VA allows qualifying applicants to put zero down.

Special note on loan obligations in a contract: Most real estate contract forms — especially those provided by REALTOR® associations — contain specific terms and conditions the buyer must meet to fulfill their loan obligations. Many of these conditions have specific deadlines that must be met. This is a significant part of the buyer's performance in the contract.

As the buyer's agent, you will need to monitor these dates and work with your client and their lender to ensure each performance date is met. A seller may make specific demands of the buyer if they feel the loan process is not proceeding as stated in the agreement. Missing these dates may cause the buyer to default on the contract and place them in a position where they lose the home.

Cash offers. If the buyer will buy the home with cash, the offer will not have a financing contingency, and they should be able to close within a week or two after the binding agreement date if the seller is agreeable. The buyer will need to provide proof of available funds to purchase the home. The seller will want some form of assurance or guarantee the buyer has the money to bring to the closing table.

The buyer should obtain a notarized letter from the financial institution holding their funds and submit it with the offer. If your buyer is going to liquidate investments such as stocks, bonds, treasury notes, etc. to purchase the property, they need to do so before making an offer. Investments can be volatile and drop in value in a short period. They might have the money at the time of the offer, but if the stock market takes a downward turn, a buyer might find themselves without the funds needed to purchase the home. I believe a cash offer should be based on the cash on-hand at the time of the offer, not when the transaction closes.

IS IT WORTH THE PRICE?

The best way to know if the offer is reasonable, and the property is worth the amount they are offering, is to get the home appraised. An appraisal is an unbiased estimate of the fair market value of what the property is worth.

If the buyer is purchasing the house with a loan, an appraisal contingency will need to be included in the offer. Cash buyers have the option of not having an appraisal. Is this wise? I don't think so. I always encourage cash buyers to get an appraisal, too, so they do not overpay for the property.

INSPECTIONS

Clients need to know the condition of the property before spending hundreds of thousands of dollars for it. Home inspections can uncover serious adverse facts affecting the condition and value of the property as well as the health of those who occupy it.

In the inspection contingency section of the offer, you should indicate how much time your buyer needs to have *all* inspections completed on the home. Inspections should include a thorough review of the electrical and plumbing systems, kitchen appliances, bathroom fixtures, its structural integrity, and exterior features including the roof, swimming pools, decks, siding, brick, septic systems, and water wells. Additionally, a licensed pest control company should inspect the house to rule out the presence of wood-destroying insects (for example, termites) or rodents.

After the inspections are completed, the buyer has two options: proceed with the purchase and remove the inspection contingency or terminate the contract and request a refund of their earnest money. If they choose to end the agreement, the seller will probably want to know the reasons why and may request copies of the buyer's inspection reports. So, as the listing agent, be prepared to submit the full inspection report to the seller and any other documentation they may want to review.

CLOSING EXPENSES

Both the buyer and seller will incur costs to close the transaction. The buyer's closing costs are pretty much tied to their loan. These include lender expenses such as origination fees, discount points, appraisal, credit report, underwriting, attorney fees, notary fees, etc. One significant closing expense is the cost associated with the property's title. These costs include the title search and mortgagee's and owner's title policies.

All of these expenses, by default, are buyer expenses. However, the buyer may need assistance in paying for some or all of these costs. If the buyer wishes the seller to pay for any closing costs, they will need to be stated in the offer. Pre-paid items such as property taxes, homeowner's insurance, and mortgage interest that will accrue between the closing date and month-end should also be included as buyer closing costs. Be specific when writing any and all seller concessions in the offer, so there is no confusion or surprises at closing.

CLOSING DATE AND POSSESSION

Two of the most critical components in an offer to purchase a home are the closing and possession dates. These two dates need to be specific, and they also should be realistic. Due to federal lending guidelines, a buyer will not be able to close on a home in less than thirty to forty-five days if they are purchasing the property with a conventional home loan. It takes time for the loan application, appraisal, employment verification, credit reports, and other required loan paperwork to be reviewed by the lender's underwriting department. FHA, VA, USDA, or other government loan products offer significant benefits for buyers, but these types of loans can take up to sixty days to close.

Closing the transaction means the house is the buyer's once the deed is signed, and the money is paid to the seller, the seller's closing attorney, or title company. Possession of the property takes place once these two events happen.

However, the seller may need to stay in the home for a specified period after closing if their next house is not ready or if they need a few days to move out of it. Buyers may want to move into the property before closing because they have closed on their previous home and moved out.

In both cases, a temporary occupancy agreement should be executed by the parties and attached to the contract. A temporary occupancy agreement, however, is *not* a lease. It is a document signed by the parties to allow temporary possession of the property.

It is designed to last no longer than a few days. If a buyer or seller would like to extend their occupancy longer, they will need to execute a residential lease with detailed terms and conditions that will provide both parties with additional protection.

OTHER TERMS AND CONDITIONS (SPECIAL STIPULATIONS)

Most real estate transactions use a pre-printed Purchase and Sale Agreement, or contract form written and supplied by either a REALTOR® association or a real estate attorney. These forms contain pre-printed language covering most of the terms and conditions considered customary in a real estate contract.

However, additional terms and conditions not contained in the boilerplate language already provided on the form may need to be added to the agreement. For example, a buyer may need to make his or her offer contingent on the sale of their current home. Or, they may need to add a contingency allowing them to seek the approval of local planning officials to rezone the property from residential use to commercial use.

As a buyer's agent, you should use caution when writing special stipulations in an offer. The language added needs to be clear, concise, legal, ethical, and constructed in a way that it would survive being contested in court. Ask your principal broker or a reputable real estate attorney to assist you in composing any additional provisions in your client's offer.

EXHIBITS, ADDENDA, AND AMENDMENTS

There may be occasions when an exhibit, addendum, or amendment needs to be included in the Purchase and Sale agreement. Agents are typically not trained on the correct use of each one and remain confused as to their purpose.

Exhibit items are not part of the offer. They are usually documents illustrating something related to the contract or documentation that would need to be executed by the parties at a later date.

Addenda are documents supplementing something in the offer such as an FHA addendum, lead-based paint disclosure, assumption agreements, temporary occupancy agreements, etc.

An **addendum** adds terms and conditions to the pre-printed language and/or special stipulations in the (offer).

Think of the addendum as an additional page to the agreement that you can use if you run out of room under the Special Stipulations section. The addendum is made a part of the Purchase and Sale Agreement, and if any terms of the addendum conflict with the terms of the Purchase and Sale Agreement, the terms of the addendum will control.

An **amendment** is used when changes need to be made to an already bound Purchase and Sale Agreement. Amendments in real estate contracts are very common. An amendment can correct an agreement or improve it. It can also be dubbed as a "modification" or "change" to any terms in the original agreement. An amendment may include anything from changing the purchase price to correcting the name of one of the buyers or changing the performance date of a contingency.

Be careful how you write a counteroffer. Any counteroffer submitted should include the terms and conditions the countering party wants stated in previous offers. If it doesn't, the terms and conditions in the original offer will stand.

Think of them this way: an exhibit is something extra to further illustrate (look at "ex" in "exhibit" to think of "extra"), an addendum "adds" to the offer (look at the first three letters of the word: "add"), and an amendment "changes" the terms of an already agreed to and bound contract.

It's best not to add agency confirmation disclosures, brokerage compensation agreements, and property condition disclosures in the "Exhibits and Addenda" section of the offer/contract due to legal issues related to the legal statute of limitations. Your managing broker can assist you in deciding which documents should be included as exhibits and addenda.

Using any of these forms incorrectly can make you look unprofessional to cooperating agents and title attorneys. You don't want to sit down at the closing table with your client and have the closing attorney inform you an amendment should have been used instead of an addendum in the transaction or an addendum should have been designated an exhibit.

That can be quite embarrassing.

TIME LIMIT OF THE OFFER

Be specific as to the date and time you want to hear back from the seller on your buyer's offer. An offer is not considered statutory if it does not have a deadline. Moreover, without a time limit noted in the offer, the seller does not have to respond to your offer and can "shop" the offer by using it as leverage against other offers they might receive.

COUNTEROFFERS

I have found a lot can happen between the original offer and any subsequent counteroffers. I did some of my best negotiations during the "back and forth" of offers and counteroffers.

Negotiations always begin with the first counteroffer. In a counteroffer, the purchase price and closing date can change as well as other terms and conditions found in the original offer. Be careful how you write a counteroffer.

Any counteroffer submitted should include the terms and conditions the countering party wants stated in previous offers. If it doesn't, the terms and conditions in the original offer will stand.

WITHDRAWING AN OFFER

Offers and counteroffers are withdrawn for various reasons. A buyer may withdraw an offer because they have "buyer's remorse" or another property that better fits their needs catches their attention. A seller may withdraw an offer because another offer has been submitted with a higher purchase price and better terms.

Withdrawing an offer can take place all the way up to right before the offer is accepted or notification of acceptance is received. In either case, a written notification needs to be sent by the buyer or seller as soon as possible informing them the offer is being withdrawn.

MAKE ONE OFFER AT A TIME

Do not make an offer on more than one home at a time, or your buyer may end up purchasing more than one property.

A few years ago, I had an agent submit an offer to me for one of my listings. After she sent the offer, she called to make sure I received it. She informed me the offer she sent was one of many her buyer had made on numerous properties. She said they would withdraw all the other offers once one was accepted on a property. Her rationale was she wanted to make sure her buyer found a house quickly.

I asked her if she was aware she was violating her fiduciary responsibility to her client and putting herself and the client in a position to be sued by several sellers if they all accepted her buyer's offer. She went very quiet. After a few seconds of silence, she asked me what to do.

I told her she should rescind her other offers and work one offer at a time. I also encouraged her to speak to her managing broker to learn how best to manage offers for her clients in the future. Even though I was not her broker, I wanted to help her to make sure she did all she could to reduce her risk of being sued or having a real estate commission complaint filed against her and her broker.

As crazy as this story sounds, this type of scenario occasionally happens, especially in tight real estate markets with low housing inventory. Buyers and their agents become desperate and behave foolishly. Never make multiple offers on multiple properties at the same time. Submit one offer on one house — period.

MULTIPLE OFFERS

In a market with a low supply of properties and a large number of buyers, it's highly likely a buyer client's offer will be one of many on a desirable property. This experience will probably happen more than once in the home-finding process.

Buyers become frustrated when they finally find their dream home only to discover the offer they make on the house is one of many the seller will receive from other eager buyers. Multiple-offer situations will result in offers way over the purchase price and with few to no contingencies. It becomes a very competitive environment for everyone involved. The thought of a buyer "getting a deal" is thrown out the window.

Keep in mind these key points when working in a multiple-offer scenario:

- The existence of multiple offers should only be disclosed with the seller's consent, according to the Standard of Practice of the REALTOR® Code of Ethics.
- The seller alone determines whether one or more of the prospective buyers will be informed that there are multiple offers on the property.
- Sellers who elect to disclose multiple offers risk a buyer walking away from a possible "bidding war."
- Alternatively, sellers may elect to leverage the existence of multiple offers to get the best price and terms.
- Escalation clauses may appear on a submitted offer. An

escalation clause states that a buyer is willing to outbid any other offers on a home by a certain amount, up to a capped price.

Personally, I do not like escalation clauses for a variety of reasons. First, is the offer an actual offer? Some attorneys have said that without a definite price in the offer, it may not meet statutory requirements.

Also, it will probably impact the property's appraisal. Escalation clauses could drive the price above market value and outside the pricing parameters used by appraisers. If there is a loan involved in the transaction, the lender will only provide financing to a buyer based on the market value of the home. In addition, an appraiser will use historical comps, not the purchase price, to determine the property's value.

Besides legal and appraisal issues, there is a strong possibility an agent might be breaching client confidentiality by disclosing information to a buyer whose offer contains an escalation clause. The buyer would need to prove they have the highest offer among all offers submitted to the seller.

If you use an escalation clause in an offer be aware the seller may come back in their counteroffer asking your buyer to resubmit an offer without the escalation clause in it.

BEFORE YOU WRITE AN OFFER

1. Make sure an agency relationship with your buyer has been established through a signed, exclusive buyer representation agreement. Also, prepare a written confirmation of this agency so it can be disclosed to the other party in the transaction.
2. Read all property disclosures carefully with your client, including the property condition disclosure, lead-based paint, and septic disclosures.
3. Ask your client's lender to provide you with a pre-approval letter you can submit with the offer. The lender may also be able to give you a loan estimate containing closing costs and pre-paid items.
4. As the buyer's agent, you should prepare a compensation agreement that can be sent to the cooperating broker/agent before the submission of an offer.

5. Review all of the offer paperwork to ensure it is correct and complete.

As a buyer's agent, you must correctly shepherd the offer process for your client. You and your buyer need to carefully think through the offer before you write it.

It's absolutely crucial that you know and understand real estate contract language backward and forward. You must be knowledgeable in the terms and conditions in the Purchase and Sale Agreement and their impact on the performance of the parties. This also includes knowing all the other supporting documentation involved in the transaction.

Be prepared to negotiate and maximize your selling skills when a seller counters your offer. As a real estate professional, your negotiation expertise is an essential part of the offer and counteroffer process.

READ AND KNOW THE DARN PAPERWORK!

Reading is fundamental. Do not underestimate the importance of reading every single word in every single document in a real estate listing and a sales transaction. You must know what the purpose is for each document and the language contained in it. Your client *will* ask you questions about something in the forms — especially the terms and conditions of the Purchase and Sale Agreement. Part of your fiduciary responsibility is helping buyer and seller clients comprehend the document they are signing and why they are signing it. Too many times I find agents will ask me questions about an issue in a transaction and it is because they have not read the contract or agency agreement. Regulatory complaints are increasing against real estate licensees because their client did not know what they were signing. You can avoid this happening to you if you will just read and understand all of the paperwork! You owe it to your client.

CHAPTER 34

The Importance of Representing a Buyer in New Construction

"We shape our buildings: Thereafter, they shape us."

— WINSTON CHURCHILL

Tom, one of my agents, had a very calm demeanor and never let anything get to him. When he called me one Saturday afternoon, he seemed pretty upset. He told me had been out of town for a few days visiting his elderly mother in Florida. Apparently, one of his active buyers wrote an offer with a builder without him knowing about it.

Tom said the builder was not paying him a selling commission, as he was not present with his buyers when they walked through the door of the model home. The onsite agent claimed he was not the "procuring cause" for the sale. Unfortunately, in this case, Tom was not the one who introduced the property to his client and initiated the offer and subsequent purchase contract with the builder.

Tom's experience is not unique. During the years, I've handled similar situations involving an agent not getting paid by a builder on a new construction contract because they did not accompany the buyer when they visited the model home to write the contract. This is why it is critical real estate agents educate buyer clients at the *beginning* of the buyer/agent relationship, so they understand the importance of not visiting new construction sites without the agent. Unfortunately, buyers will visit and write a contract because they fall in love with the home plan the builder's agent presents to them and want to get the deal sealed before it gets away.

HOW TO PREVENT THIS AND GET PAID

What must you do to make sure this doesn't happen to you? First, educate your client! You must explain to them the importance of having buyer representation in a new home construction. Second, you need to have a signed buyer representation agreement in place before an offer is made on a property, including new construction.

Third, if you want to get paid, and you are not receiving compensation from the seller/builder, the buyer needs to understand you do not work for free. Most buyer representation forms provide pre-printed language that offers a way for you to be compensated if the seller is not offering a selling commission. If not, you will need to add compensation terms to an addendum or draft a separate commission agreement.

It could become problematic when a buyer says they did not realize they had to pay you, their buyer representative, a commission if you did not receive compensation from the seller/builder. That is why it is critical you review the buyer representation agreement in detail with them.

Don't be afraid to go over the compensation sections. Remember, you are operating a business, and you get paid for your experience, knowledge, negotiating ability, and knowing how to manage complex real estate transactions. If they clearly understand what buyer representation is all about and the benefit it provides them, they will want *you* to be with them when they visit new construction home sites. They will know you "have their back" and are working in their best interest.

CHAPTER 35

How to Handle Buyer Remorse

"Remorse, the fatal egg that pleasure laid."

– WILLIAM COWPER

I have seen several transactions fall apart right after the contract has been bound as well as at the last minute because the buyer no longer wanted the house they were purchasing. Many of these were contract terminations "without cause." In other words, they did not have a legitimate or legal reason to back out. They were experiencing buyer remorse and were looking at how to walk away from the deal.

Several years ago, I listed a condominium for a friend's elderly mother who was moving into an assisted living center in Nashville. After spending several weeks preparing it for sale, the property was listed in the MLS. We received an offer from a young lady who recently moved to town the same day we put it on the market. The buyer's agent said her client was going to pay cash and forgo an inspection and appraisal. She could close in two weeks. This was good news for my client as she was on a fixed income and needed every penny she could get her hands on.

Three days before closing, I received a telephone call from the buyer's agent. She told me her buyer decided she did not want the condo and was not going to close on the transaction. Apparently, the buyer had remorse for submitting an offer on the property so quickly without consulting with her parents and fiancé.

My client was not happy, to say the least. She contacted an attorney and settled with the buyer out of court for an undisclosed sum of money. There is a happy ending, however. A few months later, we put the property back up for sale, found a qualified buyer, and closed the transaction without a hitch. My client was happy.

What causes remorse? There are numerous reasons, including:

1. **Family and friends are quick to tell them why they should not purchase the home.** Discuss with your buyers early on in the process the importance of not consulting family members or friends if they start experiencing buyer's remorse. If a parent, sibling, or friend view the home and they do not like it, anything they say to the buyer will probably be negative and cloud the buyer's perspective on their purchase.

   Tell your buyer client to remain as objective as they possibly can throughout the transaction and rely on you and other professionals to provide guidance if they begin to regret their decision. You can help them maintain the "bigger picture" point of view and remind them of the reason why they placed an offer on the home.

2. **They continue to look at homes after they sign a contract to purchase.** When the buyer sees another house online or in-person that better fits their needs, they may have second thoughts. Stop sending your buyers any automatic emails from your MLS containing new listings once they sign an agreement, and keep the excitement of their purchase in front of them so they stay focused on the home and their upcoming closing date.

3. **Some buyers feel pressure when they find themselves in a multiple-offer situation.** Due to a low inventory seller market, a buyer may feel pressured to put an aggressive offer on a house because they lost the last four or five offers they made on other properties. They feel stressed and begin to have reservations. This is a difficult one to manage with the buyer because this may have been the third, fourth, or fifth property they tried to buy.

   Remind them of the tight market and the fact they made an offer on the house because it can meet their needs. Educating the buyer early on in the buying process can help them understand buyer remorse and may help to alleviate any second-guessing on their part.

4. **The buyers don't want the property long after the end of the inspection and resolution periods.** They find other issues with

the house that were not covered in the inspection contingency release. In this situation, you need to advise the buyer they are past the contract's inspection contingency period, and if they back out there could be serious legal consequences for them.

5. **They feel you have not provided them with good counsel and guidance.** Make sure you deliver outstanding customer service and offer professional expertise on a daily basis, so they know you are walking with them through the transaction. Also, communicate with them regularly so their questions can be answered, and any of their concerns can be quickly addressed.

6. **They could be suffering from a mental or emotional illness.** Advise your principal broker when working with people who exhibit behavior that causes concern. The broker is there to help you prevent issues popping up later by way of a lawsuit or a regulatory complaint. Obviously, if a client makes you feel physically threatened or in danger, seek safety and contact 911 immediately!

POSSIBLE DEFAULT ON THE CONTRACT

Whatever the reason for a buyer's remorse, you, as their agent, have a fiduciary responsibility to discuss with your client the legal consequences of backing out of a contract without a legitimate reason(s) that would stand up in court. A discussion on breach of a real estate contract should take place early on in the home-search process or when you discuss the "Default" section of the Purchase and Sale Agreement. You can't force someone to buy a property they don't want. However, a good, clear, and honest conversation with them might lessen the chances of the buyer deciding to walk away from the transaction for no apparent reason. This is drama you and your broker don't want or need.

Buyer remorse is genuine and frequently occurs, especially with first-time homebuyers, those who lack self-confidence, and those who let their emotions get in the way of thinking clearly and objectively. When a buyer wants to back out of a deal, remind them of their original "wants and needs" list.

Encourage your buyer, letting them know you acknowledge their remorse and want to assist them in making a wise decision on whether or not to continue in the transaction. If they trust you and have confidence in your ability to represent their interests, they might be more open to seeing the deal through to closing.

If not, it is not the end of the world. Prepare the buyer for what happens if the seller decides not to release them from the agreement. Negotiate with the seller and try to terminate the contract amicably. The buyer will probably forfeit some or all of their earnest money to the seller by terminating the contract early. Once they have settled with the seller and are released, continue the search to find the buyers a house they do want to call "home."

CHAPTER 36

For Sale By Owners: Know What Makes Them Tick!

"If you think hiring a professional is expensive, wait till you hire an amateur."

Believe it or not, I once was one of those homeowners who thought they could sell their house on their own without utilizing the services of a real estate professional.

Yes, I was a FSBO (For Sale by Owner).

In fact, my experience as a FSBO was one of the reasons I decided to get my real estate license and become an agent.

Many years ago, I attempted to sell our home in Indiana myself so we could move back home to Tennessee. We did not have very much equity in the house, and we had to pay for most of the move out-of-pocket. In those days, listing agents were commanding between 7 and 8 percent in commission. In my mind, that was several thousands of dollars we could save and put toward moving expenses.

I went to the local hardware store and purchased a generic real estate "For Sale" sign to put in our front yard. I thought a sign and an ad in the local newspaper would procure enough prospective buyers to the property.

Well, it didn't, and we had to wait almost six weeks to get an offer on our house. While waiting for an offer, we showed the home at all times during the day to strangers who, for all we knew, may have been out "kicking the tires" or worse — casing the house to see if there was anything worth stealing.

Finally, we got the house under contract with a buyer who had an agent. The purchase price was much less than what we wanted. However, we needed to sell the house. The buyer's agent had recently received her real estate license and did not make the experience any easier. The contract-to-close period was a bumpy ride; the buyers had issues with their loan, and the home inspection was difficult.

Two weeks before closing, the basement of the home had water intrusion from several days of record rainfall. This concerned the buyers, and they almost walked away from the deal. We lowered the purchase price and paid for the necessary repairs and restoration work.

We made it to the closing table, and the packed moving van with all of our furniture and belongings headed south the following day. The experience of selling our home ourselves was not what we imagined it would be, and it was a stressful experience from beginning to end.

I know, from first-hand experience, that we could have avoided many issues in selling our home if we had worked with someone who was knowledgeable, who represented our interests, who was there when problems arose, and who negotiated and advocated for us. Undoubtedly, we would have sold our home quicker and received additional money at the closing table if we had used an agent.

WORKING WITH FSBO SELLERS

Once I had my real estate license, FSBOs became one of my target markets in my real estate business. Selling our property on our own allowed me to have a unique perspective on FSBOs that most real estate professionals do not understand. On the many occasions I approached unrepresented sellers, I was able to gain their trust, and more times than not, eventually list their home or assist them in purchasing their next one. FSBOs are a unique group of players in the real estate market, and most agents attempt to avoid them. Don't overlook them because they can be a viable client prospect group for you.

Going after unrepresented sellers requires strategy and patience. Consider the following:

1. **Understand the mindset of the For Sale by Owner.** There are two types of FSBOs: the "trying to save money" seller and the "do-it-yourself" seller. The first one believes they will save

thousands of dollars by not using an agent. They focus on the money paid to agents and not the value they bring to the table.

The second type may have the same desire as the first, but they believe they can sell their home without our assistance because they know everything about the process. Unfortunately, both of these types of FSBOs rarely accomplish their original objective, due to the complexity of today's real estate transactions and the ever-changing housing market.

FSBOs consistently sell their homes for about 15 to 18 percent less than homeowners who list with an agent (according to the National Association of REALTORS® *[NAR] Profile of Home Buyers and Sellers*). One reason why is that FSBOs do not competitively price their homes, nor do they have the necessary time to devote to the entire transaction process including marketing, showing the property, handling offers, and completing the required paperwork. They discover the amount of work to get their house sold is much more than they anticipated when they decided to do it themselves.

2. **FSBOs have preconceived notions about real estate agents.** Most For Sale by Owners dislike real estate agents because of a bad past experience with an agent, or their friends or family have influenced them not to use one. In order to overcome these objections, you must ask specific questions to determine if they have merit or are just products of misinformation.

   Present your value proposition in a way that erases any prejudices about us and demonstrates the benefit of using our services. Remember, you possess the experience and expertise to market their home and guide them through the transaction to a successful closing.

   As a real estate agent, your value proposition for FSBOs includes:
   - You can sell their home for more money.
   - You understand the paperwork and all the forms needed in a real estate transaction.
   - You are a full-time real estate agent. Marketing and selling homes is your job.
   - You know the local real estate market, so the home can be priced competitively.
   - You can be objective. FSBOs have a difficult time being objective because they are emotionally tied to the home.

- You can qualify prospective buyers.
- You have negotiating skills.
- You can get the deal closed.

3. **The FSBO doesn't understand the risk and liability of selling their home themselves.** Mistakes can be made in any transaction. Both unrepresented sellers and their buyers can make errors that can be costly. An attorney can close a transaction for a FSBO, but they don't carry errors and omissions (E&O) insurance for mistakes made by the seller or the buyer before closing.

    For example, if the seller advertises their property as a four-bedroom home, but the septic system construction permit specifies it can only accommodate three bedrooms, chances are the seller is going to have to pay for that error. A professional real estate agent would have caught the mistake, or their E&O insurance would cover it.

    We live and work in a litigious society. What seller wants to be a target of a lawsuit? FSBOs need to be reminded of the perilous waters they will be sailing when they try to go at it alone.

4. **FSBOs don't realize transaction paperwork can be overwhelming.** According to the *NAR Profile of Home Buyers and Sellers*, managing the paperwork in a real estate transaction is one of the most challenging tasks for a FSBO. The days of signing one or two documents to get the property under contract are in the past.

    Today, the average contract package contains close to thirty to forty pages of complex and lengthy documents. Many FSBOs don't realize they will need to complete disclosures concerning the condition of the property, the presence of possible lead-based paint, capacity and operation of their septic system, past water leaks, etc. By not completing the required documents, sellers can find themselves in violation of state and federal laws.

5. **The marketing a FSBO does for their property is limited.** Most FSBOs will advertise their home on Craigslist, Facebook, the local newspaper, and possibly the MLS, if they use an MLS discount brokerage. FSBOs do not have the experience or expertise to market their home like a real estate professional.

    According to the NAR, 42 percent of FSBOs rely on a yard sign, 32 percent depend on friends and family, and about 15 percent use social media.* Expecting neighbors and family members to spread the word has its limitations. Even paying for the house to be listed in the MLS won't be enough because there is no incentive for an agent to show a FSBO property to a prospective buyer because the seller may not offer the agent minimal compensation to bring them a buyer. What agent wants those hassles?

6. **FSBOs do not know how to qualify buyers.** One of the most significant components in the buyer representation side of our business is that we know how to adequately screen and qualify buyers. Most FSBOs will allow strangers to enter their homes, with no clue about how to ensure the buyer has the financial ability to buy it.

    Sellers do not know to ask specific questions about how the buyer is planning to pay for the home, either with a loan or with cash. I am amazed at the number of FSBOs who trust the buyer and enter into a purchase agreement without doing the necessary due diligence.

7. **Be careful when talking to a FSBO.** The words you use and the questions you ask when speaking to a seller can make or break your ability to work with them. Inman News published an article listing the four things never say to a FSBO:**
    - "You'll never sell your house on your own."
    - "I can help you improve your marketing."
    - "I'm not like other agents," and
    - "Wow, how did you come up with that price?"

    Instead, you should ask:
    - "What made you decide to sell your home on your own?"
    - "What are the best features of your home?"
    - "What type of service do you expect from your agent?"
    - "What method did you use to price your home?"

8. **Consider helping a FSBO with a "FSBO First Aid Kit."** One of the best ideas someone shared with me when I was trying to get FSBO listings was to develop and hand out a "FSBO First Aid Kit."

---

*   *2017 National Association of REALTORS® Profile of Home Buyers and Sellers*

** *Kellie Tinnin, "4 things you should never say when prospecting FSBOs," Inman, April 6, 2018, https://www.inman.com/2018/04/06/4-things-you-should-never-say-when-prospecting-fsbos/.*

This "kit" is full of resources for the seller to use in selling their home. It includes tips on how to prepare a home for sale, a guide to qualifying prospective buyers for a mortgage, how to host a successful open house, free templates for in-house brochures and flyer boxes, safety guidelines, and more.

The real benefit of providing this packet to a FSBO is to let them know I am there to help them, not hinder them. My approach is never to try to get the listing. If they reach the point where they cannot sell their home on their own, I hope I will be the first one they turn to when they seek the help of a real estate professional. And, maybe they will also use me to help them purchase their next home.

Several FSBO sellers *did* turn to me for help over the years in selling their home. Once they discovered how difficult it was to sell the property themselves, they asked me to list the property so they could get it sold.

9. **If your buyer is interested in a FSBO property, show it to them.** If you have a buyer who wants to look at a FSBO property, don't be afraid to approach the seller because their goal is to sell their home. A seller may or may not be willing to compensate you if your buyer elects to make an offer to purchase the home.

If they are willing to pay you a commission, you should provide them with a written agreement confirming the compensation between them and your broker. This agreement should be signed *prior* to showing the seller's property to your buyer.

There will always be sellers who will want to try to sell their home on their own. However, I believe there are real opportunities for agents to work with unrepresented sellers in either helping them sell their home or bringing them a ready, willing, and able buyer. Remember, if you work with FSBOs in the right way, you can provide yourself with another revenue stream and possibly an excellent source for referrals.

Creating a FSBO First Aid Kit can provide the unrepresented seller with resources to use when they are attempting to sell their home without the assistance of an agent. All the handouts can be created by you or found on Realtor.org or other real estate-related websites. Customize them to reflect your unique brand, personality, and value proposition. Include the following in the kit:

1. A personalized letter like the one below.

> Dear Homeowner,
>
> By now you have probably been contacted by a number of real estate agents who want to list your home. Well, I too am an agent, but I am not writing to ask you to list your home. Instead, I am enclosing information that will help you sell your home "by owner."
>
> As a professional REALTOR®, I know what type of commitment it takes to prepare, market, and sell a home. I admire any homeowner who is prepared to take on this challenge. So, rather than insist you need to hire me as your REALTOR®, I am going to share with you some ideas and tools that will help you sell your home.
>
> The enclosed "For Sale by Owner" First-Aid Kit includes:
>
> - Common sense security tips. When you list your property for sale you are inviting strangers to enter your home. The enclosed information will help you take sensible precautions to help keep your family safe.
> - Advice on how to make sure a potential buyer is "bankable" BEFORE you accept the offer
> - Simple, low-cost ideas to make your home more appealing to potential buyers
> - Effective marketing ideas
> - Information regarding financing options for your home. In most cases it's the financing that can make or break a quick sale. The information enclosed will help you educate potential buyers on financing options available to buy your home.
>
> In addition, to help you price your home at the maximum value, I can provide you with a free list of homes currently listed in your neighborhood, as well as a list of recent sales in the area. If you are interested in either of these lists, call me and I will send it to you free of charge.
>
> By now you are probably wondering, "Why would a real estate agent help me sell my home on my own?" There are three simple reasons:

1. Not everyone will be successful selling his or her own home. And in the event, you decide to turn the job over to a professional REALTOR®, it seems logical to expect that you will consider the agent that was working for you even before you hired him or her.

2. You will likely be purchasing a new home. Hopefully, by working to help you sell your home "by owner," you will come to realize that I am willing to work hard to earn your business.

3. Finally, your friends, relatives, and neighbors may ask you if you know a good real estate agent.

In the meantime, I offer this information, tool kit, and my support without any obligation on your part. If I can be of assistance at any point during this process, please do not hesitate to call me.

Sincerely,

John Giffen
REALTOR®

---

2. Open House registration sheet
3. Property Condition Disclosure form
4. Tips for holding a yard sale
5. Generic purchase and sale agreement
6. "Five Things to Do Before You Sell" handout
7. "Ten Things to Make Your House More Salable" handout
8. "Five Ways to Speed Up Your Sale" handout
9. "Seven Steps to Prepare for an Open House" handout
10. "Seven Things to Watch for in a Real Estate Offer" handout
11. Blank seller net sheet
12. "Moving Tips for Sellers" handout
13. "20 Low-Cost Ways to Spruce Up Your Home" handout
14. "What is 'Appraised Value'?" handout
15. "Understanding Capital Gains in Real Estate" handout
16. "Does Moving Up Make Sense?" handout
17. "Remodeling that Pays" handout
18. "12 Tips for Hiring a Remodeling Contractor" handout
19. "Tips on How to Price Your Home" handout
20. "17 Service Providers You Will Need When You Sell" handout
21. "Six Forms You Will Need to Sell Your Home" handout
22. "Is Your Buyer Qualified?" handout
23. Information on disclosing lead-based paint in the home
24. "Understanding Title and Closing" handout
25. A list of qualified home inspectors
26. Property brochures

From Contract
to Close

CHAPTER 37

Explaining the Contract-to-Close Process to Your Buyer Client

"If you can't explain it simply, you don't understand it well enough."

- ALBERT EINSTEIN

After the seller accepts your buyer's offer and the contract is bound, the contract-to-close process begins. This process has become more complex over the years, and buyers need your professional guidance, so they are well informed and do not have any surprises as they move forward in the transaction.

I created a narrative for agents to use with clients explaining the nine most important activities in the contract-to-close process. You can read a summary of the steps below, and download a copy of the narrative from DoYouHaveAMinuteBook.com to use with your clients.

Clearly explaining each one can reduce stress for the client and ensure you are carrying out your responsibilities as their agent. This information can easily be used in your buyer marketing materials educating the client on what happens after they get the house under contract.

THE NINE ACTIVITIES OF THE CONTRACT-TO-CLOSE PROCESS

Earnest money - Once the buyer and seller have agreed on the offer ("acceptance"), the first step is for the buyer through their agent to submit an earnest money check made payable to either the listing or selling real estate company or the title company handling the closing. Once this money has been received, along with the accepted and signed purchase contract and other supporting documentation, the title company begins the process of searching the title, preparing the final transaction documents, and moving toward a closing date.

Title search — A title company or real estate attorney usually serves as the escrow agent for the transaction, and more importantly, handles all the details of the closing process. They will coordinate with the buyer's and seller's agents, the buyer, the seller, and the buyer's lender to bring everything together for a smooth closing.

Perhaps the most critical function of the title company is to order a preliminary title report, which is used to confirm that the seller is the legal owner of record of the property and that there are no unpaid liens or other legal claims against the property. This could include unpaid debt to contractors, banks, the Internal Revenue Service for back federal income taxes, or unpaid real estate taxes and special assessments.

Homeowners insurance — It is the buyer's responsibility to obtain sufficient homeowners insurance coverage for their new home. In addition to having insurance as a smart financial decision to protect their new investment, a certain amount of minimum coverage (usually the purchase price) is always required by the lender to secure financing. The buyer will have to provide proof of insurance to close. The buyer's insurance agent usually coordinates with the lender directly to ensure this is completed.

Property inspection — Most states require sellers to provide a property condition disclosure that includes information about material facts, any property defects, lawsuits regarding claims to ownership of the property, etc. It will be the buyer's responsibility to obtain a professional inspection on the property that includes a general property report as to material defects, pest infestations, electrical or plumbing issues, or any other problems with the property.

The inspection report serves two critical functions: It provides useful information that helps the buyer determine whether or not they'd like to move forward and purchase the home, and it serves as a negotiation tool to work with the seller to agree upon solutions to problems before the inspection resolution period expires.

A Wood-Destroying Insect Infestation Inspection Report will also need to be generated as part of the inspection process. A pest inspector creates this report, which outlines any findings of termites, carpenter ants, or any other wood-destroying insects.

Appraisal of property — A professional appraisal is required for the buyer's lender to provide the buyer with a loan to purchase the property. The appraiser's report describes the physical characteristics of the property and the comparable property values that will be used to determine its value.

Once the appraiser has performed a detailed inspection of the property, they'll prepare a written report and determine the final dollar amount that the property is worth. As long as this amount is at least equal to the loan amount, the buyer and the lender should be good to go with moving forward in the deal.

However, in this fluid and ever-changing real estate market, I have seen issues arise from lender appraisals that are not related to the "loan to value" (LTV). So, be prepared for surprises because they might occur. On FHA and VA government-insured mortgages, an FHA- or VA-certified appraiser will produce a more comprehensive inspection and appraisal report. These particular appraisals may require repairs be made before the lender will approve the final underwriting of the loan.

Loan approval — Once all of the lender's conditions have been satisfied and all of the underwriting steps have been completed, the lender will notify the title company that the loan has been approved. The buyer will receive a closing disclosure from the lender three days before the closing date. The lender will then send the final loan documents (sometimes referred to as a "closing package") to the title company so that the buyer can sign the documents at the closing table.

Closing funds — Before the closing (usually a day or so before), the title company will confirm with both the seller and the buyer the final amount of money due and/or to be paid to the respective parties of the transaction at the closing table. This is accomplished through the preparation of a settlement statement.

The buyer's agent works with both sides of the transaction to ensure all parties have the final number in advance of the closing date. The closing funds are in the form of a bank-certified check payable directly to the title company or funded using a wire transfer or electronic payment.

The closing — It's finally time for the closing day! This is when both parties sign all the necessary closing and loan paperwork. The buyer will provide a bank certified check or wire the funds for the amount due to close the transaction.

Some markets will use one title company to handle closing paperwork for both the buyer and seller. Other markets will utilize two title companies representing each side and do "split" closings — two separate closing meetings. Many times, each side will have their own closing attorney/title company with whom they will work to finalize their part of the closing.

Final steps — Once all the documents are signed, and all monies are received, the transaction is completed, sent to the county to be recorded, and the buyer takes possession of the home.

The buyer's agent works with all parties to obtain the keys and any other required items from the seller, at which point the lockbox comes off, the signs come down, and the buyers are ready to move into their new home.

KEEP THE TRANSACTION MOVING FORWARD

One of the most important jobs we perform for our clients is managing their transaction. From the time the contract is bound to the day the deal is finalized at the closing table, we must oversee numerous tasks behind the scenes.

Several years ago, I created a transaction management form to track the progress of all of my active sales contracts. When I began using Top Producer, an Internet-based customer relationship and transaction management program, I still used the tracking form.

In fact, I customize my Top Producer transaction tracking action plans based on the information contained in this form. The form allows me to quickly reference at what stage I am in with the transaction and the items that need to be completed so we can move closer to the closing. It has become an invaluable tool for me.

Download my tracker form at DoYouHaveAMinuteBook. com and keep your transactions moving forward.

CHAPTER 38

The Home Inspection

"Every person who invests in well-selected real estate in a growing section of a prosperous community adopts the surest and safest method of becoming independent, for real estate is the basis of wealth."

— THEODORE ROOSEVELT

When I was an active principal broker, I signed the earnest money release form most frequently. Many times, the reason stated on the form for terminating the contract was "inspection issues." Every time I signed the release I always wondered if the transaction could have been saved one way or another. Did the buyer know what to expect going into the inspection? Did they remain objective and open to remedies to items in the inspection report? Did the agent influence their decision?

I have personally purchased and sold fifteen homes since the 1980s. When we purchased our fourth home, our agent provided us with some excellent counsel on home inspections. He explained the inspection was designed to evaluate the current performance of the home's systems and their features, not to evaluate cosmetic defects or design issues.

Fortunately, for us, we had a very good inspector who was upfront and honest in his review of the property. He provided us with an objective opinion and said most things could be corrected and/or remediated. Regrettably, I can't say all of the home inspectors who inspected our homes were as good and as competent as this gentleman.

I learned early on the importance of understanding home inspections and what to expect when the house was professionally inspected. It's critical that agents review the following, so their clients know what to expect during the inspection:

1. **Traditional home inspections have limitations.** Even though many inspectors are good at their jobs, they are usually not properly trained or have the experience or expertise to provide a true professional opinion on the systems and structure of a property. A typical home inspection is just one person's review of the home's systems and their function.

    Home inspectors usually aren't heating and cooling experts or professional structural engineers. A buyer should seek out licensed, specialized professionals who can properly inspect and evaluate a system or structural defect.

2. **The inspector *will* always find something wrong with the house.** I have never had a home inspector not find some issue in a home. All inspectors find *something*. However, what they find may or may not be a problem. The buyer will need to decide whether or not to investigate further to see if a real issue exists.

3. **The actual inspection report can be overwhelming.** Most inspectors use a pre-written template from an inspection computer software program to generate an inspection report. Usually containing several pages of information, most reports include the inspector's findings plus tips on interior and exterior home maintenance and other topics related to home ownership. Prepare the client for what they will receive in their email, so they won't be alarmed by all that is written in the inspector's report.

4. **More years equals more issues.** Before the home inspection, remind the buyers that they are not purchasing new construction. Existing homes will have some wear and tear on them, like high mileage on an automobile. I have learned over the years that most problems and defects in older properties can be repaired or replaced.

    Water in the crawl space, mold, fungus, broken window seals, and even radon gas can all be remediated. Don't walk away from a house if the issues found can be easily corrected either before or after the buyer closes on the property.

5. **Seek out an expert to provide a professional opinion on issues that need additional investigation.** Having an expert investi-

gate further into an issue the home inspector discovered can alleviate the buyer's concerns, so they feel comfortable in moving forward in the transaction. An additional inspection can confirm a system or structural element of the home is in good working order, or a serious issue needs to be addressed before closing the deal.

6. **Consider not using a "home inspector."** Hire a licensed electrician, plumber, roofer, and contractor to inspect the respective components of the property to see if they are sound and in good working order. It may cost a little more, but you have the licensed professionals who know what to look for when inspecting. This was how it was done years ago, and some buyers still have experts do individual systems inspections on the home they are purchasing.

7. **Don't ask the seller to address everything in the report.** Be realistic on the requested items to be repaired or replaced by the seller. Sending an exhaustive list of repairs to the seller may cause them to become angry toward the buyer (and their agent) and change the entire tone of the deal. Adversarial relationships are difficult to manage. I have seen inspection requests asking for cracked light switch plates to be replaced or a loose doorknob be tightened. These types of items can be addressed when the buyer moves into the home. Keep the list realistic, only noting the significant issues the seller should take care of before closing.

8. **Be careful with your words.** An agent should keep their opinions on inspection reports and repairs to themselves. Most clients rely on the professional counsel of their agent; however, we are not experts in knowing how particular systems in a home should function or the structural integrity of the property. Our role is to shepherd them through the inspection process. What comes out of our mouths may not be what the buyer is thinking. Our comments can cause a buyer to become concerned and possibly walk away from the deal.

9. **Maintain and promote a sense of "calm" during the inspection and resolution period.** At this point in the transaction, the emotions of the seller and the buyer, as well as their agents, can run high. It is always good to grab the client by the hand and reassure them everything is going to be okay. Tell them to take a deep breath and to remember the "bigger picture"

in their home-buying process. Give yourself this same advice. Always try to find a resolution so the transaction can move on to the next step.

The home inspection can make or break a real estate transaction. I have seen inspectors and their inspections kill a deal. If the buyer knows what to expect and understands how to navigate the inspection process, they will be more calm, rational, and objective in responding to what is discovered and whether or not to move forward in the transaction.

CHAPTER 39

What to Do When Earnest Money Becomes Non-Refundable

"For even the wise cannot see all ends."

One of my agents, Paige, asked me to assist her in resolving an earnest money dispute concerning one of her buyers. Paige's client was under contract with an independent builder, who was also the seller, in a rural area outside of Nashville. In the final counteroffer, the seller stated, "Earnest money to be non-refundable." The buyer agreed to all the terms and conditions of the offer including the earnest money going "hard." Both parties signed the Purchase and Sale Agreement, and the contract was bound. Construction commenced on the home a few weeks after the binding agreement date.

A couple of weeks before closing, several problems with the house were discovered, and the builder could not obtain a Certificate of Occupancy from the county. The seller, in the opinion of the buyer and Paige, did not perform to the terms of the contract and was possibly in default. The closing date came and went during the dispute, and no resolution was ever reached between the parties.

Paige submitted an earnest money release form to the seller requesting a refund of the earnest money. The buyer felt their earnest money should be returned to them because of non-performance on the part of the seller/builder. The builder said they did not have to return the money because the contract stated the earnest money was non-refundable. Did the seller have the right to retain the money even though they may have been in breach of the contract? Unfortunately, yes.

Whenever a buyer and seller agree to earnest money being non-refundable without condition, it is just that — non-refundable. The seller has the right to keep the money once an agreement has been reached. Most states' statutes support the earnest money becoming non-refundable once the condition of performance tied to the money is not met.

As a buyer's agent, be very careful in allowing your client to accept a contract stipulation resulting in non-refundable earnest money or deposits without condition. I'm not saying your buyer shouldn't agree to it, because it may be a stipulation they will have to accept if they want the property, but they should do so with caution.

> As a buyer's agent, be very careful in allowing your client to accept a contract stipulation resulting in non-refundable earnest money or deposits without condition.
>
> You should always attempt to place a particular condition as to what makes the earnest money non-refundable, so there are possible "outs" for your client.

We've seen this happening more frequently in Tennessee during the past several years due to the markets, especially with multiple offers. Your state may be experiencing the same market conditions and an increase in non-refundable earnest money. You should always attempt to place a particular condition as to what makes the earnest money non-refundable, so there are possible "outs" for your client.

Also, make sure they clearly understand the terms and conditions of the documents they are signing. It can become very uncomfortable for you if they think they can get their money back when, in fact, they will never see a penny of it again. And, trust me, that is not a conversation you want to have with your client.

CHAPTER 40

The Dos and Don'ts During the Mortgage Loan Process

"Do the right thing. It will gratify some
people and astonish the rest."

— MARK TWAIN

One of my agents, Janie, came into my office balling her eyes out because she had just learned her buyer could not close on her home the following day. I asked her what happened, and she said her client just quit her job and was going to accept a new one in a few weeks. The lender said she could not close because they would not be able to do a final check of her employment for underwriting before closing. The buyer lost the house. Janie was devastated.

Many years ago, I represented a couple who were purchasing an expensive home in a prestigious suburb of Nashville. We satisfied all the inspection and appraisal contingencies. A couple of weeks from closing, I received a phone call from my buyer's lender telling me we had a problem with their loan. I learned the buyer recently financed a $55,000 SUV without informing the lender. The purchase significantly changed their debt to income ratio, and they no longer qualified for the loan product that would be used to purchase their new home. The lender denied their loan, and they lost the house.

Another one of my agents, Tonya, telephoned me in distress. She told me her client's lender called to inform her the buyer's loan was being denied, and the loan officer would be emailing a loan denial letter to justify terminating the agreement. Tonya said the closing was supposed to take place in just a few days.

The buyer's loan application was in final review with the lender's underwriting department. The underwriter discovered the buyer had paid off a student loan as well as a couple of credit cards. By doing this, the buyer's credit score changed, and the lender could not underwrite the loan.

There is a happy ending to this story. The buyer was able to work with the lender using another loan product to get the transaction closed. They closed a week later than initially planned.

I share these three scenarios to encourage you to educate your buyer clients about the importance of watching what they do financially during the mortgage loan process. A borrower's decision to pay off a credit card, charge purchases to a credit card, or change their employment status can impact their ability to acquire a loan to complete the purchase of their new home.

Make sure your clients understand the following, so they can avoid mistakes impacting their credit during the loan process:

1. **Buyers should not apply for any credit after they have applied for a home loan.** Every check to a buyer's credit by a potential creditor or lender immediately impacts their credit score. Depending on what has been reported and shows up in the credit report, a buyer's credit score could drop anywhere from two to fifty points for one credit inquiry.

2. **Buyers should not pay off any collections or account "charge-offs" during the loan process.** Paying collections will reduce a buyer's credit score immediately, due to the date of the last activity becoming the most recent. If your client wants to pay off old accounts, they should ask the lender if this could be done at closing. They also need to validate that the debt is theirs and that the creditor agrees to give them a letter of deletion.

3. **Buyers should not close credit card accounts.** Closing a credit card account will alert credit-reporting agencies, and the buyer's FICO score will go up. Doing so changes the debt ratio and affects other factors in the score, including the length of credit history and amount of credit used by the cardholder. If they have to close a credit card account, they should do it after the closing, and make sure it is a more recent account.

4. **Buyers should not make charges to their credit card resulting in reaching their account limits.** Reaching a credit card's limit will immediately bring a buyer's credit score down fifty to one hundred points. Your buyer needs to keep credit card balanc-

es below 30 percent of their available limit at all times during the loan process. If your buyer decides to pay down balances, they should do it on every credit card account. This means they should make an extra payment on all of their cards at the same time.

5. **Buyers should not transfer or consolidate credit card debt to one or two credit cards.** Even though many people believe transferring credit card balances from multiple cards to one card is wise, it can negatively impact their credit score. That's because once all balances are consolidated onto one card, it appears they are maxed out on that particular card, and the credit reporting systems will penalize them accordingly. If they want to save money on credit card interest rates, they need to wait until after closing.

6. **Buyers should not do anything that will flag their credit accounts.** *Don't do anything that will cause the scoring system to raise a red flag.* Your client should not open any new credit card or charge accounts, co-sign on a loan, or change their name or address with the credit reporting companies. The less activity on their credit reports during the loan process, the better.

7. **Buyers should join a credit protection program.** Many banks and financial institutions provide credit protection programs for consumers. There are also several private "credit watch" companies online that can offer credit protection. If your buyer joins one of these programs, they can check their reports weekly, or even daily, depending on the program they select.

    The good news with these programs is your client is not penalized when they request their credit report. If an error were to appear on their statement negatively impacting their credit score, they will be made aware of it immediately and may be able to address the issue before closing on their new home.

8. **Buyers need to stay current on existing credit card and other charge accounts.** Your client should make on-time payments on their current home mortgage, college student loans, automobile loans, and other consumer loans. If a borrower is late more than thirty days, it can affect their credit score anywhere from thirty to seventy-five points.

9. **Buyers should continue to use their credit as normal.** If your

client changes any credit charging pattern, it will raise a red flag with the credit reporting agencies and their credit score could be lowered.

10. **Buyers need to maintain good communication with their mortgage loan officer.** If your client receives a notice from a creditor or collection agency that they believe may affect their credit score during the loan process, they should speak to their loan officer immediately. Their loan officer may be able to provide them with guidance and the resources they need to halt any pejorative reporting to the credit agencies.

Your buyer client needs to remember the lender will run another credit report on them before closing as part of the final loan underwriting process. If their credit score has dropped, they may no longer qualify for the loan or rate for which they initially applied. Experienced mortgage loan officers will shepherd the loan process with your client from beginning to end, so there are not any surprises before closing on the loan.

CHAPTER 41

Managing the Integrity of the Transaction

"Do what is right not what is easy."

Each real estate transaction is as different as are the people participating in it. The personalities of the clients and real estate professionals can have a bearing on whether or not the transaction goes smoothly.

I believe there are seven fundamental "rules" an agent must follow, so the transaction moves forward without delay, the interests of the client are protected, and the original objectives established by you and your client are reached. I call this "managing the integrity of the transaction." Without these critical elements, the transaction is at risk of collapsing and leaving all parties frustrated and angry in its wake. Hopefully, the following points will be helpful to you in your next transaction.

Protect the client's interests. One of the primary responsibilities you have as a licensee is to protect the interests of the client at all times, placing theirs above all others. This means you think of your client first when you negotiate an offer, an inspection repair list, closing and possession dates, or any other activity.

The only exception to this protection is when you are asked by your client to do something that could harm the other party in the transaction (the customer) or their agent. A client's interest cannot be protected when they instruct you to do something unlawful or unethical.

Also, you must never put your personal interest ahead of that of your client at any time during your agency relationship. For example, if you are negotiating an offer and the result would be an increased amount of compensation for you, you must consider the client first and negotiate in a way that keeps their interest primary — no matter what the outcome is for you. The client always comes first.

Remember the original objectives. Before I work with a buyer or seller, I discuss their goals in purchasing or selling a home. I write down each goal, make a copy for them, and keep one for myself, so we have a list we can refer back to as we progress through listing or contract.

It is very easy, especially for buyers, to get off track and go down another path instead of the one we laid out in that first meeting. Of course, people can change their minds. However, it is your responsibility to keep the client focused on their original intentions, so the outcome they are looking for is reached. Without staying true to these initial objectives, you will find yourself doing much more work in the management of the client and the transaction.

Confront any and all issues immediately when they occur. As a principal broker, I'd become frustrated with an agent who would tell me about an issue a day or two before the closing date, when it could have been resolved much earlier in the transaction. As agents, we do not like to confront others with a problem. We want everything to go smoothly, without any bumps in the road. Unfortunately, it doesn't always happen that way. When you have something come up in the transaction that could be problematic, you must deal with it immediately. Do not let anything sit and become a more significant issue.

Be honest. Honesty is an essential part of the underlying fabric of the National Association of REALTORS® Code of Ethics and Standards of Practice. As REALTORS®, we must act honestly in everything we do and be truthful in all we say. Dishonesty does nothing but cause harm to clients, customers, cooperating agents, and us.

You may be wrong. I don't like it when I'm wrong. Most people don't like being wrong. However, we cannot be right all the time. When you find yourself having to 'fess up to an issue involving a listing, a contract, or a client, be upfront and honest. Trust me, you will gain the respect of those with whom you were wrong and be more likely to preserve the relationship.

Do not let personal opinion or your emotion get in the way. Believe it or not, agents can change the course of a transaction with the words that come out of their mouths. I have seen occasions when an agent would offer a personal opinion on an issue, and it would change the client's mind. Closings are delayed or fall apart entirely because the agent injects himself or herself into an issue, creating a more significant problem than the original one.

I have also seen agents let their emotions come to the forefront when talking with other agents and brokers about a problem. The issue needs to be resolved, but the agent becomes emotional in trying to seek a resolution, and more problems arise. Emotions can quickly take away objectivity and clear thinking. Stay calm and remember you are a professional. Solve the problem; don't be the source of the problem.

Most of the time, "it will work itself out in the end"! My father gave me a piece of advice a long time ago: "Don't worry. It will work itself out in the end." And, most of the time it does. I share this advice with agents almost on a daily basis.

It is important not to let the challenges and frustrations of what you do get in the way of negotiating a contract or closing a transaction for your client. Staying calm and collected and being objective will allow you to be successful in the work you undertake for your clients, customers, and yourself. In the end, it does work itself out.

Keeping a real estate transaction from unraveling takes experience and expertise in solving problems and creating solutions that allow the buyer and seller to get to the closing. I tell agents to remember the primary goal of the parties in the deal: The seller wants to sell the house, and the buyer wants to buy the house. To make that happen, a real estate agent needs to do what they can to make sure the transaction stays together, and their client remains positive and upbeat.

CHAPTER 42

Explaining Paperless Transactions and Digital Signatures to Your Client

"We cannot solve problems with the same thinking we used when we created them."

— ALBERT EINSTEIN

One of the best things to ever happen in the real estate industry is the digital signature. Signing real estate agency agreements, sales contract forms, disclosures, disclaimers, and other forms electronically provides a great benefit to both agents and clients.

Before the Uniform Electronic Transactions Act (UETA) was adopted in 1999 and Congress passed the United States Electronic Signatures in Global and National Commerce (ESIGN) Act in 2000, all real estate documents were signed using an ink pen. During the past ten years, more brokerages and real estate professionals have incorporated electronic paperwork and digital signatures in their business.

Working in a paperless transaction environment offers many advantages. The use of manila folders and filing cabinets are no longer needed. Agents can create and send any transaction document to their clients to review and sign. Also, through the digital signature method, the client and any other signatories in the signing automatically receive a copy of the fully executed form once the signing process is complete. Agents who work for brokerages operating a paperless transaction file system can provide their compliance department with all the required documents via transaction portals such as Dotloop and Transaction Desk. Creating and managing paperwork through electronic means increases agent productivity and provides brokers with a better system for transaction compliance and file storage.

EXPLAINING DIGITAL SIGNATURES TO YOUR CLIENT

A few years ago, I learned of a court case involving a buyer's agent whose client brought legal action against her and her broker for not clearly explaining the digital signing process for documents in a real estate transaction.

The lawsuit alleged the client signed a package of contract documents electronically for a home to be constructed without knowing what they were signing. They claimed they couldn't read the documents because when they clicked on the various buttons in the signing, all the documents "flew by," (automatically scrolled down after clicking the "next" button) as they stated in their complaint.

The court determined the agent failed her fiduciary duty by not informing the client of the terms and conditions contained in the documents she sent the client for digital signature. The judge in the case said the agent had a responsibility to explain the digital signing process in detail to the client before they received a request to participate in the digital signing of their paperwork. The court ruled in favor of the client and ordered the agent to pay damages the client incurred in the transaction as well as the client's legal fees and court costs. The award was more than $100,000.

Make sure you review each document with your client before they sign them. This can eliminate any confusion the client might have about a document, as well as ensure the signing is expedited in a timely manner. When I read more details about this case, I decided to provide my agents with a document thoroughly explaining the digital signing process to their clients.

You may use the digital signature disclosure document I include in this chapter or create your own using mine as a guide.

DIGITAL SIGNATURE DISCLOSURE

Dear Client:

As we work together on your real estate transaction, you may receive one or more emails inviting you to review and sign electronic documents from our digital document signing system. The use of digital signatures allows us to process transaction documents more quickly and efficiently, especially when we need to meet a particular deadline/performance date in the transaction. Also, the digital signing process allows you to receive a complete, fully executed set of documents for your files.

We utilize the most secure and technologically advanced digital signing service available in the real estate industry. Our service meets all federal and state regulatory compliance guidelines for digital signatures and is recognized as a "true signature" of the person participating in the signing process. Once you sign a document (or documents) digitally, it will be treated as an original signature and have the same enforceability as if you had signed it in person with a pen.

THE DIGITAL SIGNING PROCESS

When we want you to sign a document digitally, you will receive an email informing you we need your signature(s). Any and all documents we send you will require your immediate attention and signature. The digital document signing system will automatically prompt you on how to establish a password and electronically "sign" the documents. Please follow the instructions on the screen to complete the signing.

VERY IMPORTANT: PLEASE READ ANY AND ALL DOCUMENTS BEFORE DIGITALLY SIGNING!

When you log in to the signing process, you will notice the system will prompt you to begin the signing. The system is designed to take you directly to the signing/initialing area(s) once you start. It is imperative you scroll through and read the document before signing/initialing so you understand its content and any terms and conditions you might be legally held to by the other signatory party. **REMEMBER, BY DIGITALLY SIGNING THE DOCUMENT(S) SENT TO YOUR EMAIL, YOU ARE CERTIFYING THAT YOU HAVE THOROUGHLY READ AND ACCEPT THE TERMS AND CONDITIONS CONTAINED WITHIN THE DOCUMENT AND ACKNOWLEDGE ITS RECEIPT.**

When the system receives all of the necessary signatures, a final, fully executed document will be available for your records via a PDF document.

Please do not hesitate to contact me if you have any questions concerning the digital signing process.

ACKNOWLEDGMENT OF THIS DISCLOSURE

By signing below, you are acknowledging you have read this disclosure and understand the importance of the digital signing process and the need to know what you are digitally signing thoroughly.

| _____ | _____ |
| Client   Date | Client   Date |

CHAPTER 43

Meeting Contract Performance Dates and Deadlines

"A perfect method for adding drama to life is to wait until the deadline looms large."

— ANONYMOUS

One of the most important topics I cover in my contract courses is the need to keep up with contract performance dates. A contract clause that emphasizes punctual performance is an essential requirement of the contract. Failure for any party to the agreement to meet a contractual deadline may result in a breach of contract, forfeiture of earnest money, unenforceable performance, and in some cases, liability for civil damages. I cannot overstress the importance of watching performance dates and ensuring your client meets every one of them.

THE MOST COMMON CONTRACT PERFORMANCE DATES

Meeting the date for performance can make all the difference in whether or not the contract remains in force or terminates by an action or inaction on the part of one of the parties. As part of your fiduciary responsibility to your client, you must know all the dates for performance in a contract, as well as the resulting consequence(s) if they are not met. The following performance requirements are in most real estate contracts:

- Time limit of offer
- Earnest money/trust money
- Appraisal
- Financial contingency/loan obligations
  - Credit report
  - Hazard insurance
  - Intent to proceed
  - Appraisal paid and ordered
- Non-financial contingency proof of funds (cash deal)
- Inspection contingency
- Response to inspection contingency
- Closing and possession dates
- Property condition disclosure
- Title and conveyance
- Final inspection
- Flood issues
- Survey issues
- Title issues
- Closing issues

HOW TO MAKE SURE YOUR CLIENT MEETS THE CONTRACT'S PERFORMANCE DATES

Failure for any party to the agreement to meet a contractual deadline may result in a breach of contract, forfeiture of earnest money, unenforceable performance, and in some cases, liability for civil damages.

*You **must** watch performance dates and ensure your client meets every one of them.*

Performance date checklist. Keeping up with contract performance dates is relatively simple. There are two easy ways to make sure the dates are met. The first one is a checklist with all the various performance dates. Many state or local REALTOR® associations provide pre-printed checklists agents can use to know when a specific contract performance component is due. These forms are great because they contain the list of performance areas included in the associated Purchase and Sale Agreement form provided by the association.

The red pen method. Another tried-and-true technique of knowing contract performance deadlines is to use a red pen (I like felt tip markers) to mark on a copy of the executed contract the due date for each contingency or performance requirement. I put the actual date in the margins of the contract where the performance deadline is noted. I check the contract on a daily basis, so I will know when a date is coming up and if I needed to "light a fire" under the cooperating agent to make sure the date is met.

TIME IS OF THE ESSENCE!

Most real estate contracts contain a phrase stating that "time is of the essence." This phrase in a real estate sales contract means that performance by one party within the time period stated in the agreement is necessary for one party to require performance by the other party. Failure to act within the time required constitutes a breach of the contract.

That just means the clock is ticking! Thus, if any party to the contract does not perform within the specified time (the drop-dead date), that party is in default, provided the non-defaulting party has made a valid notice of demand for performance.

One way to properly manage contract performance dates is to consider the contract-to-close period as a work-back schedule. In my former career in the printed packaging industry, my company's production department would schedule their customer delivery dates based on a "work-back" schedule. They would plan their production of my orders knowing they were due on a specific date.

The same method can be used when looking at performance dates. Everyone involved in a real estate transaction knows there is a closing date. So, as the parties proceed in the agreement, they need to follow each performance date knowing time is of the essence to get the deal closed.

SECTION SIX

Professionalism and Expertise

CHAPTER 44

Misrepresentation:
The Gateway to a Lawsuit

"Serious misfortunes, originating in mis-
representation, frequently flow and spread
before they can be dissipated by truth."

— GEORGE WASHINGTON

As real estate professionals, we want clients to turn to us for answers to all of their questions. We don't want to look unprofessional if we don't know the answers or have the information they need. We should be the primary source of information for a client, right?

Wrong! I have seen lawsuits and regulatory complaints arise from something an agent said to a client about matters that were clearly out of their area of expertise.

When an agent begins working with a seller or buyer client, they should provide their clients with a written statement explaining what an agent can and cannot do in a real estate transaction. This statement should be a formal disclaimer outlining the importance of utilizing other professionals for certain aspects of the sale or purchase of the client's property. We are not home inspectors, structural engineers, roofing contractors, electricians, plumbers, city planners, surveyors, or appraisers. We are licensed real estate agents who have the education and experience to assist buyers and sellers in purchasing or selling real estate.

When you start working with a client, you need to discuss with them the scope of your expertise as well as the boundaries in which you must operate. If you have established a good rapport with your client and a strong relationship forms, often they will turn to you for advice. Sometimes their request for counsel or information might be very specific and complex.

Errors and omissions (E&O) insurance is a necessity if you practice real estate. Most state real estate commissions will not issue or renew a real estate license without the applicant/licensee having a current E&O insurance policy in force. E&O policies provide comprehensive protection for claims filed against real estate professionals. There are limits, however, on what is covered, so it is important that an agent or broker check with their current insurance carrier to determine the specific terms and conditions of coverage.

One of the most frequent claims received by E&O carriers is for misrepresentation. Clients will sue agents and real estate brokerages for misrepresenting the condition of the property, failure to disclose water intrusion (flooding and leaks), and misrepresenting the value of the property. Litigation has increased over the past few years in these three areas due to misrepresentation. Millions of dollars have been paid to plaintiffs who claimed the seller, listing agent, buyer's agent, or all three did not correctly represent the condition or value of the property.

SUED FOR MISREPRESENTATION

A year or so after one of our agents, Cliff, left our brokerage for another firm, he found himself in big trouble because of misinformation he shared with a client. Cliff showed a property to his buyers who fell in love with a house on a large one-acre lot. Located directly behind the row of pine trees in the backyard was a large parcel of vacant land. Cliff's clients ask him if that particular piece of property was ever going to be developed.

He was not sure how to answer their question, but he did say that he heard the land was put in a land trust and would not be developed. Later that afternoon, Cliff's buyers elected to make an offer on the property. The offer was accepted, and the transaction closed forty-five days later. One of the reasons they wanted the home was because it backed up to a large, undeveloped piece of property.

Fast-forward one year when Cliff got a voicemail from those buyers. They were extremely upset. They informed Cliff they just learned the city commission had approved a large outdoor family entertainment center with go-carts, miniature golf, and two water-slides. Construction of the facility was to begin within a month. They reminded him of their conversation when he told them the property behind the house was in a land trust and would never be developed.

Cliff had to sit down as he began feeling faint. Two weeks later he and his broker were served with a $2 million lawsuit accusing Cliff of misrepresentation and not using reasonable skill and care as a licensed real estate agent. The next day Cliff received a complaint for misrepresentation from the state real estate commission filed by the buyers.

BE THE SOURCE OF THE SOURCE, NOT THE SOURCE

What should Cliff have done to avoid a lawsuit and a real estate commission complaint?

The answer is straightforward. When the buyers asked him about the vacant property behind their future home, he should have said he did not know if it was going to be developed or not, but the city planning and zoning commission probably could answer their question. If Cliff had encouraged them to call the city planning department to seek out any information on any future development plans for the property, he'd avoid being the source of the information and, instead, become the "source of the source" for information.

Agents can jeopardize themselves by "being the source" or coming across as an expert on a particular topic. Many times, to gain a client's trust, real estate agents will come across as being knowledgeable on *everything* asked of them by their clients. They do not want their clients and prospects to doubt their expertise and not turn to them for answers to their questions. They know their clients are more likely to use their services again and make referrals to agents they trust.

Unfortunately, when we step outside the bounds of our licensure, we put ourselves at significant risk by causing severe harm to our clients with incorrect information or indigent counsel. Also, we can lose our real estate license through disciplinary action by the state and be subject to civil lawsuits with large monetary requests.

TWO DIRTY WORDS IN REAL ESTATE:
LAWSUITS AND *COMPLAINTS*

A real estate agent can't prevent someone from filing a lawsuit or complaint against them. However, an agent can be proactive and reduce the chances of seeing one come across their desk. The following tips can help keep a subpoena or a registered letter from your state real estate commission showing up at your door:

- Resolve problems far before the closing date. Don't wait until the last minute to address problem issues.

- Don't try to be an expert at everything. Involve key professionals, such as attorneys, home inspectors, termite inspectors, appraisers, lenders, and surveyors when needed. Provide a list of several names or a copy of internet search results, but do not recommend a specific individual or firm! Keep a copy of the list you provide.

- It is generally a good idea to require agency disclosure on every transaction. Be familiar with your state laws regarding when a written agency disclosure is required, at what stage it must be completed, and who must be provided with signed copies. Typically, agency relationships should be disclosed as soon as possible, but in any event, prior to providing specific assistance to the client.

- Document conversations, recommendations, and activities in a log. It is also often helpful to document conversations by sending a brief follow-up email. Keep organized, detailed records of all real estate transactions.

- Recommend that buyers obtain a home inspection. If they decline, have them sign a form confirming this decision.

- Utilize state and/or association standard contract forms. It is wise to address items that are outside of standard form language with the client's legal counsel, or else the real estate licensee risks the unauthorized practice of law.

- Be a "source of the source." When information is obtained from a third party, it is often a good idea to disclose the source when making representations, because sometimes information from what appears to be a valid source turns out to be inaccurate. For example, if you believe a property is on city sewer based on a prior listing or a statement by the city utility office, disclose the source of your representation.

These tips are just a few of the ways an agent can reduce many legal and/or regulatory problems facing today's real estate professional. The practice of real estate is becoming more and more challenging. When an agent is aware of problems that can arise out of a transaction and the parties associated with it, they are better equipped to meet the needs of their clients.

MISREPRESENTATION REGARDING THE CONDITION OF THE PROPERTY

Property condition misrepresentation is one of the most frequent claims received by E&O insurance carriers. Clients will claim the seller or their agent did not correctly disclose specific issues concerning the condition of the property. Examples may include misrepresentation concerning water intrusion, foundation defects, the age of the home, type of flooring, state of the roof, nature of the drywall, synthetic stucco, presence of mold, etc. It is crucial a listing agent explains the importance of fully disclosing the condition of the property no matter how small the issue.

Almost every state has passed property condition laws mandating sellers give buyers specific information about the structural condition, condition of major systems in the home and other features of the property. Also, information on local government ordinances and homeowners association regulations impacting the property must be disclosed. Sellers and agents will find themselves in major distress if an adverse fact such as a structural issue or a system failure is known, and it is not fully disclosed.

MISREPRESENTATION REGARDING FLOODING OR LEAKS

A lawsuit filed by a buyer for non-disclosure of water intruding into the property is one of the most common claims received by E&O companies. Water intrusion includes flooding from rain or other exterior sources and leaks within a home. Most lawsuits from plaintiffs affected by a non-disclosure issue centered on water intrusion will seek compensation and other financial relief for structural damage to the house and the cost for repairs and restoration.

Some examples of claims in this area include:
- The seller told the listing agent that the basement floods, but the agent told the sellers not to disclose it. (Note: The E&O carrier will see a claim for a complaint filed by the buyers based on negligence, fraud, and the applicable consumer protection statute, followed by a cross-claim from the sellers.)
- The real estate agent should have known of the house's tendency to flood because of the water stains on the basement walls.

- The real estate agent told the buyer the water was wind driv-
en and came in through the roof during a hurricane, when
in actuality the house has a propensity to flood during
minor storms.

Furthermore, Article Two of the National Association of
REALTORS® Code of Ethics states: *"REALTORS® shall avoid exagger-
ation, misrepresentation, or concealment of pertinent facts relating
to the property or the transaction. REALTORS® shall not, however, be
obligated to discover latent defects in the property, to advise on matters outside the scope of their real estate license, or to disclose facts
which are confidential under the scope of the agency or non-agency
relationships as defined by state law."*

MISREPRESENTATION REGARDING THE VALUE OF THE PROPERTY

Claims alleging the misrepresentation of the value of the property
may occur in many scenarios. For example, the buyer of a home
or the mortgage lender may allege the appraisal overvalued the
subject property. In addition to appraisals, plaintiffs may allege
misrepresentation concerning broker price opinions (BPOs),
which provide a fair market value estimate of the subject property. (Note that some jurisdictions place limits on BPOs done by
licensed real estate agents.) In contrast, a seller may allege his or
her real estate agent undervalued the subject property and listed
it for too little.

An agent can easily avoid claims for misrepresenting the
value of a property. It's imperative that the agent is not the one
who determines the price for a listing. Instead, you should provide
the seller with correct and accurate quantitative information, so
they can make an informed decision on setting the sale price for
their home. Some agents will want to price the property at a lower
value to expedite the sale of the house, so that they can receive
their commission check. Besides risking litigation for improper
valuation, an agent can find themselves facing a professional standards committee for practicing unprofessionally and unethically as
it relates to property valuation. The NAR Code of Ethics Standard
of Practice 1-3 states: *"REALTORS®, in attempting to secure a listing,
shall not deliberately mislead the owner as to market value."* As a listing agent, you should provide your professional opinion on price,
but the seller should have the final say.

HOW CAN YOU AVOID A CLAIM FOR MIS-REPRESENTATION?

Unfortunately, there is no unassailable plan of action that will insulate you entirely from a claim. Even the most meticulous and conscientious real estate agent may find himself or herself involved in a dispute or lawsuit. However, you may reduce your risk of liability or exposure if you follow these general principles on disclosure of the condition of the property:

- Listing agents should have the seller complete any required property disclosure form. *This form should never be filled out by the real estate licensee.* You are responsible for ensuring the seller understands the disclosure form, and you should answer any questions they may have concerning what they need to complete or answer on the form. The licensee should never advise what should be disclosed and what should not be disclosed.
- Buyers should carefully review any property disclosures or disclaimers before reaching a binding agreement on the purchase. Like listing agents, buyer agents are responsible for ensuring the buyer clearly understands any property disclosure form and should be able to answer any questions the client may have concerning it.
- If the seller is unwilling to disclose any adverse fact they are aware of regarding the property's condition, you will need to disclose it. If they instruct you not to disclose it, you need to walk away from the listing as you are setting yourself up for a lawsuit and regulatory complaint. The same holds true for buyer agents who become aware of any issue with the property. You have an obligation to disclose this information to your buyer.

The bottom line on avoiding misrepresentation is always be truthful in your representation of the property's condition and its value.

Cliff's errors and omissions insurance carrier eventually settled out of court with the buyers for an undisclosed amount of money. The state real estate commission heard the buyers' complaint against Cliff, and he had to pay a $1,000 fine and attend continuing education classes on contracts and real estate ethics.

Ironically, a couple of years after all the dust settled for Cliff, his clients sold the property and moved out of state. The family entertainment center was built and continues to be a big hit with everyone in the community.

CHAPTER 45

How to Work as a Facilitator/Transaction Broker

"A just balance and scales are the Lord's; all the weights in the bag are his work."

Note: Terminology for a non-agency status for an agent varies throughout the country. I use the terms, facilitator *and* transaction broker, *(which are used in the State of Tennessee, where I practice), to identify an agent who is not in an agency relationship with a buyer or seller customer.*

Many years ago, before I became a real estate agent, my wife and I wanted to move to another part of town to be closer to friends, church, and work. We contacted an agent who was well known in the market as a buyer's agent but had listed several homes in our neighborhood. She visited with us to see our house and discussed how she could market the home and find the "right" buyer for it. Even though she did not have extensive experience in listing homes, we decided to list with her. Our home was on the Multiple Listing Service in a few days.

We had several showings the first couple of weeks, but no offers to purchase. Then, one Friday afternoon, she called and said she had buyers who contacted her and wanted to see the house. She showed the house to them early Friday evening. The buyers, a young couple relocating to the area from Chicago, made an offer first thing the next morning. Our agent came by the house around noon to present the offer to us. It was a full price offer with the standard contingencies.

She informed us the buyers contacted her the day before asking to see our house. They were unrepresented and did not want a buyer's agent. She asked us if she could change her agency status from "designated agent for the seller" to "facilitator/transaction broker" in order to work with both parties in the contract. We really didn't care what she did as long as she sold our home. We accepted the buyer's offer and bound the Purchase and Sale Agreement.

As soon as our agent became a facilitator, it became apparent she was having a difficult time remaining "in the middle" as a neutral third-party agent. In the days following the binding of the contract, she appeared to be assisting the buyers and "representing" their interests more than ours. And, we were the ones who offered her the opportunity to sell our home!

After the buyer's inspection was completed, we think she might have instructed the buyers what to do when the time came to submit their repair list to us. As we were reviewing their list of repairs, "our" agent suggested we reduce our price in exchange for not completing any of the repairs noted on the inspection contingency release form. She suggested this would be the best option for both sides and the quickest way to get everything "wrapped up" in the transaction. What concerned us was not the price reduction, but how she presented it to us. We felt she was representing the buyer.

Other issues came up as we progressed in the deal. We learned the agent assisted the buyers in getting a loan through her husband, who was a loan officer with a local mortgage company. She also encouraged us to let the buyers move in early because they needed to vacate their temporary housing. And, as we learned after the closing from one of our former neighbors, the buyers told several neighbors they were very appreciative of the efforts of their "agent" in getting them the house. From our perspective, we believed she was much more focused on getting the deal closed for the buyers than for us. It was clear to us she was unable to remain neutral as a facilitator.

That particular situation always comes to mind when an agent wants my opinion on changing their agency status to facilitator/transaction broker. I ask them, "Can you give up the relationship with the folks who brought you to the dance?" The answer to this question really depends on the particular agent. It is very difficult for some agents, but it's easy for others.

The real advantage of the facilitator status is it eliminates dual agency. Dual agency is when an agent represents both the buyer and the seller. Disclosed dual agency is legal in most states, but undisclosed dual agency is not. In my contract course and other classes I teach, I always joke about dual agency. I tell them, "When you hold the words, *dual agency*, up to a light, it shows the word, *lawsuit*." My advice to all agents is to stay away from dual agency and choose facilitator status.

All real estate licensees are considered facilitators until they establish an agency relationship with a seller or buyer. If you choose to act as a facilitator in the sale or purchase of a home, you can assist the two customers with various aspects of the transaction.

You can:
- provide a comparative market analysis (CMA) to the buyer
- assist both the buyer and the seller with all transaction paperwork
- coordinate all inspections on the property
- work with the lender in ensuring the appraiser has access to the home
- relay communication and requests between the buyer and seller
- coordinate the closing with the title attorney or title company
- give both the buyer and seller closing gifts

You cannot:
- recommend what price the buyer should offer for the property
- recommend which repair or replacement items from the home inspection report the buyer should submit to the seller
- share any confidential information the seller may have shared with you prior to you changing your agency status to a facilitator
- share information that would give one side an advantage over the other
- withhold information from one side of the transaction without telling the other side.

You must:
- communicate with both the buyer and the seller about any information you may obtain about the inspections, appraisal, or property itself (example: adverse facts)
- remain neutral and "stay in the middle"

CHAPTER 46

Can't We Just Get Along?
Working and Communicating With Other Real Estate Agents

"In union there is strength."

Real estate is one of the few industries that relies on communicating and cooperating with other competitors in the profession to earn a living. A cooperative spirit is at the heart of what it means to be a professional real estate agent.

In order to work with each other cooperatively, we must keep communication lines opens, respect one another as professionals, and encourage one another to maintain the integrity of what we do to meet the needs of our clients. To survive in this business, you must be able to work with other agents on an ongoing basis.

HOW TO WORK WELL WITH OTHER REAL ESTATE AGENTS

The number one complaint lodged against real estate agents by consumers and other agents is the lack of communication. In fact, our industry has a black eye with the general public when it comes to how we handle communication.

There is no question we dislike giving bad news or providing information to the other side of a transaction that may result in confrontation. No one likes confrontation. We want to avoid it. We want it to go away. Unfortunately, most times, it will not disappear.

By avoiding an important issue, a difficult subject, or complaint with the cooperating agent in your transaction, you are guaranteed to see the problem worsen. You must take care of the issue sooner rather than later so your path to closing the deal will be less cluttered with obstacles and any unnecessary drama.

Here are some helpful reminders to make sure you're doing your part as a communicative and cooperative real estate agent.

Communicate, communicate, communicate. How do you deal with an agent not responding to your telephone call, text message, or email? One of my biggest frustrations as a REALTOR® and as a principal broker is when I cannot reach the cooperating agent or, if necessary, their principal broker. *This drives me crazy*! To this day, I still get frustrated when someone does not get back to me in a timely manner.

If you feel the same, know that we're not alone. Poor communication tops the list of complaints by agents about other agents. Common grievances include poor communication involving important issues at the offer stage, during the inspection and repair/replacement resolution periods, and before the property closes. Sometimes the news at these critical points in the transaction is not always good news, but agents must communicate with one another, no matter what the issue might be. Remember, another key to good communication in our business is responding to other agents' calls and e-mails promptly and courteously.

Use this script when talking to the cooperating principal broker when you can't reach the other agent:

"Mr. Broker, I've been trying to reach Betty Agent to present an offer we have on her listing at 123 Elm Street. I was wondering how to proceed. I've tried reaching Betty on her cell via voice mail and text as well as leaving multiple messages at her office. I'm wondering if she is OK. My buyers are eager to have their offer presented. What do you recommend?"

I've had great results with this approach. It is non-threatening and will make the other broker track the agent down.

For example, what should you do when the cooperating agent won't return your calls, texts, or emails after you submit an offer to purchase?

First, call their principal broker to let them know you have been diligently attempting to contact their agent to confirm receipt of your buyer's offer. I have found when the principal broker gets involved, the absent agent usually will respond to me. Not always, but most times. Frame your conversation with the broker by letting them know the agent has not responded to you, and you are wondering if something may have happened to him or her. Your telephone call will get the broker's attention.

If you are not getting anywhere with the other broker, call your principal broker and see if he or she can assist you. Most likely, they will contact the other broker to get an answer. If this doesn't work, trust your principal broker to take the necessary action to address the situation so the agent and broker can be held accountable. This may result in speaking with an attorney to apply pressure or filing a grievance against the agent and their broker through their REAL-TOR® association's professional standards committee. This final step is very rare, and as a principal broker, I never had to reach this point. However, I was prepared to do so.

The bottom line is — *communicate!* Sometimes, it may not be the news you want to deliver to the other side, but it needs to be discussed, so a resolution is reached.

The telephone still is the best communication tool. Instead of emailing or texting, *pick up the phone and call the person!* Voice communication is much more effective and helps build trust in the relationship. Please don't hide behind lengthy emails or text messages. I cannot stand it when someone sends me a nine-paragraph email that took an hour for them to write that could easily have been handled in a three-minute phone conversation.

If you struggle with communication, add a goal to your business plan to make improvements in how you communicate. You may need to seek counsel from someone who is an excellent communicator to help you. Face your fear and develop tools that will make you a great communicator!

Do not assume the other agent is doing their job. Never assume the cooperating agent is doing something they are responsible for in the transaction affecting performance dates, contingency releases, closing and possession dates, contract extensions, etc. Many times, when we assume someone else is handling an issue, nothing happens or gets resolved. You must always follow-up with the other agent to make sure things are happening on the other side of the transaction, so the deal is not jeopardized, and the interests of your client are protected.

Show professional respect for your peers. To make it in this business, agents must have mutual respect for one another. Article 15 of the Code of Ethics states: *"REALTORS® shall not knowingly or recklessly make false or misleading statements about other real estate professionals, their businesses, or their business practices."*

Article 15 is probably the most violated article in the entire Code.

We tend to speak ill of another agent when something goes wrong, or they do something that affects our client, our transaction, or us. Bad-mouthing another person has become a common problem in society, but it does not have to be in our industry. The professionalism we espouse through the Code and within our real estate practice depends on managing the words and actions towards each other. Hold your tongue and keep your personal feelings about another agent to yourself when they have caused issues or problems.

Don't poach another agent's clients. I once fired an agent from our firm when I learned she was prospecting at other agents' open houses. She was trying to get information about the sellers, so she could contact the seller to try to steal the listing from the listing agent.

I was furious, and when I learned what she was doing, I immediately terminated her from our firm and returned her real estate license to the Tennessee Real Estate Commission with a letter from me informing the Commission what she did. To this day, I still hear of agents in our local market attempting to steal clients from other agents through prospecting and other means.

Agents need to realize there is enough business out there for everyone. Real estate agents need to procure clients through legal and ethical means and not by tactics that are incongruent with who we are as professionals. Article 16 of the Code provides several standards of practice outlining the importance of not encroaching on signed exclusive agency agreements. Contact your principal broker immediately if you discover someone is trying to take your client away from you and your firm.

Don't change the cooperative agent's compensation listing. One of the most frequent complaints I hear about other agents involves altering compensation before or after a contract is signed. A listing agent will enter the cooperating broker compensation in the Multiple Listing Service as "X," but when the agent discusses compensation at the time of the offer, the compensation is "Y."

Most MLS systems have established detailed rules on commissions and compensation. In our MLS in Middle Tennessee, the rule states: *"In filing a property with the Multiple Listing Service, the Participant is making blanket unilateral offers of compensation to the other MLS Participants, and shall therefore specify on each listing filed with the MLS, the compensation being offered to the other Participants."*

The problem we see is that listing agents are changing the compensation after a buyer's agent has procured a buyer to the broker's listing in the MLS. Changes to compensation get messy and sometimes ends up in an arbitration hearing at the local REALTOR® association. You should submit a cooperative compensation agreement to the listing broker *before* submitting an offer to purchase so there are no questions about how much you will be paid at closing.

Change your mindset. When there is an uncooperative agent on the other side of the deal who is not doing what they should be doing, you will end up doing most of the work in the transaction.

Why? The reason is pretty simple: you must always protect your client and work in their best interest. Remember, they need to sell or purchase a home. If the other side is not cooperating or doing their part in the transaction, you will have to do it.

You will need to change your mindset and take control of the situation. The other agent has dropped the ball, and now you need to pick it up and possibly carry it to the finish line. The bottom line is you cannot let your client down.

FOLLOW THE PATHWAYS TO PROFESSIONALISM

One of the best publications from the National Association of REAL-TORS® is a document titled "Pathways to Professionalism." It does not replace the Code of Ethics, as it does not have any enforceability when it comes to grievances among the REALTOR® community. However, it does provide us with an excellent guide on how we should be respectful of others and real property. I use this document in my professional ethics courses for the two-year NAR Code of Ethics training requirement. It has become an invaluable tool for my agents and me.

The following information is reprinted with permission from the current National Association of REALTORS® Code of Ethics and Arbitration Manual.

Note: While the Code of Ethics and Standards of Practice of the National Association establishes objective, enforceable ethical standards governing the professional conduct of REALTORS®, it does not address issues of courtesy or etiquette. Based on input from many sources, the Professional Conduct Working Group of the Professional Standards Committee developed the following list of professional courtesies for use by REALTORS® on a voluntary basis. This list is not all-inclusive and may be supplemented as a result of local customs and practices. These professional courtesies are intended to be used by REALTORS® on a voluntary basis and cannot form the basis for a professional standards complaint.

RESPECT FOR THE PUBLIC

1. Follow the "Golden Rule": Do unto others as you would have them do unto you.
2. Respond promptly to inquiries and requests for information.
3. Schedule appointments and showings as far in advance as possible.
4. Call if you are delayed or must cancel an appointment or showing.
5. If a prospective buyer decides not to view an occupied home, promptly explain the situation to the listing broker or the occupant.
6. Communicate with all parties in a timely fashion.
7. When entering a property, ensure that unexpected situations, such as pets, are handled appropriately.
8. Leave your business card if not prohibited by local rules.
9. Never criticize property in the presence of the occupant.
10. Inform occupants that you are leaving after showings.
11. When showing an occupied home, always ring the doorbell or knock—and announce yourself loudly before entering. Knock and announce yourself loudly before entering any closed room.
12. Present a professional appearance at all times; dress appropriately and drive a clean car.
13. If occupants are home during showings, ask their permission before using the ... bathroom.
14. Encourage the clients of other brokers to direct questions to their agent or representative.
15. Communicate clearly; don't use jargon or slang that may not be readily understood.
16. Be aware of and respect cultural differences.
17. Show courtesy and respect to everyone.
18. Be aware of—and meet—all deadlines.
19. Promise only what you can deliver—and keep your promises.
20. Identify your REALTOR® and your professional status in contacts with the public.
21. Do not tell people what you think—tell them what you know.

RESPECT FOR PROPERTY

1. Be responsible for everyone you allow to enter listed property.
2. Never allow buyers to enter listed property unaccompanied.
3. When showing property, keep all members of the group together.
4. Never allow unaccompanied access to property without permission.
5. Enter property only with permission even if you have a lock-box key or combination.
6. When the occupant is absent, leave the property as you found it (lights, heating, cooling, drapes, etc.). If you think something is amiss (e.g., vandalism), contact the listing broker immediately.
7. Be considerate of the seller's property. Do not allow anyone to eat, drink, smoke, dispose of trash, use bathing or sleeping facilities, or bring pets. Leave the house as you found it unless instructed otherwise.
8. Use sidewalks; if weather is bad, take off shoes and boots inside property.
9. Respect sellers' instructions about photographing or video graphing their properties' interiors or exteriors.

RESPECT FOR PEERS

1. Identify your REALTOR® and professional status in all contacts with other REALTORS®.
2. Respond to other agents' calls…and e-mails promptly and courteously.
3. Be aware that large electronic files with attachments…may be a burden on recipients.
4. Notify the listing broker if there appears to be inaccurate information on the listing.
5. Share important information about a property, including the presence of pets, security systems, and whether sellers will be present during the showing.
6. Show courtesy, trust, and respect to other real estate professionals.
7. Avoid the inappropriate use of endearments or other denigrating language.
8. Do not prospect at other REALTORS'® open houses or similar events.

9. Return keys promptly.
10. Carefully replace keys in the lockbox after showings.
11. To be successful in the business, mutual respect is essential.
12. Real estate is a reputation business. What you do today may affect your reputation — and business — for years to come.

CHAPTER 47

I Think I Need to Call My Broker

"Anytime you see a turtle up on top of a fence post, you know he had some help."

The principal broker's role is significant to the success of your real estate career. He or she must be able to provide advice and counsel on a wide array of topics including regulatory compliance, growing and operating your business, professional standards, and continuing education.

The broker is the one who told the state's licensing authority they would be responsible for all the activities in your real estate practice. You should be able to turn to the broker at any time, especially if there is an issue or problem you cannot resolve. They will want you to contact them when a need arises. Rely on their education, experience, and expertise to assist you when you face a challenging issue with a client, cooperating agent, or any other party involved in your transaction. They will always have a duty to protect your reputation as well as the reputation of the firm.

I became a principal broker many years ago at a firm affiliated with a national real estate franchise in Brentwood, Tennessee. I never saw myself as a managing broker. Through a series of different events that occurred at our firm with a change of ownership and personnel, I was asked to step into a leadership role and oversee the operations of one of our branch offices. I accepted the job as a managing broker and ever since then, I have enjoyed helping hundreds of agents and their clients.

When I was selling full-time as an agent, I felt called to guide and direct my clients through the process of listing and selling their home or purchasing their next one. I took this same mindset as a managing broker, except I viewed my role as shepherding agents as they managed their clients and transactions. I always told my agents they could call me with a problem or an idea anytime. As I am now in a corporate management position with our company, I still receive calls, and I always want to help wherever I can.

During the many years I served as a principal broker, I received numerous telephone calls, emails, and text messages every day from my agents on a wide variety of topics. Many of the conversations I had with my group of folks were questions about something to which they already knew the answer — they just needed my affirmation.

However, on several occasions, an agent was either backed into a corner by another agent or client or faced a roadblock to keep their transaction on track. I was always there to help them find a solution to a problem or intervene in a matter that only a managing broker could address.

WHEN IT'S TIME TO CONTACT YOUR PRINCIPAL BROKER

I would recommend you consult with your principal broker when you are faced with the following:

Contract issues. Today's real estate contracts have become very lengthy and complicated. The language used in most Purchase and Sale Agreements are designed to provide specific terms and conditions for the buyer and the seller to follow. Your broker can help you navigate through the contract and supplemental documentation, so you understand the context of what is in the agreement, as well as the implications for your client.

Agency issues. A real estate license is all about representation. Representation in real estate is created through an agency relationship. Agency can be a complex subject for an agent if they are not well versed in the various agency categories. Your principal broker understands the intricacies of agency and can assist you in deciding whether or not you should establish a designated agency relationship, change your agency status to a neutral facilitator/transaction broker, or terminate an established agency relationship with a buyer or seller.

Assisting an agent through an agency status change was something I did on a regular basis. More times than not, it involved moving from being a designated agent to becoming a facilitator. Agents need to know the advantages and disadvantages of facilitation. The broker can provide them with the proper guidance.

Terminating an agency relationship is one you will face at least once in your career. There are different reasons why clients and agents want to (or need to) stop working with each other. No matter what the issue might be, the broker needs to be involved in this process. He or she can assist you in handling the termination professionally and with minimal stress. Remember, only the principal broker can release the client from an agency agreement as the broker is the "owner" of his or her firm's listing agreements and buyer representation agreements.

Client issues. You may find yourself facing a matter with a client requiring the involvement of your principal broker. For example, there may be a difference of opinion concerning the amount of time you are spending marketing the seller's home. Or, your buyer client is upset at you because you have not been attentive to their needs.

Whatever the matter might be, ask your principal broker to work with you in resolving your client's concerns or complaints. A good managing broker can function as a mediator who can "mend fences" in the agent/client relationship so the client's goals and objectives can continue to be met.

Earnest money issues. There will be times when your client's contract falls apart. Contract termination can be due to a structural inspection that reveals significant problems with the house, or your buyer is denied a loan because they cannot get their loan application approved by the lender's underwriting department.

When a contract is terminated for a valid reason, the earnest money will need to be returned to the buyer. However, if the seller is unwilling to release the buyer from the contract and return their earnest money, you may need to ask your broker to get involved to find a solution. Quite often, I've been called upon to help when one of my agents needed to get the buyer's earnest money returned, but the seller would not sign the earnest money disbursement form.

Agents and their clients become anxious when they are unable to move on to find another home because there is not a clean release from a transaction. It was my responsibility, as my agent's broker, to encourage the agent to work out a solution with the cooperating agent. If that failed, I would call the cooperating managing broker and see if, between the two of us, we could get the matter resolved. Nine times out of ten, the broker's involvement ended the dispute, and the money was either refunded, divided between the parties, or sent to the local court through an interpleader action where the court decides who will receive the money.

Disclosure issues. I receive numerous calls from agents asking me whether or not a potential adverse fact discovered by a home inspector, the client, the agent, or a third party should be disclosed. Non-disclosure is the number one reason sellers and listing agents are sued by "injured" buyers.

If you find yourself with a question on whether or not something should be disclosed, call your broker as soon as possible. He or she will be able to provide you with what you should and should not do concerning disclosure. Don't make any decisions about disclosure if it is not crystal clear. Call your broker.

Cooperating agent issues. Not everyone in this business plays by the rules or acts civil toward one another, including cooperating agents on the other side of our transactions. I wish I had a penny for every time one of my agents called me to complain about the "other" agent involved in their deal. Sometimes the complaints are merited; other times they are not.

Either way, if you are unable to resolve a problem with a cooperating agent, you need to contact your broker. He or she can tell you what you need to do to address the matter. If another agent is not communicating with you concerning an offer or a contract issue, you should contact their principal broker first. If you don't get anywhere with them, call your broker so he or she can get in touch with the other broker to work things out.

Possible legal matters. Our work as real estate agents requires us to handle multiple legal documents on a daily basis. However, our real estate license does not allow us to practice law. If you feel you or your client are facing an issue that may require the opinion or counsel of an attorney, call your principal broker to discuss the matter. He or she will be able to work with you and an attorney in addressing anything that is outside of our scope of licensing. Most title attorneys are well versed in real estate contract law and are an excellent source for help when legal questions arise for you or your client.

Regulatory compliance/licensing issues. The practice of real estate in all states is regulated through a governmental regulatory body, usually a real estate commission. Real estate commissions were created by acts of law to protect consumers when they sell or purchase a home. Your principal broker is the one the state has said is responsible for all of your activities. Do not hesitate to contact your broker if you face an issue that may jeopardize your real estate license. Trust me, the last thing you and your broker want to do is to find yourselves in front of your state real estate commission at a disciplinary hearing.

REALTOR® association issues. As REALTORS®, through our Code of Ethics and Standards of Practice, we agree to utilize our local REALTOR® association to address grievances against one another concerning professional conduct and compensation disputes. If you feel you need to file a complaint against another REALTOR®, you should contact your principal broker for filing a grievance or request for arbitration through your association's Professional Standards Committee. Many times, your broker must participate in the process with you. Do not file *any* complaint with your association without your principal broker knowing about it. The last thing you want to do is catch your broker off guard by going around him or her with a grievance filing.

Intra-company issues. Sibling rivalry in families is a real thing, and it is not any different in the real estate industry involving two agents licensed under the same principal broker. There may be an occasion when you and another agent in your company will be the two agents involved in a transaction. Most of the time, this is a good thing because you and the other agent received the same training from your broker and will know how to manage each respective side of the transaction correctly.

However, it is possible that the two of you may not see eye-to-eye on an issue. If this happens, immediately contact your principal broker to mediate the conflict. He or she will know how to find a resolution that will allow you, the other agent, and the clients to move forward in the transaction.

Utilize the knowledge and experience of your principal broker when a need arises. They are an excellent resource to get you through tough situations with your transactions. The person who sits in the broker's office is the one you can turn to and also learn from when you need them.

CHAPTER 48

So, You Want to Be a Mentor?

"Iron sharpens iron, and one man sharpens another."

— PROVERBS 27:17

Approximately 80 percent of real estate agents leave the profession by the end of their second year of licensing. This statistic is a very sobering one in our industry. Why is the turnover so high? There are many reasons, but one I feel is at the top of the list is lack of training and supervision.

REALTORS® are independent contractors and have limited accountability with their principal broker. As someone who is not required to show up every morning for work or to attend meetings and training classes, the real estate professional — more times than not — is left swimming in the deep end of the "real estate swimming pool" without any idea on how to survive in this business.

Agent turnover could be dramatically reduced if more agents had experienced and successful colleagues walking with them as they attempt to get their business up and running after they receive their real estate license. I believe every new agent should have a mentor. In fact, mentoring can be beneficial to experienced agents who are either struggling with their business or need to reach the next level of production.

Many mentors have paid a heavy price by not understanding what all is involved in mentoring another agent. A few years ago, one of my agents, Michael, contacted me about his desire to mentor a young man who just passed his real estate license exam. I asked him why he wanted to mentor someone. He said he was looking for a buyer representative to work buyer leads he was receiving from an online lead generation company. His workload had increased, and he couldn't find the time to effectively handle the leads coming in to him. I asked him if he had the time to teach a "newbie" the ropes and learn how to be an effective and productive agent. He said he did, and I ultimately approved his mentoring the new agent.

Unfortunately, Michael was extremely busy with his clients and prospects and was unable to make the time necessary to mentor the new agent. Eventually, the mentee floundered, left the company, and joined another brokerage that could provide him "on board" training that new licensees need after they enter the business.

Mentoring is not an easy job, and it is not for everyone. It requires a considerable amount of time and energy of a senior agent. It is a commitment that, if not managed well, can take valuable time away from the mentor's business and cause their production to level off or slow down. If you are considering becoming a mentor, you need to realize what you are getting yourself into before committing to working with a new agent.

Here are a few points to consider about mentoring:

- **Commitment.** Commitment is probably the number one characteristic I look for in someone who wants to be a mentor. The first question I ask a potential mentor is, "Are you willing to commit your time, experience, and emotional energy in helping someone become as competent and successful as you?" I then advise them to think long and hard before they say "yes."

  Successful mentoring programs are built by those who are willing to spend the time and effort advising and guiding someone through the "peaks and valleys" of the real estate industry. A mentoring relationship will inevitably fail if a mentor is not willing to invest themselves in the mentee. The mentee must feel they have a dependable and reliable person who is helping them reach the next step in their career.

- **Experience.** A mentor must be successful in the real estate industry to provide the expertise needed to ensure success in a mentee. What is success? Success is tied to transaction production, professional development, technological expertise, and industry knowledge and advocacy. Someone who is a top producer probably can bring more to the table for an emerging agent than someone who closed only a handful of homes.

We always say, "The more one sells, the more one knows." Also, a mentor who is willing to spend the time and money to educate themselves through professional development and involvement in the real estate community will provide the confidence and proficiency needed to advise a new licensee properly.

- **Professionalism and ethical behavior.** What we do as real estate professionals is a noble task. We have been asked to steward the most substantial asset a person owns through the selling or purchasing process. To do this, an agent must possess the competence and skill to manage the transaction and the expectations of the client correctly. Their ability to handle multiple and sometimes difficult tasks related to property marketing, buyer representation, and transaction management is critical to ensuring the expectations of the client are met. In addition, adherence to the National Association of REALTORS® Code of Ethics and Standards of Practices enables the REALTOR® to conduct themselves and their businesses in a manner that ensures they are always following the guiding principles of the "Golden Rule" and keeping the interests of their clients before their own. The importance of professionalism must be conveyed to the protégé early on in the mentoring process for them to understand the critical role of the agent and the legal and fiduciary liabilities associated with it.
- **Encouragement.** A mentor must be an encourager. Our work as real estate agents day in and day out requires a tremendous amount of time, money, and emotional energy. We may occasionally become discouraged, especially when we feel our efforts are not paying off. The mentor must always provide ongoing encouragement to the mentee as they, themselves, once knew how it felt when they started in the business. There is "the good, the bad, and the ugly" of the business that all agents will experience at one time or another. The mentor must be someone one who can encourage others to enjoy their successes but also persevere and stay focused so that they can navigate through the difficult times.
- **Patience.** The old saying, "patience is a virtue," really is true

when it comes to mentoring someone in this business. It can be easy to get frustrated and upset at the mentee when their performance does not meet your expectations. Mentoring takes quite a bit of time and effort, and the new licensee may not "get it" the first time around. You must be willing to repeat skills and techniques more than once, so they can reach a level of competency in a particular task/skillset.

• **Selflessness.** The real estate business can be a very narcissistic one. Self-promotion and personal marketing are a standard part of the business to gain an edge on the competition. We spend a great deal of time and money marketing our services and value propositions to the market so that we can differentiate ourselves from others in the business.

As a mentor, it is not about you and what you can get out of the mentoring relationship, but about the one you are helping and how you can make them successful. A mentor must be willing to help and to put any self-serving motives aside so the mentee can benefit from what the mentor can offer them. Mentoring is more about giving than receiving.

QUESTIONS YOU NEED TO ASK BEFORE MENTORING AN AGENT

Before you enter into a mentoring relationship with a new or inexperienced real estate licensee, you need to ask yourself some fundamental and serious questions:

• Do I have the qualifications to be a mentor?
• Do I have the time and energy to mentor a new real estate licensee?
• What are the benefits of mentoring this new agent?
• What are the disadvantages of mentoring this new agent?
• How will this impact my business?
• What if the mentoring relationship fails?
• Do I really want to do this?
• Am I only focusing on the money?

Once you have answered *all* of these questions and you feel ready to move forward, meet with your principal broker or team leader to schedule a time to discuss your interest in being a mentor. His or her input will be extremely valuable as you make your final decision.

CHAPTER 49

Learning Never Stops in Real Estate

"It's what you learn after you know it all that counts."

— JOHN WOODEN

The late, great college basketball coach John Wooden once said, "If you don't have time to do it right, when will you have time to do it over?" This quote has stuck with me since I first read it more than thirty years ago. For us to get it "right," we must take the time and effort to learn the what, why, who, how, where, and when of our ever-changing profession.

We real estate agents must continually develop our professional skills and abilities in order to realize sustained growth in our businesses and see long-term success. We must be open to learning the latest knowledge on the "mechanics" of what we do in managing listings, sales contracts, transaction management, professional standards, and state and federal compliance regulations impacting our real estate license. The "business" side of what we do requires ongoing training on effective prospecting, lead generation, sales training, improving business systems and processes, client management, advertising, and marketing. Both areas can be accomplished through good professional development and continuing education.

As a certified real estate instructor and author of numerous continuing education courses, I am a strong proponent of real estate agents bettering themselves to grow professionally in order to effectively meet the needs of their clients. Whether it be National Association of REALTORS® designations or courses on real estate contracts and forms, an agent can benefit from the knowledge they will gain by taking a classroom or online education course. I believe I always profit from taking a class, even if I don't need the continuing education hours to renew my real estate broker license.

PROFESSIONAL DEVELOPMENT OPTIONS

Designations and certifications. One question agents ask on a regular basis is this: *Will earning NAR designations make an agent more money?* I believe they can if an agent utilizes the information they learned from the courses and the resources. I have several designations and certifications. Although I received the continuing education hours to renew my real estate license, I took the courses and seminars to increase my skills and abilities as a REALTOR®.

Which NAR designations are the best ones to acquire? There are many to choose from, but the following are the various designations and certifications I hold and when I earned them.

The first designation I went after was the **Accredited Buyer Representation® (ABR)** designation from the Real Estate Buyer's Agent Council (REBAC) of NAR. I chose the ABR designation as my first one because I was primarily working with buyers early on in my career. The designation gave me numerous resources to help in the buyer representation side of my business. One benefit of the ABR: Most of the materials in my buyer packets were professional pre-printed handouts REBAC provides ABR designees. I suggest you get your ABR if you haven't already done so.

The next designation I earned was the **Senior Real Estate Specialist® (SRES)** designation from the SRES Council of NAR. Right before I obtained my affiliate broker license, my father passed away as a result of a fall. He was in the beginning stages of Alzheimer's disease and had been afflicted with dementia for a couple of years before his death. As my family was dealing with his death, my mother was also diagnosed with Alzheimer's. In light of her prognosis, I decided to learn more about how agents can assist families who are facing the same issues.

The SRES designation provided me with valuable information and tools I could use when assisting seniors and their families with their real estate needs. Almost every year I was selling full-time, I was able to list a home owned by an older individual who was downsizing to an apartment, condominium, or assisted living facility. The SRES is a great designation to earn.

My principal broker and others encouraged me to earn my **Graduate, REALTOR® Institute (GRI)** designation from the Tennessee Association of REALTORS® (now known as Tennessee REALTORS®) at the three-year mark of my career. The GRI designation can be earned through your state REALTOR® association in coordination with NAR. Earning your GRI through a sixty-hour curriculum will increase your skills with comprehensive training in legal and regulatory issues, technology, professional standards, and the real estate sales process. The curriculum is developed by state REALTOR® associations, and GRI courses are offered on an ongoing basis.

A few years later, I earned my **Certified Residential Specialist® (CRS)** designation from the Council of Residential Specialists affiliated with NAR. The council is now known as Residential Real Estate Council (RREC). The CRS designation is the highest credential awarded to residential sales agents, managers, and brokers. There are specific production and education requirements to earn the CRS. Less than 3 percent of all REALTORS® have earned the CRS designation. Like many of the other NAR designations, the RREC provides CRS designees with a wide array of printed materials and tools to use when working with prospects and clients. One of the most significant benefits CRS designees receive is the CRS Referral Network where CRS designees throughout North America can refer clients to each other.

I also hold the **Certified Real Estate Brokerage Manager (CRB)** designation from the Council of Real Estate Brokerage Managers. The CRB designation is designed for those who are in management positions with a real estate firm. This designation allows managing brokers or real estate brokerage owners to add specialized management skills to their knowledge base.

In addition to my designations, I have numerous NAR certifications including the **Short Sales and Foreclosure Resource (SFR), e-PRO,** and **Broker Price Opinion Resource (BPOR)** certifications. A complete list of available NAR designations and certifications is available at www.realtor.org.

Continuing education courses. If you are like me, you are required to take a certain number of continuing education classes during each state licensing renewal cycle. Local and state REALTOR®

associations, as well as independent and distance education course providers, offer numerous options. Beyond the specific courses your state requires for you to renew your real estate license, I encourage you to take classes that interest you or allow you to enhance your unique value proposition.

Most classroom and online course providers offer an array of classes including contracts, agency, ethics, risk awareness, property valuation, home inspections, title issues, business planning, etc. The list is large, and there is something for everyone.

Some of the best CE courses offered are those that are relevant to today's real estate industry issues and applicable to current standards of real estate practice. Every state requires courses and instructors be reviewed and approved by the state real estate commission or real estate regulatory agency.

In my home state of Tennessee, the quality of the course material and the competency of the instructor's knowledge in the subject matter are reviewed carefully by the Tennessee Real Estate Commission. Their review process is comprehensive and thorough, so it meets the Commission's standards for real estate license renewal and the licensee's overall professional development.

A WORD ON DISTANCE (ONLINE) EDUCATION

Distance education continues to grow as a choice for continuing education as more agents see the benefits of taking classes at their own pace as their busy schedule allows. Some real estate agents, especially those who have been in the business for quite some time, are skeptical of online classes. For many years, I was, too. However, the providers have done a good job of developing relevant content and improving course delivery methods. Now, I believe distance education is another quality option for licensees who need CE credit hours or want to learn something new to make them a better agent.

The International Distance Education Certification Center (IDECC) in association with the Association of Real Estate License Law Officials (ARELLO) ensures the delivery of all online courses are of the highest quality and meet all state regulatory continuing education requirements for license renewal. The qualifications IDECC has for curriculum designers and online instructors are very stringent. I am a Certified Distance Education Instructor (CDEI) and provide consulting services to two of the largest online course providers in the country. I can assure you the process IDECC uses to certify online courses and instructors is much more demanding than most state regulatory continuing education guidelines for classroom courses.

Webinars. Although most webinars do not provide continuing education credit, they do offer another avenue for agents to receive information on topics ranging from new selling techniques to developing social media platforms. Many webinars are free and can be viewed online through live streaming or in a pre-recorded format.

Seminars and conferences. My professional development has also included attendance at local, state, and national REALTOR® seminars and conferences. These events always provide a wide array of speakers on various topics on how to grow your business, industry trends, technology, team building, etc. If you are part of a large brokerage or one that is affiliated with a national franchise, you may have an opportunity each year to attend your company's annual meeting. Seminars and conferences also provide an excellent networking opportunity for agents. I always enjoy meeting and interacting with other agents to discover what they are doing in their real estate business. If I can pick up one or two ideas to help me in my business, the cost of attending the meeting or conference is well worth the expense.

You should continuously be learning new ideas, concepts, and techniques that can help you expand your business and make you a better real estate professional. Our industry must have competent and knowledgeable individuals practicing real estate with the highest level of professionalism supported by ethical and moral principles. Professional development accomplishes this through live classroom and online continuing education, as well as industry-related conferences and seminars. My advice to you is to make professional development an essential part of your business plan. Look at your calendar over the next couple of months and make room in it for a class, seminar, or webinar in a subject area you want to learn more about or add to your current knowledge base.

CHAPTER 50

Surviving an Ever-Changing Real Estate World

"By failing to prepare, you are preparing to fail."

Have you ever heard the expression, "The one thing in this world that is constant is change"? Well, this saying holds true for the ever-changing real estate industry.

The changes real estate agents have experienced over the past few years have been dramatic, especially in technology and company business models. New trends are emerging every day, and real estate agents and their brokers must not only know what is happening right now, but they must also anticipate what may occur in the future. I believe changes on the horizon will create a significant paradigm shift in how you and the other two million real estate agents in North America market and sell property.

I have been studying real estate industry trends for quite some time. The industry is changing so fast it is difficult at times to keep up. The transformation now taking place in real estate is supported by technological innovation and a vast influx of money from venture capitalists who believe real estate is worth the risk. In the years ahead, the manner in which an agent markets and sells houses and interact with clients could be radically different. Real estate agents, national real estate companies, local brokerages, technology companies, and other affiliated entities will have to modify their business models, or they will be left behind in the dust of the new reality of real estate.

THE FUTURE OF REAL ESTATE:
TECHNOLOGY AND NEW BROKERAGE MODELS

Whether we like it or not, technology is here to stay. Buyers and sellers are increasingly utilizing the internet via their laptops, tablets, and smartphones to locate properties, find an agent, or both. One emerging technology is artificial intelligence (AI). AI is no longer something seen in the movies or on television. It is real. We use AI every day through our phones with Apple's Siri and Google's Alexa.

Many believe AI will, to some degree, automate many processes in the real estate industry. Digital property transactions and closings will accelerate the entire home-selling and purchasing process allowing for additional closings and reducing the entire contract-to-close period. Customer Relationship Management (CRM) systems, designed with advanced technologies and predictive analytics, will be much more active in automatic lead generation and transaction management.

I believe agents will still play a vital role in assisting a seller in selling their house or a buyer in purchasing a home. However, in the years ahead, agents will become project managers, advisors, and transaction facilitators (not the non-agency definition) instead of the ones who are considered the gatekeepers of the real estate transaction holding all the information the consumer is seeking. Agents will need to change their unique value proposition and their business plans to adapt and remain relative to the consumer's real estate experience.

I believe as time goes on, we will eliminate a large number of agents from the industry due to their inability to accept the changes ahead and the new reality we all will face.

THE FUTURE OF REAL ESTATE

I believe agents will still play a vital role in assisting a seller in selling their house or a buyer in purchasing a home. However, in the years ahead, agents will become project managers, advisors, and transaction facilitators (not the non-agency definition) instead of the ones who are considered the gatekeepers of the real estate transaction holding all the information the consumer is seeking. Agents will need to change their unique value proposition and their business plans to adapt and remain relative to the consumer's real estate experience.

FINDING AN AGENT ONLINE IS INCREASING

More homebuyers are finding their real estate agent online through national real estate search sites such as Zillow, Trulia, and Realtor.com. Through expensive agent marketing programs offered by these sites and others, buyers now can pick and choose from available agents listed on a search results page or through an agent search portal on the website. Many experts believe buyers finding an agent online will happen more often than through personal referrals from family, friends, or co-workers.

I still feel referrals from those we know will always be an essential part of how we generate new business. I encourage you to *never* depend on technology to provide you with all of your business.

TRADITIONAL BROKERAGES WILL FADE AWAY

Leading real estate industry experts agree that the traditional brokerage model is dying and will not be around too much longer. "Traditional" models are those that compensate agents on a split of the gross commission from the closing. Many charge additional fees for the use of office space, copier, computers, etc. With the many changes taking place in technology and consumer participation in online home and agent searches, the traditional broker will more than likely see their demise if they don't make some fundamental changes.

Today, many traditional firms are providing more services for their agents including lead generation, marketing and branding services, health benefits, etc. to remain viable and relevant in their local market. In order for these firms to sustain their existence, compensation models will have to change, and overhead be trimmed. The large, spacious offices of traditional brokers offering multiple amenities for their agents, as well as prime locations, will have to be abandoned for more efficient and cost-effective workspaces.

Consumers want and expect less complex real estate transactions. Agents affiliated with traditional brokerages are unable to provide more straightforward transactions because the broker has substantial control over commissions and other fees charged to the agent's client. Continuing to pursue large split commission models from days long gone will guarantee the death and burial of some very well known real estate brokerages. So far, few brokers have responded to the changes taking place now and what will be coming their way in the not-so-distant future.

THE EMERGENCE OF THE MODERN DISCOUNT BROKER

Discount real estate brokers have been around for some time. However, as the overall brokerage business model is evolving, a new group of companies offering discounted services called Modern Discount Brokerages (MDB) have emerged. They are not the typical "$199" outfit that will list a property on the MLS, provide the seller with a cardboard sign, and tell them "good luck." These new companies are very well organized, well funded, and have the technology, systems, and processes in place to provide a full-service consumer experience at a much lower cost than the traditional brokerage.

The most successful MDBs are backed by venture capital and operate on a regional or national scale. MDBs have a central base of operations, allowing them to control overhead. Some will have agents who are W2 employees as well as independent contractors.

MDBs are leveraging technology and systems to lower costs while providing full-spectrum services to consumers for fees well below traditional rates. They are very customer-centric providing consumer-focused tools, virtual tours, simplified transaction management and marketing and branding with the client in mind. They utilize a flat-fee structure designed to handle both sides of the transaction. To be profitable, they must have massive transaction production supported by distinct processes.

The result of the emergence and widespread acceptance of these models is that the industry will split into two tiers:
- High-touch, full-service, full commission, agent-led brokerage models, and
- Low-cost, system-led, technology-controlled MDB models

Brokerages who do not offer exceptional customer service or a strong brand presence probably cannot compete with the national MDBs who provide similar services at a much lower cost.

THE DIRECT BUYER (THE I-BUYER)

A new breed of homebuyers in the real estate marketplace are investors that use automated valuation models (AVMs) and other technology to make quick offers on properties, will close in a matter of days — not weeks — and then resell them. They are growing because of the influx of venture capital and other investment funding. Their purchases take place online and directly from the homeowner, usually at a small discount. Some will pay a referral fee, typically 1 percent, to real estate agents.

The i-buyer companies are connecting a small group of large, qualified investors to prospective buyers, for a fee. Homeowners who use a direct buyer company to sell their home will more often than not get less money for it than they would by listing it with a real estate agent. However, they will receive their money much faster and with less risk. A seller must decide whether speed and convenience trump potential increase net returns on the home sale. These are two elements that may become increasingly important as market conditions change.

THE NEW REAL ESTATE PARADIGM

Did you know real estate is a significant component of the U.S. economy? Our industry accounts for nearly one-fifth of the U.S. Gross Domestic Product (GDP), even though it has been slow to change and operates as if it was 1975. Investors are now noticing our "sluggishness" and infusing it with lots of money. Billions of dollars are being used to either acquire existing companies or create new ones and utilize the latest technology to address the needs of the consumer.

I believe we will continue to see a large number of brokerage firm mergers and acquisitions in the years ahead. Traditional brokerages will not be able to compete and survive in the climate of a rapidly changing industry. Companies will either be forced to merge their operations or shut their doors. The players who have the money are gaining substantial market share and are becoming a dominant force in shaping how real estate is sold in the U.S. This trend will only continue.

Efficiency and professionalism of real estate brokerage operations have never been as significant as they are now, given the necessity for speed in adapting to rapidly changing market conditions and the revolution catalyzed by technology, as well as the immense influx of venture capital funding that is reshaping the industry.

We real estate agents have done a poor job communicating our value proposition to the consumer. Whether we like it or not, the term "REALTOR®" no longer has the distinction it once had with buyers and sellers. Consumers are bypassing real estate professionals by going online to get available property information and attempting to manage their listing or real estate transactions themselves.

We must reimagine the relationships between agents, brokers, and technology so that we focus on benefits to the consumer. For us to remain relevant, we must show our value in the client relationship and convey the benefits of using our services. There will be no need for us to assist a consumer if they cannot see what we can do for them in selling or purchasing a home.

John M. Giffen is an award-winning real estate broker, manager, agent, author, and real estate educator. He holds numerous industry designations and certifications, including the Certified Real Estate Brokerage Manager (CRB) and Certified Residential Specialist (CRS) designations from the National Association of REALTORS® and the GRI (Graduate, REALTOR® Institute) designation from Tennessee REALTORS®. He also has earned the Certified Distance Education Instructor (CDEI) designation from the International Distance Education Certification Center affiliated with the Association of Real Estate License Law Officials (ARELLO). He is the Director of Broker Operations for Benchmark Realty, LLC, one of the fastest-growing independent real estate companies in North America.

John is a Tennessee Real Estate Commission-approved course provider and instructor, as well as the author of several continuing education courses on real estate contracts, agency, licensing issues, buyer representation, property marketing, real estate ethics, transaction behavior, and real estate business development. He works closely with Tennessee REALTORS® and other state-approved real estate providers in developing new courses for license renewal. John is a consultant with two of the largest distance education providers in the country assisting them with curriculum design and development. He has authored the Tennessee REALTORS® Residential, Commercial, and Principal Broker Core courses required for license renewal in Tennessee.

In 2014, John was named "REALTOR® of the Year" by the Williamson County Association of REALTORS®. He is a multi-million-dollar REALTOR® and has received numerous awards and accolades for his sales production over the years, including "Rookie of the Year" by his first real estate brokerage.

John and his wife, Michelle, have three adult children and reside in Franklin, Tennessee.

CPSIA information can be obtained
at www.ICGtesting.com
Printed in the USA
LVHW101918100319
610158LV00001B/1/P